Collins

Webster's

175 YEARS OF DICTIONARY PUBLISHING

easy learning

ENGLISH

VOCABULARY

HarperCollins Publishers
Westerhill Road
Bishopbriggs
Glasgow
G64 2QT

First edition 2012

Reprint 10 9 8 7 6 5 4 3 2 1 0

© HarperCollins Publishers 2012

ISBN 978-0-00-745054-1

Collins ® is a registered trademark of
HarperCollins Publishers Limited

www.collinslanguage.com

A catalogue record for this book is
available from the British Library

Typeset by Davidson Publishing
Solutions, Glasgow

Printed in Great Britain by Clays Ltd,
St Ives plc

Editorial staff

Senior editors:
Penny Hands
Kate Wild

Project management:
Lisa Sutherland

Contributors:
Sandra Anderson
Katharine Coates
Jennifer Craig
Kate Mohideen
Jane Solomon
Elspeth Summers

For the publisher:
Lucy Cooper
Kerry Ferguson
Elaine Higgleton

contents

contents

Collins Webster's Easy Learning English Vocabulary is designed for anyone who wants to broaden their knowledge of English words in key everyday situations. Whether you need English at work, at school or college, or for a vacation, *Collins Webster's Easy Learning English Vocabulary* offers you the information you require in a clear and accessible format.

This book is divided into 50 subject areas. These cover such topics as "air travel," "business," "food and drink," and "science," arranged in alphabetical order. This arrangement by subject area helps you to learn related words and phrases together. In this way, you can always be sure of using the right word in the right context.

Within each topic, vocabulary is divided into nouns, verbs, adjectives, adverbs, phrases, and idioms. Each word is defined in relation to the topic in question. For example, in "air travel," the meaning that is given for the word *connection* is:

"a plane that leaves after another one arrives and allows you to continue your journey by changing from one to the other."

In "computers and the internet," on the other hand, *connection* is defined in terms of its computer-related sense:

"a link between a computer and a network."

For each topic, there are plenty of authentic example sentences from the Collins corpus. These show you how words and phrases are used in real English.

At the end of the book, there are additional sections on place names and people, numbers, measurements, times, and dates. There is also an alphabetical index, and a list of irregular verbs.

We hope that this book will help you to expand your knowledge of English vocabulary in a wide range of situations. For more information about Collins dictionaries, visit us at **www.collinslanguage.com**.

Topics are organized in alphabetical order.

air travel

Each topic is divided into word classes. These include nouns, verbs, adjectives, adverbs, phrases, and idioms.

Common British words are shown.

Where a noun has an irregular plural form, this is shown below the main form.

The main form of the word is in bold.

These symbols show you how to say the word. See page vii for an explanation of these.

The meaning of each word is given as it relates to the topic.

Short phrases show you how the word is used in context.

Examples from the corpus show how words and phrases are used in real English.

Phrasal verbs and other verb phrases are shown at the end of each verb section.

Where a word has more than one meaning that relates to the topic, each meaning is given.

NOUNS

aeroplane (BRIT)		see **airplane**
aircraft (pl **aircraft**)	[ɛ͡ərkræft]	a plane or a helicopter
airline	[ɛ͡ərlaɪn]	a company that carries people or goods in planes
airplane	[ɛ͡ərpleɪn]	a plane: a vehicle with wings and engines that can fly (In British English, use **aeroplane**)
airport	[ɛ͡ərpɔrt]	a place where planes come and go, with buildings and services for passengers
air-traffic controller	[ɛ͡ər træfɪk kəntroʊlər]	someone whose job is to organize where planes go
aisle	[aɪl]	the long narrow passage between the rows of seats on a plane
arrivals	[əraɪvlz]	the part of an airport where passengers get off planes; wait in arrivals
bag	[bæg]	a container made of plastic, leather, or cloth used for carrying things
baggage	[bægɪdʒ]	same as **luggage**
baggage claim	[bægɪdʒ kleɪm]	the place where you collect your baggage after your flight; go to baggage claim (In British English, use **baggage reclaim**)
baggage reclaim (BRIT)		see **baggage claim**
boarding card (BRIT)		see **boarding pass**
boarding pass	[bɔrdɪn pæs]	a ticket that you must show when you get on a plane (In British English, use **boarding card**)
bureau de change (BRIT)		see **currency exchange**

EXAMPLES

Most low-cost airlines do not serve food.
We checked in early and walked around the airport.
Please do not leave bags in the aisle.
The police said the incident occurred last weekend in arrivals at Terminal 3.

check in		to tell the person at an airport desk that you have arrived
check something in		to give your luggage to the person at an airport desk; check in luggage
delay	[dɪleɪ]	to make something later than expected; The flight is delayed.
depart	[dɪpɑrt]	to leave
fly	[flaɪ]	**1** to travel somewhere in an aircraft **2** when a pilot flies a plane, they make it move through the air
hijack	[haɪdʒæk]	to illegally take control of a plane
land	[lænd]	**1** when a plane lands, it comes down to the ground after moving through the air **2** when a pilot lands a plane, it comes down to the ground after moving through the air
search	[sɜrtʃ]	to look carefully in a place for something; search someone's luggage
take off		when an aircraft takes off, it leaves the ground and starts to fly

IPA Symbols

Vowel	Sounds
ɑ	calm, ah
æ	act, mass
ɑɪ	dive, cry
ɑʊ	out, down
ɛ	met, lend, pen
eɪ	say, weight
ɪ	fit, win
i	feed, me
ɒ	lot, spot
oʊ	note, coat
ɔ	claw, more
ɔɪ	boy, joint
ʊ	could, stood
u	you, use
ʌ	fund, must
ə	the first vowel in about
i	second vowel in very
u	second vowel in actual

Consonant	Sounds
b	bed, rub
d	done, red
f	fit, if
g	good, dog
h	hat, horse
k	king, pick
l	lip, bill
ᵊl	handle, panel
m	mat, ram
n	not, tin
ᵊn	hidden, written
p	pay, lip
r	run, read
s	soon, bus
t	talk, bet
v	van, love
w	win, wool
x	loch
y	yellow, you
z	zoo, buzz
ʃ	ship, wish
ʒ	measure, leisure
ŋ	sing, working
tʃ	cheap, witch
θ	thin, myth
ð	then, bathe
dʒ	joy, bridge

Notes

Stress is shown by a line below the stressed syllable. For example, in the word *accomplish*, /əkɒmplɪʃ/, the second syllable is stressed.

air travel

NOUNS

aeroplane (BRIT)   *see* **airplane**

aircraft [ɛərkræft]   a plane or a helicopter
(PL) **aircraft**

airline [ɛərlaɪn]   a company that carries people or goods in planes

airplane [ɛərpleɪn]   a plane: a vehicle with wings and engines that can fly (*In British English, use* **aeroplane**)

airport [ɛərpɔrt]   a place where planes come and go, with buildings and services for passengers

air-traffic controller [ɛər træfɪk kəntroʊlər]   someone whose job is to organize where planes go

aisle [aɪl]   the long narrow passage between the rows of seats on a plane

arrivals [əraɪvəlz]   the part of an airport where passengers get off planes; *wait in arrivals*

bag [bæg]   a container made of plastic, leather, or cloth used for carrying things

baggage [bægɪdʒ]   same as **luggage**

baggage claim [bægɪdʒ kleɪm]   the place where you collect your baggage after your flight; *go to baggage claim* (*In British English, use* **baggage reclaim**)

baggage reclaim (BRIT)   *see* **baggage claim**

boarding card (BRIT)   *see* **boarding pass**

boarding pass [bɔrdɪŋ pæs]   a ticket that you must show when you get on a plane (*In British English, use* **boarding card**)

bureau de change (BRIT)   *see* **currency exchange**

EXAMPLES

Most low-cost airlines do not serve food.

We checked in early and walked around the airport.

Please do not leave bags in the aisle.

The police said the incident occurred last weekend in arrivals at Terminal 3.

business class	[bɪznɪs klæs]	seats that are cheaper than first class but more expensive than economy class; *in business class*
cabin	[kæbɪn]	the part of a plane where people sit
cabin crew	[kæbɪn kru]	the people whose job is to look after passengers on a plane; *The cabin crew were very nice.*
captain	[kæptɪn]	the person who is in charge of a plane
cargo hold	[kɑrgoʊ hoʊld]	the place in a plane where goods or luggage are stored (*In British English, use* **hold**)
car hire (BRIT)		*see* **car rental**
car rental	[kɑr rɛntᵊl]	paying money to borrow a car, for example when you are going on holiday (*In British English, use* **car hire**)
carry-on luggage	[kæri ɒn lʌgɪdʒ]	the bags that you take with you in the cabin, rather than your checked bags; *lots of carry-on luggage* (*In British English, use* **hand luggage**)
checked luggage	[tʃɛkt lʌgɪdʒ]	the bags that you have stored in the cargo hold of the aircraft, rather than your carry-on bags
check-in	[tʃɛk ɪn]	the desk that you go to in an airport to say that you have arrived; *Go to check-in at once.*
connection	[kənɛkʃᵊn]	a plane that leaves after another one arrives and allows you to continue your journey by changing from one to the other

EXAMPLES

We had seats in business class on the flight from London to Los Angeles.

Ask cabin crew or see leaflet for details.

This piece of luggage will have to go in the cargo hold.

The price includes flights, car rental, and accommodation.

How many pieces of carry-on luggage can I take on the plane?

The airline will transport a bicycle for free if it's counted as one of your pieces of checked luggage.

We got to the airport and went straight to check-in.

My flight was late and I missed my connection.

customs	[kʌstəmz]	the place at an airport where you have to show certain goods that you have bought in another country, and, if necessary, pay tax on them
customs duty	[kʌstəmz duti]	tax that you pay when bringing certain goods into a country from another country
currency exchange	[kɜrənsi ɪkstʃeɪndʒ]	an office where you can buy and sell different currencies (*In British English, use* **bureau de change**)
departures	[dɪpɑrtʃərz]	the part of an airport where you wait before you get on a plane; *He was standing in departures.*
duration	[dʊəreɪʃ°n]	the length of time that something lasts
economy class	[ɪkɒnəmi klæs]	the cheapest seats on a plane; *in economy (class)*
emergency exit	[ɪmɜrdʒ°nsi ɛgzɪt, ɛksɪt]	a place where you leave a plane if there is an emergency, such as a crash or a fire
entrance	[ɛntrəns]	the door or gate where you go into a place
escalator	[ɛskəleɪtər]	a set of moving stairs
e-ticket	[i tɪkɪt]	short for "electronic ticket": a ticket that is stored on a computer rather than on paper
exit	[ɛgzɪt, ɛksɪt]	the door that you use to leave a public building
fare	[fɛər]	the money that you pay for a journey in a plane
first class	[fɜrst klæs]	the best and most expensive seats on a plane; *in first class*
flight	[flaɪt]	a trip in an aircraft

EXAMPLES

We walked through customs.

You must pay customs duty on these goods.

Please go to departures.

You must keep your mobile phone switched off for the duration of the flight.

Margarita sat in economy class on the flight to Bucharest.

Take the escalator to the second floor.

Our flight was delayed by three hours because of fog.

There were no direct flights to San Francisco, so we had to change planes in Chicago.

flight attendant	[flaɪt ətɛndənt]	a person whose job it is to look after passengers on a plane and to give them food and drink
flight number	[flaɪt nʌmbər]	the unique number that is given to each flight
gate	[geɪt]	a place where you leave an airport and get on a plane
hand luggage (BRIT)		*see* **carry-on luggage**
helicopter	[hɛlikɒptər]	an aircraft with long blades on top that go around very fast
hold (BRIT)		*see* **cargo hold**
ID card	[aɪ di kɑrd]	a card with your name, date of birth, and photograph on it that shows who you are
information desk	[ɪnfərmeɪʃən dɛsk]	a place where you can ask for information about your flight
jet lag	[dʒɛt læg]	the feeling of being very tired when you fly between two places where the time is different; *suffering from jet lag*
jumbo jet	[dʒʌmbou dʒɛt]	a large plane that can carry several hundred passengers
landing	[lændɪŋ]	the act of bringing a plane back down on to the ground; *a smooth landing*; *a bumpy landing*
layover	[leɪouvər]	a short stay in a place between parts of a journey (*In British English, use* **stopover**)
luggage	[lʌgɪdʒ]	the bags that you take with you when you travel; *lots of luggage*
luggage label	[lʌgɪdʒ leɪbəl]	a piece of plastic with your name, address, and phone number that you attach to your luggage in case it gets lost

EXAMPLES

I asked the flight attendant for a glass of water.

He is on flight number 776 from Beijing.

I had terrible jet lag for three days after my vacation.

We made a layover in Bangkok to break up the journey between London and Brisbane.

How many pieces of luggage are you checking in?

Why does Ingrid need so much luggage for a short stay?

parachute	[pærəʃut]	a large piece of thin material that a person attaches to their body when they jump from an aircraft to help them float safely to the ground
passenger	[pæsɪndʒər]	a person who is traveling in a plane, but who is not flying it or working on it
passport	[pæspɔrt]	an official document that you have to show when you enter or leave a country
pilot	[paɪlət]	a person who controls an aircraft
plane	[pleɪn]	a vehicle with wings and engines that can fly
plane crash	[pleɪn kræʃ]	an accident in which a plane hits another plane or hits the ground
propeller	[prəpɛlər]	a part of an aircraft that turns around very fast and makes the aircraft move
reservation	[rɛzərveɪʃ°n]	a seat on a flight that an airline keeps ready for you
runway	[rʌnweɪ]	a long road that a plane travels on before it starts flying
seat	[sit]	something that you can sit on
seat belt	[sit bɛlt]	a long belt that you fasten around your body to keep you safe when you are on a plane
security	[sɪkyʊərɪti]	**1** everything that is done to protect a place; *Security has been increased.* **2** the place in an airport where your bags are checked; *go through security*
stopover *(BRIT)*		*see* **layover**
suitcase	[sutkeɪs]	a case for carrying your clothes when you are traveling
take-off	[teɪk ɔf]	the beginning of a flight, when a plane leaves the ground; *a smooth take-off*

EXAMPLES

Could I see your passport and boarding pass, please?

You are in seat 35C.

Please fasten your seat belts during take-off and landing.

World leaders have announced plans to tighten up airline security.

What time is take-off?

terminal	[tɜrmɪnᵊl]	a place where people begin or end a flight
ticket	[tɪkɪt]	a small piece of paper that shows that you have paid for a flight
timetable	[taɪmteɪbᵊl]	a list of the times when planes arrive and depart
tourist	[tʊərɪst]	a person who is visiting a place on vacation
travel agency	[trævᵊl eɪdʒənsi]	a business that sells vacations
traveler	[trævələr]	**1** a person who is on a trip **2** a person who travels a lot (*In British English, use* **traveller**)
traveller (*BRIT*)		*see* **traveler**
tray table	[treɪ teɪbᵊl]	a small table that is attached to the back of the seat in front of you on a plane
trip	[trɪp]	a journey that you make to a particular place and back again
trolley	[trɒli]	a large container with wheels that you use at an airport for moving heavy luggage
window	[wɪndoʊ]	a space in the side of a plane that you can see through
wing	[wɪŋ]	one of the long flat parts at the side of a plane that support it while it is flying

VERBS

board	[bɔrd]	to get into a plane to travel somewhere
book	[bʊk]	to arrange and pay for a flight; *book a ticket*; *book a flight*
cancel	[kænsᵊl]	to say that something that has been planned will not happen; *cancel a flight*

EXAMPLES

We left the airport terminal and looked for the taxi rank.
Terminal 1 will handle Air Canada's domestic flights.
I'm taking a short trip to France.
I pushed my luggage trolley toward the "Nothing to Declare" sign.
Can I have a window seat, please?
I boarded the plane to Dubai.
British Airways canceled several flights because of the bad weather.

check in		to tell the person at an airport desk that you have arrived
check something in		to give your luggage to the person at an airport desk; *check in luggage*
delay	[dɪleɪ]	to make something later than expected; *The flight is delayed.*
depart	[dɪpɑrt]	to leave
fly	[flaɪ]	**1** to travel somewhere in an aircraft **2** when a pilot flies a plane, they make it move through the air
hijack	[haɪdʒæk]	to illegally take control of a plane
land	[lænd]	**1** when a plane lands, it comes down to the ground after moving through the air **2** when a pilot lands a plane, it comes down to the ground after moving through the air
search	[sɜrtʃ]	to look carefully in a place for something; *search someone's luggage*
take off		when an aircraft takes off, it leaves the ground and starts to fly

ADJECTIVES

airsick	[ɛərsɪk]	feeling sick during a flight because of the movement of the plane
direct	[dɪrɛkt, daɪ-]	used to describe a flight that goes from one place to another without stopping
domestic	[dəmɛstɪk]	used to describe flights between airports in the same country
duty-free	[dutifri]	duty-free goods are sold at airports or on planes at a cheaper price than usual because they are not taxed; *duty-free perfume*

EXAMPLES

Flight BA201 will depart from gate 21 in 30 minutes.

We are flying over London.

The Boeing 737 was hijacked after taking off from London yesterday.

The plane took off twenty minutes late.

international	[ɪntərnæʃənᵊl]	used to describe flights between airports in different countries
on time	[ɒn taɪm]	not late or early; at the expected time; *The flight is on time.*

ADVERBS

on board	[ɒn bɔrd]	on an aircraft
on time	[ɒn taɪm]	not late or early; at the expected time; *arrive on time*

PHRASE

nothing to declare	used to describe the area of customs that you walk through if you do not have to pay customs duty on any goods

EXAMPLE
The plane landed on time, at eleven thirty.

the animal world

ANIMALS

animal [ænɪməl] **1** a creature such as a dog or a cat, but not a bird, fish, insect, or human
2 any living creature, including a human

ant [ænt] a small crawling insect that lives in large groups

bat [bæt] a small animal, like a mouse with wings, that sleeps upside down during the day and comes out to fly at night

bear [bɛər] a large, strong wild animal with thick fur and sharp claws

bee [bi] a yellow and black striped flying insect that makes a sweet food (called honey) and can sting you

bird [bɜrd] an animal with feathers and wings

bull [bʊl] **1** a male animal of the cow family
2 a male animal of some other animal families, such as elephants and whales

butterfly [bʌtərflaɪ] an insect with large colored wings

calf [kæf] a young cow
  (PL) **calves** [kævz]

camel [kæməl] an animal with one or two large lumps on its back

cat [kæt] a small animal covered with fur, that people in some countries keep as a pet

caterpillar [kætərpɪlər] a small animal with a long body, that develops into a butterfly

cockroach [kɒkroʊtʃ] a large brown insect that likes to live in places where food is kept

cod [kɒd] a large fish with white flesh

cow [kaʊ] a large female animal that is kept on farms for its milk

crab [kræb] a sea animal with a shell and ten legs. Crabs usually move sideways.

crocodile	[krɒkədaɪl]	a large animal with a long body, a long mouth, and sharp teeth. Crocodiles live in rivers in hot countries.
deer (PL) **deer**	[dɪər]	a large wild animal that eats grass and leaves. Male deer usually have antlers (= large horns that look like branches).
dog	[dɔg]	an animal that people in some countries keep as a pet, or use to guard buildings
donkey	[dɒŋki]	an animal like a small horse with long ears
duck	[dʌk]	a bird that lives near water
eagle	[igᵊl]	a large bird that eats small animals
eel	[il]	a long, thin fish that looks like a snake
elephant	[ɛlɪfənt]	a very large grey animal with a long nose called a trunk
fish (PL) **fish**	[fɪʃ]	an animal that lives and swims in water, that people eat as food
fly	[flaɪ]	a small insect with two wings
fox	[fɒks]	a wild animal that looks like a dog, and has red fur and a thick tail
frog	[frɔg]	a small animal with smooth skin, big eyes, and long back legs that it uses for jumping. Frogs live in or near water.
giraffe	[dʒɪræf]	a large African animal with a very long neck, long legs, and dark spots on its body
goat	[goʊt]	an animal that has horns, and hairs on its chin that look like a beard
goose (PL) **geese**	[gus] [gis]	a large bird like a duck with a long neck
grasshopper	[græshɒpər]	an insect that jumps high into the air and makes a sound with its long back legs
hedgehog	[hɛdʒhɒg]	a small brown animal with sharp points covering its back
hen	[hɛn]	a female chicken

EXAMPLE
Where did you catch the fish?

hippopotamus (PL) **hippopotamuses, hippopotami**	[hɪpəpɒtəməs] [hɪpəpɒtəmaɪ]	a very large animal with short legs and thick skin, that lives in and near rivers
horse	[hɔrs]	a large animal that people can ride
insect	[ɪnsɛkt]	a very small animal that has six legs. Most insects have wings.
jellyfish (PL) **jellyfish**	[dʒɛlifɪʃ]	a sea animal that has a clear soft body and that can sting you
kangaroo	[kæŋgəru]	a large Australian animal. A female kangaroo carries her baby in a pocket (called a pouch) on her stomach.
kitten	[kɪtᵊn]	a very young cat
ladybird	[leɪdibɜrd]	a small round insect that is red or yellow with black spots
lamb	[læm]	a young sheep
lion	[laɪən]	a large wild cat that lives in Africa. Lions have yellow fur, and male lions have manes (= long hair on their head and neck).
lizard	[lɪzərd]	a small animal with a long tail and rough skin
lobster	[lɒbstər]	a sea animal that has a hard shell and eight legs
mammal	[mæmᵊl]	an animal that feeds its babies with milk
mole	[moʊl]	a small animal with black fur, that lives under the ground
monkey	[mʌŋki]	an animal that has a long tail and can climb trees
mosquito	[məskitoʊ]	a small flying insect that bites people and animals
moth	[mɔθ]	an insect that has large wings and is attracted by lights at night
mouse (PL) **mice**	[maʊs] [maɪs]	a small animal with a long tail
octopus (PL) **octopuses, octopi**	[ɒktəpəs] [ɒktəpəs]	a soft sea animal with eight long arms

ostrich	[ɔstrɪtʃ]	a very large bird that cannot fly
owl	[aʊl]	a bird with large eyes that is active at night
oyster	[ɔɪstər]	a large flat shellfish that people often eat raw
panda	[pændə]	a large animal from China with black and white fur
parrot	[pærət]	a tropical bird with a curved beak and very bright feathers
penguin	[pɛŋgwɪn]	a black and white bird that lives in very cold places, that can swim but cannot fly
pet	[pɛt]	an animal that you keep in your home
pig	[pɪg]	a farm animal with a fat body and short legs, that is kept for its meat
pony	[poʊni]	a small or young horse
puppy	[pʌpi]	a young dog
rabbit	[ræbɪt]	a small animal that has long ears and lives in a hole in the ground
rat	[ræt]	an animal that has a long tail and looks like a large mouse
rhinoceros (PL) **rhinoceroses, rhinoceros, rhinoceri**	[raɪnɒsərəs] [raɪnɒsəraɪ]	a large animal from Asia or Africa with a horn on its nose
salmon (PL) **salmon**	[sæmən]	a large fish with silver skin and pink flesh
seagull	[sigʌl]	a common type of bird with white or grey feathers, that lives near the sea
seal	[sil]	a large animal with a rounded body and short fur, that eats fish and lives near the sea
shark	[ʃɑrk]	a very large fish that often has very sharp teeth and may attack people
shellfish (PL) **shellfish**	[ʃɛlfɪʃ]	a small sea creature with a shell

EXAMPLES
We don't have any pets.

snail [sneɪl] a small animal with a long soft body, no legs, and a round shell on its back

snake [sneɪk] a long, thin animal with no legs, that slides along the ground

species [spiʃiz] a related group of plants or animals;
(PL) **species** *a species of fish*; *an endangered species*

spider [spaɪdər] a small animal with eight legs

squid [skwɪd] a sea animal that has a long soft body and many soft arms (called tentacles)

squirrel [skwɜrəl] a small animal with a long thick tail, that lives mainly in trees

stag [stæg] an adult male deer
(PL) **stag, stags**

swan [swɒn] a large white bird with a very long neck, that lives on rivers and lakes

tadpole [tædpoʊl] a small water animal that looks like a black fish, and that develops into a frog or a toad

tiger [taɪgər] a large wild animal of the cat family. Tigers are orange with black stripes.

toad [toʊd] a small brown or green animal with long legs, that lives in water

tortoise [tɔrtəs] an animal with a shell on its back, that moves very slowly

turkey [tɜrki] a large bird that is kept on a farm for its meat

wasp [wɒsp] an insect with wings, and yellow and black stripes across its body. Wasps can sting people.

whale [weɪl] a very large mammal that lives in the sea

wolf [wʊlf] a wild animal that looks like a large dog
(PL) **wolves** [wʊlvz]

worm [wɜrm] a small animal with a long, thin body, no bones and no legs

zebra [zibrə] a wild horse with black and white stripes, that lives in Africa

PARTS OF ANIMALS

antenna	[æntɛnə]	one of the two long, thin parts attached to
(PL) **antennae,**	[æntɛnaɪ]	the head of an insect, that it uses to feel
antennas		things with
antler	[æntlər]	one of the two horns that are shaped like branches on the head of a male deer
beak	[bik]	the hard, pointed part of a bird's mouth
claw	[klɔ]	the thin, hard, pointed part at the end of the foot of a bird or an animal
coat	[koʊt]	an animal's fur or hair
feather	[fɛðər]	one of the light soft things that cover a bird's body
fur	[fɜr]	the thick hair that grows on the bodies of many animals
hair	[hɛər]	the short threads that grow on the bodies of many animals
hoof	[hʊf, huf]	one of the hard parts of the feet of horses,
(PL) **hooves**	[hʊvz, huvz]	cows and some other animals
horn	[hɔrn]	one of the hard pointed things that grow from an animal's head
mane	[meɪn]	the long, thick hair that grows from the neck of some animals
paw	[pɔ]	the foot of an animal such as a cat, a dog, or a bear
shell	[ʃɛl]	the hard part that covers the back of an animal such as a snail or a tortoise, and protects it
snout	[snaʊt]	the long nose of an animal such as a pig
tail	[teɪl]	the long thin part at the end of an animal's body
trunk	[trʌŋk]	the long nose of an elephant

EXAMPLES

Cat hair makes me sneeze.
He heard the sound of horses' hooves behind him.
The kitten was black, with white paws.

tusk	[tʌsk]	a very long, curved, pointed tooth that grows beside the mouth of an elephant
wing	[wɪŋ]	one of the two parts of the body of a bird or an insect, that it uses for flying

PLACES WHERE ANIMALS ARE FOUND

aquarium	[əkwɛ̱əriəm]	**1** a building where fish and sea animals are kept and people can go to look at them **2** a glass box filled with water, in which people keep fish as pets
cage	[ke̱ɪdʒ]	a structure made of metal bars where you keep birds or animals
field	[fi̱ld]	a piece of land where animals are kept
kennel	[kɛ̱nəl]	a small house for a dog
nest	[nɛ̱st]	the place where a bird, a small animal, or an insect keeps its eggs or its babies; *build a nest*
web	[wɛ̱b]	the thin net that a spider makes in order to catch insects
zoo	[zu̱]	a park where animals are kept and people can go to look at them

OTHER ANIMAL NOUNS

bite	[ba̱ɪt]	a painful mark on your body where an animal, a snake, or an insect has bitten you
collar	[kɒ̱lər]	a band of leather or plastic that you can put around the neck of a dog or a cat
egg	[ɛg]	a round object that contains a baby bird, insect, snake, or fish; *lay an egg*
sting	[stɪŋ]	a painful mark on your body where an insect has stung you
trap	[træp]	a piece of equipment for catching animals

EXAMPLES

A canary was singing in a cage.
How do you treat a wasp sting?
The rabbit was caught in a trap.

VERBS

NOISES ANIMALS MAKE

baa	[ba]	when a sheep baas, it makes its typical sound
bark	[bark]	when a dog barks, it makes its typical short, loud sound
buzz	[bʌz]	when a bee or another insect buzzes, it makes its typical rough continuous sound
growl	[graʊl]	when a dog or another animal growls, it makes a low sound in its throat, usually because it is angry
hiss	[hɪs]	when an animal such as a snake or a cat hisses, it makes a sound like a long "s"
meow	[miaʊ]	when a cat meows, it makes its typical sound (*In British English, use* **miaow**)
miaow (*BRIT*)		*see* **meow**
moo	[mu]	when a cow moos, it makes its typical long, low sound
neigh	[neɪ]	when a horse neighs, it makes its typical loud sound
purr	[pɜr]	when a cat purrs, it makes a low sound with its throat because it is happy
quack	[kwæk]	when a duck quacks, it makes its typical sound
roar	[rɔr]	when a lion roars, it makes its typical loud sound
snort	[snɔrt]	when an animal snorts, it breathes air noisily out through its nose

WAYS IN WHICH ANIMALS MOVE

crawl	[krɔl]	when an insect or animal crawls somewhere, it moves there very slowly

EXAMPLES

Our dog always barks at the postman.
Bees buzzed in the flowers.
The cat sat on the sofa, purring happily.

fly	[flaɪ]	when a bird or an insect flies, it moves through the air
gallop	[gæləp]	when a horse gallops, it runs very fast so that all four legs are off the ground at the same time
hop	[hɒp]	when a bird or an animal hops, it moves by jumping on both of its feet or all four of its feet together
roam	[roʊm]	when an animal roams, it moves freely around an area
slither	[slɪðər]	when a snake slithers, it moves along the ground, sliding from side to side
swim	[swɪm]	when a fish swims, it moves through water
trot	[trɒt]	when an animal such as a horse trots, it moves fairly fast, taking quick small steps
wag	[wæg]	when a dog wags its tail, it moves it from side to side

OTHER ANIMAL VERBS

bite	[baɪt]	if a snake or an insect bites you, it makes a mark or a hole in your skin with a sharp part of its body
feed	[fid]	**1** when you feed an animal, you give it food to eat **2** when an animal feeds, it eats or drinks something
graze	[greɪz]	when an animal grazes, it eats the grass or other plants that are growing in a particular place
hibernate	[haɪbərneɪt]	when an animal hibernates, it spends the winter in a state like a deep sleep
hunt	[hʌnt]	to chase and kill wild animals for food or as a sport

EXAMPLES
The bird flew away as I came near.
The horse trotted around the field.

| **sting** | [stɪŋ] | if an insect stings you, a pointed part of it is pushed into your skin so that you feel a sharp pain |

ADJECTIVES

stray	[streɪ]	far away from home, or not having a home; *a stray dog*
tame	[teɪm]	not afraid of humans
wild	[waɪld]	living in nature, and not taken care of by people; *a wild animal*

EXAMPLES
The deer never became tame; they ran away if you went near them.

art and photography

NOUNS

art [ɑrt]
1 pictures or objects that are created for people to look at; *an art gallery*
2 the activity of creating pictures or objects for people to look at; *an art class*

art gallery [ɑrt gæləri]
a place where people go to look at art

artist [ɑrtɪst]
someone who draws, paints, or creates works of art

background [bækgraʊnd]
the part of a picture that is behind the main things or people in it

brush [brʌʃ]
an object with a lot of bristles or hairs attached to it, that you use for painting

camera [kæmrə]
a piece of equipment for taking photographs or making films

canvas [kænvəs]
a piece of strong, heavy material that you paint on

clay [kleɪ]
a type of earth that is used for making things such as pots and bricks; *a clay pot*

collage [kəlɑʒ]
a picture that you make by sticking pieces of paper or cloth on a surface

design [dɪzaɪn]
1 the process of planning and drawing things; *studying design*
2 a drawing that shows how something should be built or made; *drawing a design*
3 a pattern of lines or shapes that is used for decorating something; *a floral design*

designer [dɪzaɪnər]
a person whose job is to design things; *a fashion designer*

digital camera [dɪdʒɪtᵊl kæmrə]
a camera that produces digital pictures that can be stored on a computer

easel [izᵊl]
a stand that supports a picture while an artist is working on it

---

EXAMPLES

He studied art and design.
I looked at the man in the background of the photograph.
My brother has a talent for design.
The tablecloths come in three different designs.

exhibition	[ɛksɪbɪʃ°n]	a public event where you can see art or interesting objects
foreground	[fɔrgraʊnd]	the part of a picture that seems nearest to you
frame	[freɪm]	the wood, metal, or plastic border around a picture or photograph
graphics	[græfɪks]	drawings, pictures, or symbols, especially when they are produced by a computer
illustration	[ɪləstreɪʃ°n]	a picture, design, or diagram in a book
landscape	[lændskeɪp]	a painting that shows a scene in the countryside
logo	[loʊgoʊ]	a special design that an organization puts on all its products; *a corporate logo*
oil paint	[ɔɪl peɪnt]	a thick paint that artists use
oil painting	[ɔɪl peɪntɪŋ]	a picture that has been painted using oil paints
paint	[peɪnt]	a colored liquid that you put onto a surface with a brush
painter	[peɪntər]	an artist who paints pictures
painting	[peɪntɪŋ]	**1** a picture that someone has painted; *a famous painting* **2** the activity of painting pictures; *I enjoy painting.*
pattern	[pætərn]	an arrangement of lines or shapes that form a design
photograph	[foʊtəgræf]	a picture that you take with a camera; *take a photograph*
photographer	[fətɒgrəfər]	someone who takes photographs
photography	[fətɒgrəfi]	the skill or process of producing photographs

---

EXAMPLES

The game's graphics are very good, so you can see things clearly.
He is very good at painting flowers.
The carpet had a pattern of light and dark stripes.

picture	[pɪktʃər]	1 a drawing or painting; *paint a picture* 2 a photograph; *take a picture*
portrait	[pɔrtrɪt, -treɪt]	a painting, drawing, or photograph of a particular person
poster	[poustər]	a large picture that you stick on a wall
pottery	[pɒtəri]	the activity of making pots, dishes, and other objects from clay; *pottery classes*
primary color	[praɪmɛri kʌlər, -məri]	one of the three colors (red, yellow, and blue) that you can mix together to produce other colors (*In British English, use* **primary colour**)
primary colour (*BRIT*)		*see* **primary color**
sculptor	[skʌlptər]	an artist who makes works of art out of stone, metal, or wood
sculpture	[skʌlptʃər]	1 a piece of art that is made into a shape from a material like stone or wood 2 the art of creating sculptures from materials like stone or wood
sketch	[skɛtʃ]	a drawing that you do quickly, without a lot of details
statue	[stætʃu]	a large model of a person or an animal, made of stone or metal
still life	[stɪl laɪf]	1 a painting or drawing of an arrangement of objects such as flowers or fruit 2 the type of painting or drawing that shows an arrangement of objects such as flowers or fruit
watercolor	[wɔtərkʌlər]	1 a coloured paint that is mixed with water and used for painting pictures 2 a picture that has been painted with watercolors (*In British English, use* **watercolour**)
watercolour (*BRIT*)		*see* **watercolor**

EXAMPLES

She drew a picture with a piece of colored chalk.
Paul did a quick sketch in pencil.

VERBS

design	[dɪzaɪn]	to make a detailed plan or drawing that shows how something should be made
draw	[drɔ]	to use a pencil or a pen to make a picture
frame	[freɪm]	to put a picture or photograph in a frame; *a framed photograph*
paint	[peɪnt]	to produce a picture using paint
sketch	[skɛtʃ]	to make a quick drawing, without a lot of details

EXAMPLES

Monet painted hundreds of pictures of water lilies.

bikes

NOUNS

back light (BRIT)		see **tail light**
bell	[bɛl]	a metal object on a bicycle that makes a ringing sound
bicycle	[baɪsɪkəl]	a vehicle with two wheels that you ride by sitting on it and using your legs to make the wheels turn
bike	[baɪk]	**1** a bicycle **2** a motorcycle
bike lane	[baɪk leɪn]	a section of a road that is marked for cyclists to use; *stay in the bike lane* (In British English, use **cycle lane**)
bike path	[baɪk pæθ]	a special path that cyclists can use separately from cars and other vehicles; *ride on the bike path* (In British English, use **cycle path**)
brake	[breɪk]	the part of a bicycle that makes it go more slowly or stop; *put the brakes on*
chain	[tʃeɪn]	a line of connected metal rings that turn the wheels of a bicycle
crossbar	[krɔsbɑr]	the horizontal bar between the handlebars and the saddle of a bicycle
cycle lane (BRIT)		see **bike lane**
cycle path (BRIT)		see **bike path**
cycling	[saɪklɪŋ]	the activity of riding a bicycle
cyclist	[saɪklɪst]	someone who rides a bicycle
fall	[fɔl]	an occasion when you move quickly to the ground by accident; *have a bad fall*
fender	[fɛndər]	a curved piece of metal or plastic above a bicycle wheel that protects the cyclist from dirt or water see **mudguard**

EXAMPLES

"How did you get there?" – "I went by bike."
"How did you get here?" – "I came by bike."
We rode along the bike path through the forest.

flat	[flæt]	a small leak in a tire that has been made by a sharp object; *have a flat*; *fix a flat* (*In British English, use* **puncture**)
flat tire	[flæt taɪər]	a tire that has no air in it (*In British English, use* **flat tyre**)
flat tire repair kit	[flæt taɪər rɪpɛər kɪt]	the tools and materials you need to repair a flat tire (*In British English, use* **puncture repair kit**)
flat tyre (*BRIT*)		*see* **flat tire**
frame	[freɪm]	the metal part of a bicycle between the wheels, handlebars, and saddle
front light (*BRIT*)		*see* **head light**
gears	[gɪərz]	the system of wheels with teeth that are driven by a chain on a bicycle, making it easier or more difficult to pedal
handlebars	[hændəlbɑrz]	a curved metal bar with handles at each end that you use to steer a bicycle
head light	[hɛd laɪt]	a white light on the front of a bicycle (*In British English, use* **front light**)
helmet	[hɛlmɪt]	a hat made of a hard material, that you wear to protect your head
hub	[hʌb]	the center of a wheel
inner tube	[ɪnər tub]	a rubber tube containing air that is inside a tire; *a spare inner tube*
motorcycle	[moʊtərsaɪkəl]	a large heavy bicycle with an engine
mountain bike	[maʊntən baɪk]	a type of bicycle with a strong frame and thick tires
mudguard	[mʌdgɑrd]	a curved piece of metal or plastic above a bicycle wheel that protects the cyclist from dirt or water *see* **fender**
padlock	[pædlɒk]	a metal lock that you use for fastening two things together

EXAMPLES
On hills, you use low gears.
Cyclists should always wear helmets.

pedal	[pɛdᵊl]	one of the two parts that you push with your feet to make a bicycle move
pump	[pʌmp]	a machine that you use to fill a tire with air; *a bicycle pump*
puncture (BRIT)		see **flat**
puncture repair kit (BRIT)		see **flat tire repair kit**
reflector	[rɪflɛktər]	a small piece of special plastic on the front or back of a bicycle that becomes bright when light shines on it
ride	[raɪd]	a journey on a bicycle; *go for a ride*
saddle	[sædᵊl]	a seat on a bicycle or a motorcycle
speed	[spid]	**1** how fast something moves or is done; *increase/decrease your speed* **2** very fast movement or travel; *travel at speed*
spoke	[spoʊk]	a bar that connects the outer ring of a wheel to the center
tail light	[teɪl laɪt]	a red light on the back of a bicycle (*In British English, use* **back light**)
tire	[taɪər]	a thick round piece of rubber that fits around the wheels of bicycles (*In British English, use* **tyre**)
tyre (BRIT)		see **tire**
valve	[vælv]	the part of a bicycle pump that controls the flow of air
wheel	[wil]	one of the two large round objects on a bicycle that allow it to move along the ground

[VERBS]

bike	[baɪk]	to ride a bicycle (*In British English, use* **cycle**)

EXAMPLES
My bike's got a flat tire.
I need a new front/back wheel.
Every day he biked to work.

brake	[breɪk]	to make a vehicle go more slowly or stop
change gear		to make the chain of a bicycle move to another gear wheel; *change into first gear*
cycle (*BRIT*)		*see* **bike**
pedal	[pɛdəl]	to push the pedals of a bicycle around with your feet to make it move; *pedal faster/ more slowly*
pump up a tire		to fill a tire with air (*In British English, use* **pump up a tyre**)
pump up a tyre (*BRIT*)		*see* **pump up a tire**
ride	[raɪd]	to sit on a bicycle, control it, and travel on it
signal	[sɪgnəl]	to make a movement that tells other people which way you intend to go; *to signal right/left*
stop	[stɒp]	to slow down and no longer move

ADJECTIVES

rusty	[rʌsti]	covered with rust (= a red-brown substance that can form on metal when it gets wet)
shiny	[ʃaɪni]	bright and reflecting light

EXAMPLES
Belinda braked suddenly.
When you ride a bike, you exercise all your leg muscles.

boats, water, and the coast

NOUNS

anchor	[æŋkər]	a heavy object that you drop into the water from a boat to stop it moving away
bank	[bæŋk]	a raised area of ground along the edge of a river
bay	[beɪ]	a part of a coast where the land goes in and forms a curve
beach	[biːtʃ]	an area of sand or stones next to a lake or the sea; *at the beach*
boat	[boʊt]	a vehicle that people use to travel on water; *a fishing boat*; *a rowing boat*; *a sailing boat*; *a motor boat*
bridge	[brɪdʒ]	a structure that is built over a river so that people or vehicles can cross from one side to the other
cabin	[kæbɪn]	a small room on a boat
canal	[kənæl]	a long narrow river made by people for boats to travel along
canoe	[kənuː]	a small, narrow boat that you move through the water using a paddle
captain	[kæptɪn]	the person who is in charge of a ship
cargo	[kɑrgoʊ]	the things that a ship is carrying
cliff	[klɪf]	a high area of land with a very steep side next to the sea
coast	[koʊst]	the land that is next to the sea or ocean
cruise	[kruːz]	a holiday that you spend on a ship
current	[kɜrənt]	a steady flow of water; *a strong current*

EXAMPLES

The bay is surrounded by steep cliffs.
We walked along the beach.
We went there by boat.
The ship was carrying a cargo of bananas.
We drove along the coast.
James and his wife went on a cruise around the world.
The couple were swept away by a strong current.

deck	[dɛk]	one of the floors of a ship
dock	[dɒk]	an area of water beside land where ships go so that people can get on or off them
ferry	[fɛri]	a boat that regularly takes people or things a short distance across water
fisherman	[fɪʃərmən]	a person who catches fish as a job or for sport
harbor	[hɑrbər]	an area of water next to the land where boats can safely stay (*In British English, use* **habour**)
harbour *(BRIT)*		*see* **habor**
horizon	[həraɪzᵊn]	the line that appears between the sky and the sea; *on the horizon*
island	[aɪlənd]	a piece of land that is completely surrounded by water
jet ski™	[dʒɛt ski]	a small machine like a motorcycle that travels on water
kayak	[kaɪæk]	a covered canoe
lake	[leɪk]	a large area of water with land around it
lifebelt *(BRIT)*		*see* **life preserver**
lifeboat	[laɪfboʊt]	a boat that is used for saving people who are in danger at sea
lifeguard	[laɪfgɑrd]	a person who works at a beach and helps people when they are in danger
life preserver	[laɪf prɪzɜrvər]	a large ring that you can hold onto to stop you from going under water (*In British English, use* **lifebelt**)
lighthouse	[laɪthaʊs]	a tower that is built near or in the sea, with a flashing lamp that warns ships of danger
mouth	[maʊθ]	the place where a river goes into the sea
navy	[neɪvi]	the people who fight for a country at sea

EXAMPLES

We went on a luxury ship with five passenger decks.
The next ferry departs at 7 o'clock.
The fishing boats left the harbor.
A small boat appeared on the horizon.
Her son was in the Navy.

oar	[ɔr]	a long pole with one flat end that you use for rowing a boat
ocean	[oʊʃⁿn]	**1** one of the five very large areas of salt water on the Earth's surface; *the Indian Ocean* **2** same as **sea**; *The ocean was calm.*
paddle	[pædⁿl]	a short pole with two flat ends that you use for rowing a small boat
pebble	[pɛbⁿl]	a small, smooth stone
pond	[pɒnd]	a small area of water
port	[pɔrt]	**1** an area of water next to land where ships arrive and leave. It is larger than a harbor. **2** a town by the sea where ships arrive and leave
quay	[ki]	a long structure built next to water where boats can stop
river	[rɪvər]	a long line of water that flows into the sea
sail	[seɪl]	a large piece of cloth on a boat, that catches the wind and moves the boat along
sailing	[seɪlɪŋ]	the activity or sport of sailing boats; *go sailing*
sailor	[seɪlər]	**1** someone who works on a ship **2** someone who sails a boat for pleasure
sand	[sænd]	a powder made of very small pieces of stone that you find on most beaches
sea	[si]	**1** the large area of salty water that covers the Earth's surface; *The sea was calm.* **2** a large area of salty water that is part of an ocean or is surrounded by land; *the North Sea*
seaside	[sisaɪd]	an area that is close to the sea, especially where people go for their vacations; *at the seaside*

EXAMPLES

We swam in the river.
I live by the sea.
Ayr is a seaside town on the west coast of Scotland.
We spent a day at the seaside.

seaweed	[siwid]	a plant that grows in the sea
shell	[ʃɛl]	the hard part of a small sea creature that you find on beaches
ship	[ʃɪp]	a very large boat that carries people or goods
shore	[ʃɔr]	the land along the edge of the sea or a lake
speedboat	[spidboʊt]	a boat that can go very fast because it has a powerful engine
stream	[strim]	a small narrow river
submarine	[sʌbmərin]	a type of ship that can travel below the surface of the sea
surfboard	[sɜrfbɔrd]	a long narrow board that people use for surfing
swimmer	[swɪmər]	**1** someone who swims, especially for sport or pleasure; *He's a fast swimmer.* **2** someone who is swimming; *There are swimmers in the lake.*
swimming	[swɪmɪŋ]	the activity of swimming, especially as a sport or for pleasure; *go swimming*
tide	[taɪd]	the change in the level of the sea towards the land and away from the land that happens twice a day; *at low/high tide*
voyage	[vɔɪɪdʒ]	a long trip on a boat
water	[wɔtər]	a clear, thin liquid that has no color or taste. It falls from clouds as rain.
wave	[weɪv]	a higher part of water on the surface of the sea, caused by the wind blowing on the water
yacht	[yɒt]	a large boat with sails or a motor, used for racing or for leisure trips

---

EXAMPLES
We walked along the shore.
I'm going to buy a surfboard and learn to surf.
They began the long voyage down the river.
Waves crashed against the rocks.

VERBS

board	[bɔrd]	to get onto a boat in order to travel somewhere
dive	[daɪv]	1 to jump into water with your arms and your head going in first
		2 to go under the surface of the sea or a lake, using special equipment for breathing
drown	[draʊn]	to die under water because you cannot breathe
float	[floʊt]	to stay on the surface of a liquid, and not sink
launch	[lɔntʃ]	to put a boat into water
navigate	[nævɪgeɪt]	to find the direction that you need to travel in, using a map or the sun, for example
row	[roʊ]	to make a boat move through the water by using oars
sail	[seɪl]	to move over water on a boat
sink	[sɪŋk]	to go below the surface of the water
steer	[stɪər]	to control a boat so that it goes in the direction that you want
surf	[sɜrf]	to ride on big waves using a special board
swim	[swɪm]	to move through water by making movements with your arms and legs

ADJECTIVES

calm	[kɑm]	not moving much; *The sea was calm.*
coastal	[koʊstəl]	in the sea or on the land near the coast

EXAMPLES

We went diving to look at fish.
Garbage floated on the surface of the river.
The Titanic was launched in 1911.
We sailed across the bay.
The boat hit the rocks and began to sink.
Do you like swimming?
Coastal areas were flooded.

marine	[mərin]	relating to the sea or living in the sea; *marine animals*
rough	[rʌf]	with a lot of waves; *The sea was rough.*
sandy	[sændi]	covered with sand
seasick	[sisɪk]	feeling sick on a boat

EXAMPLES
Nha Trang has a beautiful sandy beach.
Do you get seasick?

body

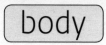

NOUNS

PARTS OF THE BODY

ankle	[æŋkᵊl]	the part of your body where your foot joins your leg
arm	[ɑrm]	one of the two parts of your body between your shoulders and your hands
artery	[ɑrtəri]	one of the tubes in your body that carry blood from your heart to the rest of your body
back	[bæk]	the part of your body from your neck to your waist that is on the opposite side to your chest
blood	[blʌd]	the red liquid that flows inside your body
body	[bɒdi]	all your physical parts
bone	[boʊn]	one of the hard white parts inside your body
bottom	[bɒtəm]	the part of your body that you sit on
brain	[breɪn]	the organ inside your head that controls your body and allows you to think and to feel things
breast	[brɛst]	one of the two soft, round parts on a woman's chest that can produce milk to feed a baby
calf (PL) **calves**	[kæf] [kævz]	the thick part at the back of your leg, between your ankle and your knee
cheek	[tʃik]	one of the two sides of your face below your eyes
chest	[tʃɛst]	the top part of the front of your body
chin	[tʃɪn]	the part of your face below your mouth
ear	[ɪər]	one of the two parts of your body that you hear sounds with
elbow	[ɛlboʊ]	the part in the middle of your arm where it bends
eye	[aɪ]	one of the two parts of your body that you see with

EXAMPLES

"What color are your eyes?" – "I have blue eyes."

eyebrow	[aɪbraʊ]	one of the two lines of hair that grows above your eyes
eyelash	[aɪlæʃ]	one of the hairs that grows on the edges of your eyelids
eyelid	[aɪlɪd]	one of the pieces of skin that covers your eyes when they are closed
face	[feɪs]	the front part of your head
feature	[fitʃər]	any part of your face, such as your eyes, your nose, or your mouth
finger	[fɪŋgər]	one of the long thin parts at the end of each hand
fist	[fɪst]	your hand with your fingers closed tightly together
flesh	[flɛʃ]	the soft part of your body that is between your bones and your skin
foot (PL) **feet**	[fʊt] [fit]	the part of your body that is at the end of your leg, and that you stand on
forehead	[fɔrhɛd, fɔrɪd]	the front part of your head between your eyebrows and your hair
fringe (BRIT)		see **bangs**
hair	[hɛər]	**1** the fine threads that grow on your head; *I have black hair.* **2** the short threads that grow on your body; *He has hair on his chest.*
hand	[hænd]	the part of your body at the end of your arm that you use for holding things
head	[hɛd]	the top part of your body that has your eyes, mouth, and brain in it
heart	[hɑrt]	the part inside your chest that makes the blood move around your body
heel	[hil]	the back part of your foot, just below your ankle

EXAMPLES

Sarah made a gesture with her fist.

The doctor felt my forehead to see if it was hot.

"What color is your hair?" – "I have light brown hair."

Your hair looks nice – have you had it cut?

hip	[hɪp]	one of the two areas or bones at the sides of your body between the tops of your legs and your waist
jaw	[dʒɔ]	the top and bottom bones of your mouth
kidney	[kɪdni]	one of the two organs in your body that remove waste liquid from your blood
knee	[ni]	the part in the middle of your leg where it bends
leg	[lɛg]	one of the long parts of your body that you use for walking and standing
lips	[lɪps]	the two soft outer parts at the edge of your mouth
liver	[lɪvər]	the large organ in your body that cleans your blood
lung	[lʌŋ]	one of the two large organs inside your chest that you use for breathing
mouth	[maʊθ]	the part of your face that you use for eating or speaking
muscle	[mʌsəl]	one of the parts inside your body that connect your bones, and that help you to move
nail	[neɪl]	the thin hard part that grows at the end of each of your fingers and toes
neck	[nɛk]	the part of your body between your head and the rest of your body
nose	[noʊz]	the part of your face above your mouth, that you use for smelling and breathing
organ	[ɔrgən]	a part of your body, for example your brain or your heart, that has a particular purpose
rib	[rɪb]	one of the 12 pairs of curved bones that surround your chest
shoulder	[ʃoʊldər]	one of the two parts of your body between your neck and the tops of your arms

EXAMPLES
She bites her nails.

shin	[ʃɪn]	the front part of your leg between your knee and your ankle
skeleton	[skɛlɪtⁿn]	all the bones in your body
skin	[skɪn]	the substance that covers the outside of your body
spine	[spaɪn]	the row of bones down your back
stomach	[stʌmək]	**1** the organ inside your body where food goes when you eat it; *a full stomach* **2** the front part of your body below your waist; *lie on your stomach*
thigh	[θaɪ]	the top part of your leg, above your knee
throat	[θroʊt]	**1** the back of your mouth and inside your neck, where you swallow **2** the front part of your neck
thumb	[θʌm]	the short thick part on the side of your hand next to your four fingers
toe	[toʊ]	one of the five parts at the end of your foot
tongue	[tʌŋ]	the soft part inside your mouth that moves when you speak or eat
tooth (PL) **teeth**	[tuθ] [tiθ]	one of the hard white objects in your mouth, that you use for biting and eating
vein	[veɪn]	a thin tube in your body that carries blood to your heart
voice	[vɔɪs]	the sound that comes from your mouth when you speak or sing
waist	[weɪst]	the middle part of your body
wrist	[rɪst]	the part between your hand and your arm that bends when you move your hand

DESCRIBING PEOPLE

age	[eɪdʒ]	the number of years that you have lived
bangs	[bæŋz]	hair that is cut so that it hangs over your forehead: *short bangs* (In British English, use **fringe**)
beard	[bɪərd]	the hair that grows on a man's chin and cheeks
complexion	[kəmplɛkʃⁿn]	the natural color of the skin on your face; *a pale complexion*

expression	[ɪksprɛʃən]	the way that your face looks at a particular moment; *a shocked expression*
false teeth	[fɔls tiθ]	artificial teeth that someone wears if they do not have their natural teeth
freckles	[frɛkəlz]	small light-brown spots on someone's skin
fringe (BRIT)		*see* **bangs**
gesture	[dʒɛstʃər]	a movement that you make with a part of your body, especially your hands, to express emotion or information; *make a gesture*
glasses	[glæsɪz]	two pieces of glass or plastic in a frame, that some people wear in front of their eyes to help them to see better; *wear glasses*
hairstyle	[hɛərstaɪl]	the way that your hair is cut or arranged; *a new hairstyle*
height	[haɪt]	your size from your feet to the top of your head; *a man of average height*
measurement	[mɛʒərmənt]	the size around a part of your body, that you need to know when you are buying clothes; *your hip/waist/chest measurement*
mole	[moʊl]	a natural dark spot on someone's skin
moustache (BRIT)		*see* **mustache**
mustache	[mʌstæʃ]	the hair that grows between a man's nose and mouth (*In British English, use* **moustache**)
pimple	[pɪmpəl]	a small red lump or mark on someone's skin (*In British English, use* **spot**)
scar	[skɑr]	a mark that is left on someone's skin after a wound gets better
size	[saɪz]	how big or small something is
smile	[smaɪl]	an expression on your face when you curve up the corners of your mouth because you are happy or you think that something is funny; *give a smile*

EXAMPLES

He has short red hair and freckles.
"What size are you?" – "Size ten."
He was smiling.

spot *(BRIT)*		*see* **pimple**
tears	[tɪərz]	drops of liquid that come from your eyes when you cry
weight	[weɪt]	how heavy a person or thing is
wrinkles	[rɪŋkəlz]	lines that form on your face when you grow old

VERBS

grow	[groʊ]	to gradually become bigger
look	[lʊk]	to seem to have a particular quality; *He looks sad.*
look like		to have a particular appearance; *What does he look like?*
weigh	[weɪ]	to have a particular weight; *She weighs 140 pounds.*

THINGS PEOPLE DO WITH THEIR BODIES

blow your nose		to force air out of your nose in order to clear it
cry	[kraɪ]	to have tears coming from your eyes, usually because you are sad
fold your arms		to put one arm under the other and hold them over your chest
go red		if you go red, your face becomes red because you feel embarrassed
have your hair cut		if you have your hair cut, someone uses scissors to make your hair shorter

---

EXAMPLES

I've got a big pimple on my nose.
He had tears in his eyes.
She has put on weight.
He has lost weight.
His face was covered with wrinkles.
Sara has grown a lot.
She was crying.

nod	[nɒd]	to move your head up and down to say "yes"
shake hands with someone		to say hello or goodbye to someone by holding their right hand in your right hand and moving it up and down
shake your head		to move your head from side to side to say "no"
shrug	[ʃrʌg]	to move your shoulders up to show that you do not know or care about something
smile	[smaɪl]	to curve up the corners of your mouth because you are happy or you think that something is funny
wave at someone		to hold your hand up and wave it from side to side in order to say hello or goodbye to someone

SENSES

feel	[fiːl]	**1** to experience a particular physical feeling; *I feel cold.* **2** used for describing the way that something seems when you touch it or experience it; *This room feels cold.* **3** to touch something with your hand, so that you can find out what it is like; *feel someone's forehead* **4** to be aware of something because you touch it or it touches you; *feel the wind on your face*
hear	[hɪər]	to become aware of a sound through your ears
see	[siː]	to notice something using your eyes

EXAMPLES

"Are you okay?" I asked. She nodded and smiled.

Claude shook hands with David.

"Did you see Magda?" Anna shook her head.

I can hear music.

It's too dark – I can't see anything.

smell	[smɛl]	**1** to have a quality that you notice by breathing in through your nose; *This flower smells sweet.*
		2 to notice something when you breathe in through your nose; *I can smell smoke.*
taste	[teɪst]	**1** to have a particular flavor that you notice when you are eating or drinking; *This soup tastes delicious.*
		2 to notice the flavor of something that you are eating or drinking; *I can taste salt in this soup.*
touch	[tʌtʃ]	to put your hand onto something

BODY POSITIONS

crouch	[kraʊtʃ]	to bend your legs so that you are close to the ground
kneel	[niːl]	to bend your legs and rest with one or both of your knees on the ground
lie	[laɪ]	to be in a flat position, and not standing or sitting; *lie on the ground*
lie down		to move your body so that it is flat on something, usually when you want to sleep or rest
sit	[sɪt]	to have the lower part of your body resting on a chair and the upper part straight
sit down		to move your body down until you are sitting on something
stand	[stænd]	to be on your feet
stand up		to move so that you are on your feet
stretch	[strɛtʃ]	to put your arms or legs out very straight

EXAMPLES
She reached down and touched her toes.
I crouched down to stroke the dog.
John was lying on the sofa.
Why don't you go upstairs and lie down?
Tom sat down beside me.
He yawned and stretched.

ADJECTIVES

bald	[bɔld]	with no hair, or very little hair, on the top of your head
beautiful	[byutɪfəl]	very attractive to look at
big	[bɪg]	large in size
blind	[blaɪnd]	unable to see
blonde	[blɒnd]	**1** blonde hair is pale or yellow; *She has blonde hair.* **2** someone who is blonde has pale or yellow hair; *She is blonde.*
curly	[kɜrli]	shaped in curves; *curly hair*
dark	[dɑrk]	black or brown; *dark hair*; *dark eyes*
deaf	[dɛf]	unable to hear anything or unable to hear very well
disabled	[dɪseɪbəld]	having an injury or a condition that makes it difficult for you to move around
dyed	[daɪd]	if you have dyed hair, you have changed the color of your hair using a special substance
fair	[fɛər]	fair hair is pale or yellow; fair skin is very pale
fat	[fæt]	weighing too much
handsome	[hænsəm]	having an attractive face
old	[ould]	**1** having lived for many years; not young; *an old man* **2** used for talking or asking about someone's age; *six years old*
overweight	[ouvərweɪt]	weighing more than is healthy or attractive
pretty	[prɪti]	attractive and pleasant
short	[ʃɔrt]	not tall

EXAMPLES

She was a beautiful woman with fine features.

"How old are you?" – "I'm 34."

"What does she look like?" – "She is short, and has curly blonde hair."

skinny	[skɪni]	extremely thin or too thin
slim	[slɪm]	thin in an attractive way
small	[smɔl]	not large in size or amount
straight	[streɪt]	not bending or curving; *straight hair*
tall	[tɔl]	**1** of a greater height than other people; *a tall woman*
		2 used when you are asking or talking about someone's height; *How tall are you?*
thin	[θɪn]	having no extra fat on your body
ugly	[ʌgli]	very unpleasant to look at
young	[yʌŋ]	not having lived for very long

EXAMPLES
A slim young girl was standing in the middle of the room.
He is taller than you.
She is 5 feet 4 inches tall.
He was a tall, thin man with a grey beard.

business

accounts	[əkaunts]	records of all the money that a business receives and spends
ad	[æd]	information that tells you about something such as a product, an event, or a job (*In British English, use* **advert**)
advert (BRIT)		*see* **ad**
advertising	[ædvərtaızıŋ]	the business of creating information that tells people about a product in order to persuade them to buy it; *an advertising campaign*; *an advertising agency*
agent	[eıdʒənt]	someone whose job is to do business for another person or company
AGM	[eı dʒi ɛm]	short for "annual general meeting": a meeting that a company has once a year to discuss the previous year's activities and accounts
boom	[bum]	an increase in the number of things that people are buying; *an economic boom*; *a boom in tourism*
brand	[brænd]	a product that has its own name and is made by a particular company
budget	[bʌdʒıt]	the amount of money that you have available to spend

EXAMPLES
I work in advertising.
You are buying direct, rather than through an agent.
What is your favorite brand of coffee?
Our company does not have a large budget for training.

business	[bɪznɪs]	**1** work that is related to producing, buying and selling things; *do business with someone* **2** used to talk about how many products a company is selling; *Business is good.* **3** an organization that produces and sells goods or that provides a service; *a hairdressing business*
CEO	[si i oʊ]	short for "chief executive officer": the person who is responsible for the management of the whole company
chair	[tʃɛər]	the person in charge of a company or an organization
client	[klaɪənt]	a person who pays someone for a service
commerce	[kɒmɜrs]	the buying and selling of large amounts of things
company	[kʌmpəni]	a business that sells goods or services
competition	[kɒmpɪtɪʃᵊn]	the activities of companies that are trying to sell more products than each other
consumer	[kənsumər]	someone who buys something or uses a service
corporation	[kɔrpəreɪʃᵊn]	a large business or company
costs	[kɔsts]	the amount of money that you must spend in order to run your business
customer	[kʌstəmər]	someone who buys something from a shop or a website; *customer services*; *customer relations*
deal	[dil]	an agreement or an arrangement in business; *do a deal*

EXAMPLES

They worried that German companies would lose business.

My brother runs a thriving furniture business.

The government is not doing enough to help small and medium-sized businesses.

A lawyer and his client were sitting at the next table.

The company owes money to more than sixty banks.

They faced competition from new online companies.

We need to cut costs.

The supermarket wants to attract new customers.

debt	[dɛt]	**1** money that you owe to someone; *a $50,000 debt* **2** the state of owing money; *be in debt*
director	[dɪrɛktər, daɪ-]	one of the people who control a company or an organization, and meet regularly to make important decisions
executive	[ɪgzɛkyətɪv]	someone who has an important job at a company
firm	[fɜrm]	same as **company**
growth	[groʊθ]	increase in profits or sales
management	[mænɪdʒmənt]	**1** the control of a business **2** the people who control a business
manager	[mænɪdʒər]	someone who runs a business or part of a business
market	[mɑrkɪt]	the people who want to buy a particular product
market research	[mɑrkɪt rɪsɜrtʃ]	the business activity of finding out about what people want, need, and buy
marketing	[mɑrkɪtɪŋ]	the business of deciding how to sell a product, for example what price it is, where it is sold, and how it is advertised
meeting	[mitɪŋ]	an event in which a group of people come together to discuss things or make decisions
PR	[pi ɑr]	short for "public relations": the part of a company's work that is concerned with getting people to like the company
product	[prɒdʌkt]	something that you make or grow in order to sell it

EXAMPLES

They are still paying off their debts.

Many firms were going out of business.

The zoo needed better management rather than more money.

The market for organic wines is growing.

There were meetings between senior management and staff.

This mobile phone is one of our most successful products.

profit	[prɒfɪt]	the amount of money that you gain when you sell something for more than it cost to make it; *make a profit*
promotion	[prəmoʊʃən]	an attempt to make a product successful or popular, especially by advertising
publicity	[pʌblɪsɪti]	information that attracts the public's attention to a person or a product
retail	[riteɪl]	the activity of selling goods directly to the public
sales	[seɪlz]	the quantity of a product that is sold
shareholder	[ʃɛərhoʊldər]	someone who owns shares in a company
stocks and shares	[stɒks ənd ʃɛərz]	the parts of company that people buy in order to invest money in the company
supervisor	[supərvaɪzər]	someone who is in charge of activities or people
trade	[treɪd]	the activity of buying and selling goods
turnover	[tɜrnoʊvər]	the value of the goods or services that are sold by a company during a particular period of time

VERBS

advertise	[ædvərtaɪz]	to tell people about a product or a service in newspapers, on television, on signs, or on the internet
break even		to make enough money to pay for costs, but not enough to make a profit
buy	[baɪ]	to get something by paying money for it
employ	[ɪmplɔɪ]	to pay someone to work for a person or a company

EXAMPLES

The group made a profit of $1.05 million.

Texas has a long history of trade with Mexico.

The company had a turnover of $3.8 million last year.

The airline hopes to break even next year and make a profit the following year.

They bought shares in US-AIR.

The firm employs 800 staff.

expand	[ɪkspænd]	**1** to become bigger, with more people, goods or activities; *Our business expanded.* **2** to make something larger; *expand services*
go out of business		if a company goes out of business, it stops trading because it does not have enough money
improve	[ɪmpruv]	to get better or to make something get better
invest	[ɪnvɛst]	to put money into a business, in order to try to make a profit from it
launch	[lɔntʃ]	to start selling a new product to the public
manage	[mænɪdʒ]	to control a business
market	[mɑrkɪt]	to advertise and sell a product
negotiate	[nɪgouʃieɪt]	to talk about a situation in order to reach an agreement
owe	[ou]	to have to pay money to someone; *owe someone money*
sell	[sɛl]	to let someone have something that you own in return for money

ADJECTIVES

bankrupt	[bæŋkrʌpt]	not having enough money to pay your debts; *go bankrupt*
commercial	[kəmɜrʃəl]	relating to the buying and selling of things
medium-sized	[midiəm saɪzd]	not large and not small; *a medium-sized firm*
online	[ɒnlaɪn]	using the internet to sell goods; *an online service*; *online retailing*; *online shopping*
private	[praɪvɪt]	not owned by the government

EXAMPLES

I want to expand my business.
Many airlines could go out of business.
We need to improve performance.
The firm launched a new clothing range.
If the firm cannot sell its products, it will go bankrupt.
New York is a center of commercial activity.

profitable	[prɒfɪtəbəl]	making a profit
senior	[siːnyər]	having an important job in an organization
small	[smɔl]	not large in size or amount; *a small business*
thriving	[θraɪvɪŋ]	successful

IDIOMS

at the cutting edge	involved in the most exciting and new developments
blue-sky thinking	new creative ideas
think outside the box	to think in a new and creative way

EXAMPLES

Drug manufacturing is the most profitable business in America.

This company is at the cutting edge of technology.

cars and road travel

NOUNS

accelerator (BRIT)		see **gas pedal**
accident	[æksɪdənt]	when a vehicle hits something and causes injury or damage
ambulance	[æmbyələns]	a vehicle for taking people to hospital; *call an ambulance*
bonnet (BRIT)		see **hood**
boot (BRIT)		see **trunk**
brake	[breɪk]	the part in a vehicle that you press with your foot to make the vehicle go more slowly or stop
breakdown	[breɪkdaʊn]	an occasion when a vehicle stops working; *have a breakdown*
bumper	[bʌmpər]	a heavy bar at the front and back of a vehicle that protects the vehicle if it hits something
bus	[bʌs]	a large motor vehicle that carries passengers; *a school bus*; *a tour bus*; *a double-decker bus*; *catch a bus*
car	[kɑr]	a motor vehicle with space for about five people; *drive/park a car*; *a sports car*; *a racing car*; *a police car*
car park (BRIT)		see **parking lot**
caravan	[kærəvæn]	a large vehicle that is pulled by a car. You can sleep and eat in a caravan on vacation.
clutch	[klʌtʃ]	the part of a vehicle that you press with your foot before you move the gear shift
coach	[koʊtʃ]	a comfortable bus that travels between cities or takes people on long journeys; *a coach tour/trip*
crossroads	[krɔsroʊdz]	a place where two roads cross each other

---

EXAMPLES

There's been an accident.
Six people were injured in the accident.
He missed his last bus home.
They arrived by car.
The car won't start.

dashboard	[dæʃbɔrd]	the part of a car in front of the driver, where most of the controls are
direction	[dɪrɛkʃ°n, daɪ-]	the general line that you move in when you are going to a place
directions	[dɪrɛkʃ°nz, daɪ-]	instructions that tell you how to get somewhere; *give someone directions*
distance	[dɪstəns]	the amount of space between two places; *travel a short/long distance*
driver	[draɪvər]	someone who drives a bus, a car, or a train, for example
driver's license	[draɪvərz laɪs°ns]	a document showing that you are legally allowed to drive (*In British English, use* **driving licence**)
driving licence (BRIT)		*see* **driver's license**
engine	[ɛndʒɪn]	the part of a vehicle that produces the power to make it move
fire engine	[faɪər ɛndʒɪn]	a large vehicle that carries firemen and equipment for putting out fires
flat	[flæt]	a small hole in a tire that has been made by a sharp object (*In British English, use* **puncture**)
garage	[gərɑʒ]	**1** a building next to your house where you keep your car **2** a public building where you can park your car **3** a place where cars are repaired
gas	[gæs]	the fuel that you use in vehicles to make the engine work (*In British English, use* **petrol**)
gas pedal	[gæs pɛd°l]	the part in a vehicle that you press with your foot to make the vehicle go faster (*In British English, use* **accelerator**)

EXAMPLES

You're going in the wrong direction.
He gave us directions to the hospital.
Do you have a driver's license?
He got into the driver's seat and started the engine.

gas station	[gǽs steɪʃ°n]	a place where you buy fuel for your vehicle (*In British English, use* **petrol station**)
gear	[gɪər]	a part of an engine that changes power into movement
gear shift	[gɪər ʃɪft]	the lever in a vehicle that you use to change gear (*In British English, use* **gear stick**)
gear stick (*BRIT*)		*see* **gear shift**
handbrake	[hǽndbreɪk]	the brake in a car that you pull with your hand to stop it moving, for example, when you have parked
headlights	[hɛdlaɪts]	the large lights at the front of a vehicle
highway	[haɪweɪ]	a wide road that allows vehicles to travel very fast over a long distance (*In British English, use* **motorway**)
hood	[hʊd]	the front part of a car that covers the engine (*In British English, use* **bonnet**)
horn	[hɔrn]	an object in a vehicle that makes a loud noise, and that you use as a warning of danger
indicator (*BRIT*)		*see* **turn signal**
journey	[dʒɜrni]	an occasion when you travel from one place to another
lane	[leɪn]	**1** a narrow road, especially in the countryside; *a country lane* **2** a part of a road that is marked by a painted line; *the fast lane*
license plate	[laɪs°ns pleɪt]	a sign on the front and back of a vehicle that shows its registration number (*In British English, use* **number plate**)
lorry (*BRIT*)		*see* **truck**

EXAMPLES

The car was in fourth gear.
Yesterday, traffic was light on the highway.
It's a 3-hour journey.
Have a good journey!

make	[meɪk]	the name of the company that made a particular car; *a make of car*
motorbike	[moʊtərbaɪk]	same as **motorcycle**; *ride a motorbike*
motorcycle	[moʊtərsaɪkᵊl]	a vehicle with two wheels and an engine
motorway (BRIT)		*see* **highway**
number plate (BRIT)		*see* **license plate**
oil	[ɔɪl]	a smooth, thick liquid that is used for making machines work
one-way street	[wʌn weɪ strit]	a street where vehicles can only go in one direction
parking lot	[pɑrkɪŋ lɒt]	an area or building where people can leave their cars (*In British English, use* **car park**)
parking space	[pɑrkɪŋ speɪs]	a place where you can park your car
passenger	[pæsɪndʒər]	someone who is traveling in a vehicle but is not driving it
pedestrian	[pɪdɛstriən]	someone who is walking, especially in a town or city
petrol (BRIT)		*see* **gas**
petrol station (BRIT)		*see* **gas station**
puncture (BRIT)		*see* **flat**
rear-view mirror	[rɪər vyu mɪrər]	the mirror on the front window of a vehicle that allows you to see behind the vehicle
registration number	[rɛdʒɪstreɪʃᵊn nʌmbər]	the official numbers and letters at the front and back of a vehicle
road	[roʊd]	a long piece of hard ground that cars travel on
road sign	[roʊd saɪn]	a flat metal object at the side of a road that gives information to drivers

---

EXAMPLES

"What make of car do you drive?" – "A Honda."

Where's the nearest parking lot?

We drove around for 20 minutes trying to find a parking space.

Mr. Smith was a passenger in the car when it crashed.

Take the road to Detroit.

roof rack	[rʊf ræk]	a metal frame on top of a car where you can put things such as suitcases
roundabout (BRIT)		see **traffic circle**
seat belt	[sit bɛlt]	a strap in a car that you put across your body to protect you in an accident
service station	[sɜrvɪs steɪʃᵊn]	a place along a highway where you can buy gas and food
side-view mirror	[saɪd vyu mɪrər]	one of the two mirrors on each side of a car (In British English, use **wing mirror**)
spare part	[spɛər pɑrt]	a part that you can buy to replace an old or broken part of a vehicle
speed	[spid]	how fast something moves
speed camera	[spid kæmrə]	a piece of equipment that takes pictures of vehicles if they are going too fast
speed limit	[spid lɪmɪt]	the maximum speed that you are legally allowed to drive at
speedometer	[spidɒmɪtər]	a piece of equipment in a car that shows how fast you are driving
street	[strit]	a road in a city or a town
taxi	[tæksi]	a car that you can hire, with its driver, to take you where you want to go; *take/catch a taxi*
tire	[taɪər]	a thick round piece of rubber that fits around the wheels of cars (In British English, use **tyre**)
traffic	[træfɪk]	all the vehicles that are moving along roads in a particular area; *heavy traffic*; *oncoming traffic*
traffic circle	[træfɪk sɜrkᵊl]	a circle in the road where several roads meet, which vehicles must drive round until they reach the road they need (In British English, use **roundabout**)

EXAMPLES

Don't forget to put on your seat belt.
There was hardly any traffic on the road.
There is heavy traffic between Junctions 14 and 18.

traffic jam	[træfɪk dʒæm]	a long line of vehicles that cannot move because there is too much traffic, or because the road is blocked
traffic lights	[træfɪk laɪts]	a set of red, yellow, and green lights that show you when to stop and when to move forward
traffic warden	[træfɪk wɔrdᵊn]	someone whose job is to make sure that vehicles are parked legally
trailer	[treɪlər]	a large container on wheels that is pulled by a truck or other vehicle
transport (BRIT)		see **transportation**
transportation	[trænspər-teɪʃᵊn]	a system for taking people or things from one place to another in a vehicle; road/air/rail transportation (In British English, use **transport**)
truck	[trʌk]	a large vehicle that is used for transporting goods by road (In British English, use **lorry**)
trunk	[trʌŋk]	the space at the back of a car that is used for carrying things in (In British English, use **boot**)
turn signal	[tɜrn sɪgnəl]	a flashing light on a vehicle that tells you when the vehicle is going to turn left or right (In British English, use **indicator**)
tyre (BRIT)		see **tire**
van	[væn]	a vehicle like a large car or a small truck with space for carrying things in the back
vehicle	[viɪkᵊl]	a machine that carries people or things from one place to another
wheel	[wiɪl]	**1** one of the round objects under a vehicle that allows it to move along the ground; the front/back wheel **2** the round object on a vehicle that you turn to make the vehicle go in different directions; a steering wheel
windscreen (BRIT)		see **windshield**

EXAMPLES

He opened the trunk and put my bags in.
There are too many vehicles on the road.

windshield	[wɪndʃild]	the glass window at the front of a vehicle (*In British English, use* **windscreen**)
wing mirror (*BRIT*)		*see* **side-view mirror**

VERBS

accelerate	[æksɛləreɪt]	to go faster
brake	[breɪk]	to use the brakes in order to make a vehicle stop or slow down
break down		to stop working; *The car broke down.*
crash	[kræʃ]	if a vehicle crashes, it hits something and is damaged
drive	[draɪv]	**1** to control the movement and direction of a vehicle; *Can you drive?* **2** to take someone somewhere in a vehicle; *I'll drive you home.*
give way (*BRIT*)		*see* **yield**
hitch-hike	[hɪtʃhaɪk]	to ask people to drive you somewhere, by standing by the side of a road and holding out your thumb
overtake (*BRIT*)		*see* **pass**
park	[pɑrk]	to stop a vehicle and leave it somewhere
pass	[pæs]	to go past another vehicle that is going in the same direction (*In British English, use* **overtake**)
skid	[skɪd]	to slide sideways
slow down		to reduce the speed you are driving at
speed	[spid]	to drive faster than the speed limit

EXAMPLES

A dog ran across the road and I braked quickly.
I crashed into the back of a truck.
We were driving at 70 miles an hour.
I'll drive you to work.
Jeff hitch-hiked to New York.
You should slow down when you are passing a cyclist.
The car skidded on the icy road.
You're going too fast – slow down.

speed up		to start driving more quickly
start up		when an engine starts up, it starts working
steer	[stɪər]	to control a vehicle so that it goes in the direction you want
stop	[stɒp]	to not move any more
tow	[toʊ]	to pull another vehicle along behind
travel	[trævəl]	to go from one place to another, often to a place that is far away
yield		to let another vehicle go before you (*In British English, use* **give way**)

PHRASES

"Construction"	if a road sign says "Construction," it means that people are fixing the road (*In British English, use* **"Roadworks"**)
"No entry"	if a road sign says "No entry," you must not go along that road
"Roadworks" (*BRIT*)	*see* **"Construction"**

EXAMPLES

Eric started the car and drove off.

People often travel hundreds of miles to get here.

He uses the truck to tow his trailer.

celebrations and ceremonies

NOUNS

baptism	[bæptɪzəm]	a ceremony in which a person is baptized
bar mitzvah	[bɑr mɪtsvə]	a ceremony for a Jewish boy on his thirteenth birthday
bat mitzvah	[bɑt mɪtsvə]	a ceremony for a Jewish girl on her thirteenth birthday
birth	[bɜrθ]	the time when a baby is born; *the birth of our daughter*
birthday	[bɜrθdeɪ, -di]	a date when you celebrate the day that you were born
bride	[braɪd]	a woman on her wedding day
cemetery	[sɛmətɛri]	a place where dead people are buried
ceremony	[sɛrɪmoʊni]	a formal event
christening	[krɪsᵊnɪŋ]	a ceremony in which members of a church welcome a baby and give it a name
Christmas	[krɪsməs]	the period around the 25th December, when Christians celebrate the birth of Jesus Christ; *at Christmas*
Christmas Day	[krɪsməs deɪ]	the 25th of December; *on Christmas Day*
Christmas Eve	[krɪsməs iv]	the 24th of December; *on Christmas Eve*
death	[dɛθ]	the end of a person's life
Easter	[istər]	a Christian festival in March or April when people celebrate Jesus Christ's return to life; *at Easter*
engagement	[ɪngeɪdʒmənt]	an agreement to get married to somebody
Father's Day	[fɑðərz deɪ]	a day when you give a card or present to your father to show that you love him; *on Father's Day*

EXAMPLES

I'm going to my grandson's baptism tomorrow.
It's my birthday today.
I'm going to the cemetery to visit my grandma's grave.
I always visit my parents at Christmas.

festival	[fɛstɪvəl]	a time when people celebrate a special event
festivities	[fɛstɪvɪtiz]	events that are organized in order to celebrate something
fireworks	[faɪərwɜrks]	things that fly up into the air and explode, making bright colors in the sky; *a fireworks display*
funeral	[fyunərəl]	a ceremony in which the body of a dead person is buried or cremated
gift	[gɪft]	same as **present**
graduation	[grædʒueɪʃən]	a ceremony for students when they have completed their studies at a university or college
grave	[greɪv]	a place in the ground where a dead person is buried
greeting card	[gritɪŋ kɑrd]	a folded card with a message inside that you give to someone on a special occasion (*In British English, use* **greetings card**)
greetings card (BRIT)		*see* **greeting card**
groom	[grum]	a man on his wedding day
Hanukkah	[hɑnəkə]	a festival in November or December when Jewish people remember a special time when a temple was given back to them; *during Hanukkah*
honeymoon	[hʌnimun]	a vacation that a man and woman take after their wedding
invitation	[ɪnvɪteɪʃən]	a written or spoken request to go to a party or a ceremony
Lent	[lɛnt]	the forty days before Easter, when some Christians stop doing something that they enjoy; *during Lent*

EXAMPLES

The Christmas festivities lasted for more than a week.
We watched the fireworks from our balcony.
I need to choose a gift for my mom's birthday.
We went to Paris for our honeymoon.
We received an invitation to their wedding.
Maureen gave up chocolate for Lent.

marriage [mærɪdʒ] **1** the relationship between a husband and wife; *a happy marriage*
2 same as **wedding**; *a marriage ceremony*

Mother's Day [mʌðərz deɪ] a day when you give a card or present to your mother to show that you love her; *on Mother's Day*

New Year's Day [nu yɪərz deɪ] the day when people celebrate the start of the year; *on New Year's Day*

New Year's Eve [nu yɪərz iv] the last day of the year; *on New Year's Eve*

occasion [əkeɪʒən] an important event, ceremony, or celebration; *a special occasion*

party [pɑrti] an event where you enjoy yourself with friends doing things like eating or dancing; *have a party*

Passover [pæsoʊvər] a festival in March or April when Jewish people celebrate a special time when God helped them; *during Passover*

present [prɛzənt] something that you give to someone on a special occasion

procession [prəsɛʃən] a line of people or vehicles that follows one another as part of a ceremony

public holiday [pʌblɪk hɒlɪdei] a day when most of the shops, businesses, and schools in a country are closed, often to celebrate a particular event

Ramadan [ræmədɑn] the ninth month of the Muslim year, when Muslims celebrate the time that God spoke the words of their holy book; *during Ramadan*

retirement [rɪtaɪərmənt] the time when you stop work; *a retirement party*

Thanksgiving [θæŋksgɪvɪŋ] a holiday in November when families in America have a special meal together to celebrate all the good things in their lives; *on Thanksgiving*

EXAMPLES

We have New Year's Day off from work.
I'm having a party on Friday night – would you like to come?
The store is closed on Sundays and public holidays.

Valentine's Day	[væləntaɪnz deɪ]	the 14th of February, when you give a card or flowers to the person you love; *on Valentine's Day*
wake	[weɪk]	an event before or after a funeral when friends and family remember the person who died
wedding	[wɛdɪŋ]	a ceremony when two people get married
wedding anniversary	[wɛdɪŋ ænɪvɜrsəri]	a date when you celebrate the day you got married; *our 10th wedding anniversary*

VERBS

baptize	[bæptaɪz]	to touch someone with water, to show that they have become a member of the Christian church; *baptize a baby*
be born		when a baby is born, it comes out of its mother's body at the beginning of its life
bury	[bɛri]	to put the body of a dead person into a grave and cover it with earth
celebrate	[sɛlɪbreɪt]	to do something enjoyable for a special reason; *celebrate your birthday*
cremate	[krɪmeɪt]	to burn the body of a dead person
die	[daɪ]	to stop living
fast	[fæst]	to not eat any food for a period of time
get engaged		**1** when two people get engaged, they agree to marry each other; *Sue and Rishi got engaged.* **2** when you get engaged to someone, you agree to marry them; *I got engaged to my boyfriend.*

EXAMPLES

We went out for dinner on Valentine's Day.
This necklace was an anniversary present from my husband.
My sister was born in 1995.
We're celebrating the birth of our baby boy.
My dad died two years ago.
We fasted during Ramadan.

get married

1 when two people get married, they become husband and wife; *John and Linda got married.*
2 when you get married to someone, you become their husband or wife; *John got married to Linda.*

invite	[ɪnvaɪt]	to ask someone to come to an event; *invite someone to a party*
marry	[mæri]	same as **get married**
organize	[ɔrgənaɪz]	to plan or arrange something; *organize a party*
turn	[tɜrn]	to reach a particular age; *turn 40*
wish	[wɪʃ]	to express the hope that someone will be lucky or happy; *wish someone a happy birthday*

[PHRASES]

Happy birthday!

you say 'Happy birthday!' to someone when you meet them on their birthday

Happy Christmas! *(BRIT)*

see **Merry Chirstmas**

Merry Christmas!

you say "Merry Christmas!" to people when you meet them on Christmas Day

---

EXAMPLES
Let's invite some friends over for dinner.
My brother has just turned 17.

clothes

NOUNS

bathing suit	[beɪðɪŋ sut]	a piece of clothing that women and girls wear when they go swimming (*In British English, use* **swimsuit**)
belt	[bɛlt]	a strip of leather or cloth that you wear around your waist
bikini	[bɪkini]	a piece of clothing with two parts, that women wear for swimming
blouse	[blaʊs]	a shirt for a girl or a woman
boots	[buts]	shoes that cover your whole foot and the lower part of your leg; *a pair of boots*
bra	[brɑ]	a piece of underwear that women wear to support their breasts
button	[bʌtᵊn]	a small hard object that you push through holes (= buttonholes) to fasten your clothes
cap	[kæp]	a soft, flat hat with a curved part at the front
cardigan	[kɑrdɪgən]	a sweater that opens at the front like a jacket
clothes	[kloʊz, kloʊðz]	the things that people wear, such as shirts, coats, pants, and dresses
clothing	[kloʊðɪŋ]	same as **clothes**
coat	[koʊt]	a piece of clothing with long sleeves that you wear over other clothes when you go outside
collar	[kɒlər]	the part of a shirt or coat that goes around your neck
dress	[drɛs]	**1** a piece of clothing that covers a woman's or girl's body and part of her legs; *a black dress* **2** a particular type of clothing; *people in traditional dress*
dressing gown	[drɛsɪŋ gaʊn]	a long, loose piece of clothing that you wear over your night clothes when you are not in bed

EXAMPLES

He was dressed in a shirt, dark pants, and boots.
Isabel's striped dress suited her very well.

fashion	[fæʃ°n]	**1** the activity or business that involves styles of clothing and appearance; *a fashion designer*; *a fashion show* **2** a style of clothing that is popular at a particular time; *the latest fashion*
gloves	[glʌvz]	pieces of clothing that you wear on your hands, with a separate part for each finger; *a pair of gloves*
hat	[hæt]	a thing that you wear on your head
high heels	[haɪ hilz]	women's shoes that have high heels (= raised parts on the bottom of the shoe)
hood	[hʊd]	the part of a coat that you can pull up to cover your head
jacket	[dʒækɪt]	a short coat with long sleeves
jeans	[dʒinz]	pants that are made of strong cotton cloth
jumper *(BRIT)*		*see* **sweater**
kaftan	[kæftæn]	a long loose piece of clothing with long sleeves, that some men in Arab countries wear
kimono	[kɪmoʊnə, -noʊ]	a long piece of clothing shaped like a coat, that some Japanese people wear
knickers *(BRIT)*		*see* **panties**
nightdress	[naɪtdrɛs]	a loose dress that a woman or girl wears in bed
pajamas	[pədʒɑməz]	loose pants and a top that people wear in bed (*In British English, use* **pyjamas**)
panties	[pæntiz]	a piece of underwear for women and girls, that covers the area between the waist and the legs (*In British English, use* **knickers**)
pants	[pænts]	a piece of clothing that covers the body from the waist downwards, and that covers each leg separately; *a pair of pants* (*In British English, use* **trousers**)
pantyhose	[pæntihoʊz]	a piece of tight clothing that covers the lower body, worn by women, girls, and dancers; *a pair of pantyhose*

EXAMPLES

People were standing outside in their pajamas.

pattern	[pǽtərn]	an arrangement of lines or shapes that form a design
pocket	[pɒkɪt]	a part of a piece of clothing that you can put things in
pyjamas *(BRIT)*		*see* **pajamas**
sandals	[sǽndəlz]	light shoes that you wear in warm weather
sari	[sɑri]	a piece of clothing that some Indian women wear, consisting of a long piece of material that you wrap around your body
scarf (PL) **scarves**	[skɑrf] [skɑrvz]	a piece of cloth that you wear around your neck or head
shirt	[ʃɜrt]	a piece of clothing with a collar and buttons, that you wear on the top part of your body
shoelaces	[ʃuleɪsɪz]	thin pieces of material that go through holes in shoes in order to make the shoes tighter
shoes	[ʃuz]	things made of leather or another strong material, that you wear on your feet over socks
shorts	[ʃɔrts]	pants with very short legs; *a pair of shorts*
size	[saɪz]	one of a series of particular measurements for clothes and shoes
skirt	[skɜrt]	a piece of clothing for women and girls that hangs down from the waist and covers part of the legs
sleeve	[sliv]	one of the two parts of a piece of clothing that covers your arms
slippers	[slɪpərz]	loose, soft shoes that you wear indoors
sneakers	[snikərz]	shoes that people wear for running and other sports, or with informal clothes (*In British English, use* **trainers**)

EXAMPLES

He put on a pair of sandals and walked down to the beach.
I take size 38 in shoes.
I need a new pair of shoes.
What size do you wear?
What shoe size are you?

socks	[sɒks]	pieces of clothing that cover your feet and ankles and that you wear inside shoes
suit	[suːt]	a jacket and pants or a jacket and skirt that are both made from the same cloth
sweater	[swɛtər]	a warm piece of clothing that covers the top part of your body (*In British English, use* **jumper**)
swimming trunks	[swɪmɪŋ trʌŋks]	shorts that men and boys wear when they go swimming
swimsuit (*BRIT*)		*see* **bathing suit**
tie	[taɪ]	a long narrow piece of cloth that you wear around your neck with a shirt
tights	[taɪts]	a piece of tight clothing that covers the lower body, worn by women, girls, and dancers; *a pair of tights*
top	[tɒp]	[INFORMAL] a piece of clothing, for example a blouse or a shirt, that you wear on the upper part of your body
trainers (*BRIT*)		*see* **sneakers**
trousers (*BRIT*)		*see* **pants**
T-shirt	[tiː ʃɜrt]	a cotton shirt with short sleeves and no collar or buttons
turban	[tɜrbən]	a long piece of cloth that Sikh, Hindu, and Muslim men wrap around their heads
underpants	[ʌndərpænts]	underwear, that covers the area between the waist and the top of the legs
underwear	[ʌndərwɛər]	clothes that you wear next to your skin, under your other clothes
uniform	[yuːnɪfɔrm]	the special clothes that some people wear to work, and that some children wear at school
vest	[vɛst]	a piece of clothing without sleeves that people usually wear over a shirt (*In British English, use* **waistcoat**)
waistcoat (*BRIT*)		*see* **vest**

EXAMPLES

He was wearing a dark business suit.

zip (BRIT)		*see* **zipper**
zipper	[zɪpər]	a long metal or plastic object with two rows of teeth that join together, and a small part that you pull in order to open and close clothes or bags (*In British English, use* **zip**)

VERBS

dress up		to put on different clothes in order to look like someone else, for fun
fit	[fɪt]	to be the right size for you
get changed		to take off some or all of your clothes, and put on different clothes
get dressed		to put on your clothes
get undressed		to take off your clothes
put something on		to put a piece of clothing onto your body
suit	[sut]	to make you look attractive
take something off		to take a piece of clothing off your body
wear	[wɛər]	to have something such as clothes, shoes, or jewelry on your body
zip	[zɪp]	to fasten something such as a piece of clothing using its zipper

EXAMPLES

My son dressed up as a cowboy for the fancy dress party.
The dress fit me perfectly.
When I get home from school I get changed.
In the morning I get dressed.
Sarah got dressed quickly and went to work.
In the evening I get undressed.
He put his shirt on.
That suits you.
Jason took off his jacket and loosened his tie.
You need to wear warm clothes when you go out today.

ADJECTIVES

casual	[kæʒuəl]	worn at home or on vacation, and not at work or on formal occasions
checked (*BRIT*)		*see* **checkered**
checkered	[tʃɛkərd]	with a pattern of small squares, usually of two colors (*In British English, use* **checked**)
fashionable	[fæʃənəbəl]	**1** popular at a particular time; *fashionable clothes* **2** wearing fashionable clothes; *a fashionable woman*
formal	[fɔrməl]	formal clothes are worn on serious or official occasions
long	[lɔŋ]	measuring a great distance from one end to the other; *a long coat*
old-fashioned	[oʊld fæʃənd]	no longer fashionable or modern
short	[ʃɔrt]	measuring only a small amount from one end to the other; *a short skirt*
smart	[smɑrt]	**1** clean and neat, and wearing attractive clothes; *You look smart.* **2** neat and attractive, and worn at work or on slightly formal occasions; *a smart suit*
spotted	[spɒtɪd]	having a pattern of spots (= small round colored areas); *a spotted handkerchief*
striped	[straɪpt]	having a pattern of stripes (= long lines of different colors); *a pair of striped pajamas*
tight	[taɪt]	small, and fitting closely to your body; *a tight skirt*
trendy	[trɛndi]	fashionable and modern

EXAMPLES
He wore formal evening dress to the dinner.
That's very smart.

college and university

NOUNS

art school [ɑrt skul] a college where people study subjects such as painting and photography

arts [ɑrts] subjects such as history, literature, and language, which are not scientific

assignment [əsaɪnmənt] a task that you are given to do as part of your studies

bachelor's degree [bætʃələrz dɪgri] a first university degree that usually lasts four years

campus [kæmpəs] an area of land that contains the main buildings of a university or college

college [kɒlɪdʒ] same as **university**

course [kɔrs] a series of lessons on a particular subject; *complete a course*

coursework [kɔrswɜrk] work that students do during a course, rather than in exams

degree [dɪgri] **1** a course of study that you do at a university or college; *do a degree* **2** the qualification that you get when you have passed this course; *have a degree*

department [dɪpɑrtmənt] one of the sections in a university or college; *the English Literature department*

discussion section [dɪskʌʃən sɛkʃən] a class at a college or university in which the teacher or TA and a small group of students discuss a topic (*In British English, use* **tutorial**)

diploma [dɪploumə] the qualification that you get when you have completed a course of study at a university or college; *have a diploma*

distance learning [dɪstəns lɜrnɪŋ] a system of education in which people study at home

EXAMPLES

We have to do written assignments as well as fieldwork.

Cars are not allowed on campus.

Joanna is doing business studies at a local college.

I did a course in computing.

He was awarded a diploma in social work.

dorms	[dɔrmz]	buildings or rooms where students live (*In British English, use* **student accommodation**)
essay	[ɛseɪ]	a short piece of writing on a subject
exam	[ɪgzæm]	a formal test you take to show your knowledge of a subject
examination	[ɪgzæmɪneɪʃ°n]	[FORMAL] same as **exam**
faculty	[fæk°lti]	a group of related departments in a university; *the Faculty of Arts*
fieldwork	[fildwɜrk]	the activity of gathering information about something in the real world, rather than studying it in a classroom
finals	[faɪn°lz]	the tests students take at the end of a university or college course; *take your finals*
graduate	[grædʒuɪt]	a student who has completed a course at a college or university
graduation	[grædʒueɪʃ°n]	a special ceremony for students when they have completed their studies at a university or college
grant	[grænt]	an amount of money given to a person or to an organization for a special purpose
halls of residence (*BRIT*)		*see* **residence hall**
honors degree	[ɒnərz dɪgri]	a type of university degree which is of a higher standard than an ordinary degree (*In British English, use* **honours degree**)
honours degree (*BRIT*)		*see* **honors degree**
invigilator (*BRIT*)		*see* **proctor**
law school	[lɔ skul]	a school people go to after college where they study to become lawyers
lecture	[lɛktʃər]	a talk that someone gives in order to teach people about a particular subject
lecturer	[lɛktʃərər]	a teacher at a university or college
major	[meɪdʒər]	the main subject that someone is studying

EXAMPLES

We had to write an essay on Shakespeare.
He is a lecturer in the Geography department of Moscow University.

master's degree	[mæstərz dɪgri]	a second university degree, that usually lasts one or two years
medical school	[mɛdɪkəl skul]	a college where people study to become doctors and nurses
natural sciences	[nætʃərəl saɪənsɪz, nætʃrəl -]	subjects such as physics, biology, and chemistry, that are concerned with the physical world
PhD	[pi eɪtʃ di]	**1** short for "Doctor of Philosophy": the highest degree in a particular subject; *working on a PhD* **2** the qualification that you get when you have passed this degree; *have a PhD*
plagiarism	[pleɪdʒərɪzəm]	the practice of copying someone else's work and pretending that you did the work
proctor	[prɒktər]	someone who checks that an exam starts and finishes at the correct time, and that there is no cheating (*In British English, use* **invigilator**)
prospectus	[prəspɛktəs]	a document that gives details about a college or university and the courses it provides
reading list	[ridɪŋ lɪst]	a document that a lecturer gives to students, with suggestions for books that they should read for a particular class
research	[rɪsɜrtʃ, risɜrtʃ]	work that involves studying something and trying to discover facts about it
residence hall	[rɛzɪdəns hɔl]	buildings with rooms or suites, usually built by universities or colleges, in which students live during the term (*In British English, use* **halls of residence**)
scholarship	[skɒlərʃɪp]	an amount of money that is given to someone who has achieved good results, so that they can continue studying

---

EXAMPLES

He has a master's degree in Business Administration.

Marc has a PhD in Linguistics.

Phuong was awarded a scholarship to study business management at the University of Luton.

school	[skul]	1 a department of a university or college; *the School of Humanities* 2 same as **university**
semester	[sɪmɛstər]	half of a college or university year
seminar	[sɛmɪnɑr]	a class at a college or university in which the teacher and a small group of students discuss a topic
social sciences	[souʃəl saɪənsɪz]	subjects such as sociology and politics, that are concerned with society
student	[studᵊnt]	a person who is studying at a university or a college
student accommodation (BRIT)		*see* **dorms**
student loan	[studᵊnt loun]	an amount of money that students can borrow from the government; *apply for a student loan*
student union	[studᵊnt yunyən]	1 an organization in a university or college that helps students 2 a building where this organization has an office, and where there is usually a shop and a coffee bar
syllabus	[sɪləbəs]	a list of subjects that are covered in a university or college course
TA	[ti eɪ]	short for "teaching assistant": a postgraduate student who teaches seminars or leads discussion sections for lecture classes at a college or university
technical college	[tɛknɪkᵊl kɒlɪdʒ]	a college where you can study practical subjects, often in order to do a particular job
term	[tɜrm]	one of the periods of time that a college or university year is divided into
test	[tɛst]	an exam that you take to show your knowledge of a subject; *take a test*

EXAMPLES

Please read this chapter before next week's seminar.

thesis	[θisɪs]	a long piece of writing based on your own ideas and research, that you do as part of a degree
(PL) **theses**	[θisis]	
tuition fees	[tuɪʃ°n fiz]	the money that you pay to be taught at a university or college
tutor	[tutər]	a private teacher who meets with students outside of normal classes to help them keep up with the materials covered in class
tutorial (BRIT)		*see* **discussion section**
undergraduate	[ʌndər-grædʒuɪt]	a university or college student who has not yet attained their Bachelor's degree
university	[yunɪvɜrsɪti]	a place where you can study for a degree, and where people do academic research
viva	[vivə]	a university examination in which a student answers questions by speaking rather than writing
vocational course	[voʊkeɪʃənᵊl kɔrs]	a course that someone does in order to do a particular job

VERBS

enrol	[ɪnroʊl]	to officially join a class
graduate	[grædʒueɪt]	to complete your studies at college or university
invigilate (BRIT)		*see* **proctor**
proctor	[prɒktər]	to check that an exam starts and finishes at the correct time, and that no-one cheats (*In British English, use* **invigilate**)
register	[rɛdʒɪstər]	to put your name on an official list, in order to be able to take a particular class

EXAMPLES

He was awarded his PhD for a thesis on industrial robots.

The government are planning to increase tuition fees.

She went to a university where she got a BA and then an MA.

She graduated with a degree in English and Drama from Northwestern University.

What do you want to do after you graduate?

| **study** | [stʌdi] | to spend time learning about a particular subject |
| **work** | [wɜrk] | to do an activity that uses a lot of your time or effort |

academic	[ækədɛmɪk]	relating to the work done in universities and colleges; *an academic journal*
full-time	[fʊl taɪm]	relating to a course that takes up the whole of each normal working week; *a full-time program*; *a full-time student*
part-time	[pɑrt taɪm]	relating to a course that takes up only part of each day or week; *a part-time course*; *a part-time student*

EXAMPLES
She spends most of her time studying.
He studied History and Geography at college.
Their academic standards are high.

colors

NOUNS AND ADJECTIVES

beige	[beɪʒ]	(having) a pale brown color
black	[blæk]	1 (having) the color of the sky at night 2 black coffee or tea has no milk in it
blue	[blu]	(having) the color of the sky on a sunny day
brown	[braʊn]	(having) the color of earth or wood
cream	[krim]	(having) a yellowish-white color
gold	[goʊld]	(having) a bright yellow color that is often shiny
green	[grin]	(having) the color of grass or leaves
gray	[greɪ]	(having) the color of ashes, or clouds on a rainy day (*In British English, use* **grey**)
grey (BRIT)		*see* **gray**
navy blue	[neɪvi blu]	(having) a very dark blue color; *a navy blue suit*
orange	[ɔrɪndʒ]	(having) a color between red and yellow
pink	[pɪŋk]	(having) a color between red and white
purple	[pɜrpəl]	(having) a color between red and blue
red	[rɛd]	(having) the color of blood or of a tomato
silver	[sɪlvər]	(having) a shiny and pale grey color
turquoise	[tɜrkwɔɪz]	(having) a light greenish-blue color
white	[waɪt]	1 (having) the color of snow or milk 2 white wine is a pale-yellow color 3 white coffee or tea has milk in it
yellow	[yɛloʊ]	(having) the color of lemons or butter

EXAMPLES

Blue suits you.

"What color are your eyes?" – "Blue."

I bought some blue shoes.

"What color is your hair?" – "Brown."

The room is decorated in soft browns and creams.

She has green eyes.

Do you have this t-shirt in green?

"What's your favorite color?" – "Red."

You look good in white.

ADJECTIVES

bright	[braɪt]	strong and noticeable in color; *a bright red dress*
dark	[dɑrk]	close to black, or containing some black; *dark brown hair*
light	[laɪt]	pale in color; *light brown hair*
pale	[peɪl]	not strong or bright in color; *pale blue eyes*
rich	[rɪtʃ]	dark in color and pleasant to look at
soft	[sɔft]	not bright, and pleasant to look at

VERBS

blush	[blʌʃ]	to become red in the face because you are ashamed or embarrassed
change color		to become a different color (*In British English*, use **change colour**)
change colour (*BRIT*)		*see* **change color**
go red		to become red in the face because you are embarrassed or angry
paint	[peɪnt]	to cover a wall or an object with paint; *paint something blue*

PHRASES

a black eye	a dark area of skin around your eye where someone has hit you

EXAMPLES

She's wearing a light blue t-shirt.
The leaves on the trees are changing color.
Mom went red in the face with anger.
He had a black eye, and several cuts on his face.

computers and the internet

attachment	[ətætʃmənt]	a file that you send with an email
blog	[blɒg]	a website that describes the daily life and thoughts of the person who writes it
broadband	[brɔdbænd]	a very fast method of sending a lot of information at the same time over the internet
browser	[brauzər]	a piece of software that allows you to search for information on the internet
bug	[bʌg]	a mistake in a computer program
CD	[si di]	short for "compact disc": a disc for storing music or computer information
CD-ROM	[si di rɒm]	a CD that stores information that you can read using a computer
chat	[tʃæt]	a way of communicating with friends by exchanging written messages using the internet; *internet chat*
computer	[kəmpyutər]	an electronic machine that stores and deals with large amounts of information; *a computer game*; *a computer system*
connection	[kənɛkʃᵊn]	a link between a computer and a network; *an internet connection*
cursor	[kɜrsər]	a small line on a computer screen that shows where you are working
data	[deɪtə, dætə]	information that can be used by a computer program
database	[deɪtəbeɪs, dætə-]	a collection of information on a computer that is stored in such a way that you can use it and add to it easily

---

EXAMPLES

Many internet users now have a broadband connection at home.

You need an up-to-date web browser.

There is a bug in the software.

A CD-ROM can hold huge amounts of data.

desktop	[dɛsktɒp]	the images that you see on a computer screen when the computer is ready to use
disk	[dɪsk]	a flat metal object that stores information and can be put into a computer
disk drive	[dɪsk draɪv]	the part of a computer that holds a disk
document	['dɒkjəmənt]	a piece of text that is stored on a computer
email	[iːmeɪl]	**1** short for "electronic mail": a system of sending written messages from one computer to another; *send a file by email* **2** a written message that you send by computer; *send an email*
email address	[iːmeɪl ədrɛs]	a combination of letters and symbols that identifies where emails are sent
file	[faɪl]	a collection of information that you keep on your computer
folder	[foʊldər]	a group of files that are stored together on a computer
font	[fɒnt]	a set of letters of the same style and size
hacker	[hækər]	a person who illegally gets access to another computer
hard disk	[hɑrd dɪsk]	the part inside a computer where data and programs are stored
hard drive	[hɑrd draɪv]	the part inside a computer that contains the hard disk
hardware	[hɑrdwɛr]	things in computer systems such as the computer, the keyboard and the screen, rather than the programs
home page	[hoʊm peɪdʒ]	the main page of a website
I.T.	[aɪ 'tiː]	short for "information technology": the study and practice of using computers
icon	[aɪkɒn]	a picture on a computer screen that you can choose, in order to open a particular program

EXAMPLES

You can rearrange the icons on your desktop.
You can cut and paste whole paragraphs from one document to another.
Could you email David Ferguson and arrange a meeting?
The company needs people with I.T. skills.

inbox [ɪnbɒks] the place where your computer stores emails that people have sent to you

ink cartridge [ɪŋk kɑrtrɪdʒ] a container of ink that you put in a printer

the internet [ði ɪntərnɛt] the network that connects computers all over the world

italics [ɪtælɪks] letters and numbers that slope to the right; *This sentence is in italics.*

key [ki] one of the buttons that you press in order to operate a computer

keyboard [kibɔrd] the set of keys that you press in order to operate a computer

laptop [læptɒp] a small computer that you can carry with you

memory [mɛməri] the part of a computer where it stores information

memory stick [mɛməri stɪk] a small object for storing information that you can carry with you and use in different computers

menu [mɛnyu] a list of choices on a computer screen, showing things that you can do using a particular program; *a drop-down menu*

modem [moʊdəm, -dɛm] a piece of equipment that uses a telephone line to connect computers

monitor [mɒnɪtər] the part of a computer that contains the screen

mouse [maʊs] an object that you use to do things on a computer without using the keyboard

mouse mat *(BRIT)* *see* **mouse pad**

mouse pad [maʊs pæd] a flat piece of plastic that you rest a mouse on (*In British English, use* **mouse mat**)

network [nɛtwɜrk] a system of connected computers

operating system [ɒpəreɪtɪŋ sɪstəm] a system in a computer that controls all the other programs

---

EXAMPLES

I had 50 emails in my inbox.
I found all the information I needed on the internet.

password	[pǽswɜrd]	a secret word or phrase that allows you to use a computer system
PC	[pi si]	short for "personal computer": a computer that people use at school, at home or in an office
printer	[príntər]	a machine for printing copies of computer documents on paper
printout	[príntaʊt]	a piece of paper with information from a computer printed on it
program	[próʊgræm, -grəm]	a set of instructions that a computer uses to do a particular task
screen	[skrin]	a flat surface on a computer where you see pictures or words
social networking	[sóʊʃəl nɛ́twɜrkɪŋ]	the activity of contacting friends and making new friends on particular websites
software	[sɔ́ftwɛər]	computer programs
spam	[spǽm]	advertising messages that are sent automatically by email to large numbers of people
spreadsheet	[sprɛ́dʃit]	a program that deals with numbers, and is mainly used for financial planning
USB	[yu ɛs bi]	short for "Universal Serial Bus": a way of connecting equipment to a computer; *a USB port*
username	[yúzərneɪm]	the name that you type onto your screen each time you open a particular program or website
virus	[váɪrəs]	a program that enters a computer system and changes or destroys the information that is there

EXAMPLES

The printer plugs into the computer's USB port.

I clicked the mouse and a message appeared on the screen.

Have you used a social networking site such as MySpace or Facebook?

The software allows you to browse the internet on your mobile phone.

You should protect your computer against viruses.

the web	[ðə wɛb]	a computer system that helps you find information. You can use it anywhere in the world.
web address	[wɛb ədrɛs]	the location of a website on the internet, for example, http://www.harpercollins.com
webcam	[wɛbkæm]	a camera on a computer that produces images that can be seen on a website
website	[wɛbsaɪt]	a set of information on the internet about a particular subject
window	[wɪndoʊ]	one of the work areas that a screen can be divided into

VERBS

back something up		to make a copy of a computer file that you can use if the original file is lost; *back up a file*
boot up a computer		to make a computer start working
browse	[braʊz]	to search for information on the internet; *browse the internet*
click	[klɪk]	to press one of the buttons on a mouse in order to make something happen on the screen; *click on a link*
copy	[kɒpi]	to make a new version of a file or disk that is exactly the same as the old one; *copy a file*
crash	[kræʃ]	used for saying that a computer or a program suddenly stops working; *The computer crashed.*
cut and paste		to move words or pictures on a computer from one place to another place
delete	[dɪliːt]	**1** to remove a file or document from a computer; *delete a file* **2** to remove text from a document; *delete a paragraph*

EXAMPLES

Go over to your computer and boot it up.
My computer crashed for the second time that day.
The report was too long so I deleted a few paragraphs.

download	[daʊnloʊd]	to copy a file, a program, or other information from a bigger computer, a network or the internet to your own computer
email	[iːmeɪl]	to send a message from one computer to another; *email someone*
format	[fɔːrmæt]	to change the arrangement of the text of a document
key something in		to put information into a computer using the keyboard; *key in data*
log in		to type your username and password so that you can start using a computer or website
log off		to stop using a computer or website by clicking on an instruction
print	[prɪnt]	to use a machine to produce a copy of a computer file on paper; *print ten copies of a document*
program	[proʊɡræm, -ɡrəm]	to give a computer a set of instructions so that it can do a particular task; *program a computer*
save	[seɪv]	to give a computer an instruction to store some information; *save your work*
scroll	[skroʊl]	to move the text on a computer screen up or down to find the information that you need; *scroll down the page*
zip	[zɪp]	to make a file smaller so that you can send it to someone using the internet

EXAMPLES

You can download software from this website.

She turned on her computer and logged in.

This is how to zip files so that you can send them via email.

[ADJECTIVES]

bold	[boʊld]	letters and numbers that are bold are thicker and darker than ordinary ones; *bold capitals*
desktop	[dɛsktɒp]	of a convenient size for using on a desk or a table; *a desktop computer*
electronic	[ɪlɛktrɒnɪk, i-]	using electricity and small electrical parts
offline	[ɒflaɪn]	not connected to the internet; *The computer is offline.*
online	[ɒnlaɪn]	1 available on the internet; *an online store* 2 connected to the internet; *people who are online*
portable	[pɔrtəbᵊl]	designed to be carried or moved around
wireless	[waɪərlɪs]	using radio waves (= a form of power that travels through the air) instead of wires; *a wireless connection*

[ADVERBS]

offline	[ɒflaɪn]	not using the internet; *work offline*
online	[ɒnlaɪn]	using the internet; *search online*

[IDIOM]

surf the net	to spend time looking at different websites on the internet

---

EXAMPLES

Your computer is currently offline.
I buy most of my clothes online.
Some teenagers spend hours surfing the net.

cooking

barbecue [bɑrbɪkyu] a piece of equipment that you use for cooking outdoors

blender [blɛndər] a piece of electrical equipment for mixing liquids and soft foods together or for turning fruit or vegetables into liquid

bottle opener [bɒtᵊl oʊpənər] a metal tool for removing tops from bottles

broiler [brɔɪlər] the part of a oven where you cook food under strong heat (*In British English, use* **grill**)

cake tin [keɪk tɪn] **1** a metal container that you use for baking a cake
2 a metal container that you put a cake in to keep it fresh

can opener [kæn oʊpənər] a tool for opening tins of food (*In British English, use* **tin opener**)

chopping board [tʃɒpɪŋ bɔrd] a flat piece of wood or plastic that you chop meat or vegetables on

coffee maker [kɔfi meɪkər] a machine for making coffee

cook [kʊk] someone who prepares and cooks food

cooker (*BRIT*) *see* **stove**

corkscrew [kɔrkskru] a tool for pulling corks out of bottles

dish [dɪʃ] a wide shallow container with no cover, that you use for cooking and serving food

food processor [fud prɒsɛsər] a piece of electrical equipment for mixing or chopping food, or for turning food into liquid

fork [fɔrk] a tool with a handle and three or four long metal points at the end, that you use for eating and cooking

frying pan [fraɪɪŋ pæn] a flat metal pan with a long handle, that you use for frying food

grater [greɪtər] a tool with a rough surface, that you use for cutting food into very small pieces

---

EXAMPLES

My mom is a good cook.

grill	[grɪl]	**1** a flat frame of metal bars that you can use to cook food over a fire **2** (BRIT) see **broiler**
hob (BRIT)		see **stove top**
kettle	[kɛtᵊl]	a metal container with a lid and a handle, that you use for boiling water
knife	[naɪf]	a tool with a handle and a sharp flat piece of metal, that you use for eating and cooking; *a carving knife*; *a bread knife*
ladle	[leɪdᵊl]	a large, round, deep spoon with a long handle, that you use for serving soup
microwave	[maɪkroʊweɪv]	an oven that cooks food very quickly using electric waves
mixing bowl	[mɪksɪŋ boʊl]	a large bowl that you use for mixing ingredients
oven	[ʌvᵊn]	a piece of equipment for cooking that is like a large metal box with a door
pan	[pæn]	a round metal container with a long handle, that you use for cooking food
peeler	[pilər]	a tool for removing the skin from fruit and vegetables; *a potato peeler*
pot	[pɒt]	a deep round container that you use for cooking soup and other food
recipe	[rɛsɪpi]	a set of instructions telling you how to cook something
rolling pin	[roʊlɪŋ pɪn]	a long wooden tool that you roll over dough in order to make it flat
saucepan	[sɔspæn]	a deep metal cooking pot, usually with a long handle and a lid
scale	[skeɪl]	a piece of equipment that you use for weighing food (*In British English, use* **scales**)
scales (BRIT)		see **scale**

EXAMPLES
Put the dish in the oven for 40 minutes.
No salt is required in this recipe.

sieve	[sɪv]	a tool with a fine metal net, that you use for separating food from liquids
spatula	[spætʃələ]	a tool like a knife with a wide flat blade, that you use for lifting hot food
spoon	[spuːn]	a tool with a handle and a part like a shallow bowl, that you use for eating and cooking; *a wooden spoon*
stove	[stoʊv]	a piece of kitchen equipment that you use for cooking food (*In British English, use* **cooker**)
stove top	[stoʊv tɒp]	the top part of a cooker where you put pans (*In British English, use* **hob**)
toaster	[toʊstər]	a piece of electrical equipment that you use to heat bread
timer	[taɪmər]	a piece of equipment that you use for measuring how long you need to cook something for
tin opener *(BRIT)*		*see* **can opener**
tongs	[tɒŋz]	a tool consisting of two connected pieces of metal, that you use for picking up food
whisk	[wɪsk]	a tool for stirring eggs or cream very fast; *an electric whisk*; *a hand whisk*

VERBS

bake	[beɪk]	to cook food in an oven without extra oil or liquid
beat	[biːt]	to mix food quickly with a spoon or a fork; *beat an egg*
boil	[bɔɪl]	**1** to heat water until bubbles appear and the water starts to change into steam; *boil water* **2** to cook food in boiling water; *boil potatoes*

EXAMPLES

We bought a new stove.

Put the pan on the stove top, add flour, and cook for one minute.

Beat the eggs with a wooden spoon.

Gradually bring the sauce to the boil.

bring something to the boil		to heat liquid until it boils
broil	[brɔɪl]	to cook food under a broiler (*In British English, use* **grill**)
carve	[kɑrv]	to cut slices from meat; *carve the meat*
chop	[tʃɒp]	to cut something into pieces with a knife *chop the vegetables*
cook	[kʊk]	to prepare and heat food
fry	[fraɪ]	to cook food in hot fat or oil
grill		**1** to cook food on metal bars above a fire or barbecue or under a grill **2** (BRIT) *see* **broil**
mash	[mæʃ]	to press food to make it soft
melt	[mɛlt]	to heat a solid food so that it becomes a liquid
peel	[pil]	to remove the skin of fruit or vegetables
prepare	[prɪpɛər]	to get food ready
roast	[roʊst]	to cook meat or other food in an oven or over a fire
serve	[sɜrv]	to give people food and drinks
slice	[slaɪs]	to cut food into thin pieces; *slice the mushrooms*
stir	[stɜr]	to mix a liquid in a container using a spoon
weigh	[weɪ]	to measure how heavy something is
whisk	[wɪsk]	to stir eggs or cream very fast

EXAMPLES

Carve the beef into thin slices.
Chop the butter into small pieces.
Mash the bananas with a fork.
Top with whipped cream and serve.
Serve the soup with crusty bread.
Helen sliced the cake.

ADJECTIVES		
baked	[beɪkt]	cooked in the oven without extra oil or liquid; *a baked potato*
boiled	[bɔɪld]	cooked in boiling water; *a boiled egg*
chopped	[tʃɒpt]	cut into pieces with a knife; *a tin of chopped tomatoes*
fried	[fraɪd]	cooked in hot fat or oil; *fried rice*
grated	[greɪtɪd]	cut into very small pieces using a grater; *grated cheese*
mashed	[mæʃt]	pressed until soft; *mashed potatoes*
medium	[mi̱diəm]	used for describing meat that is cooked so that the inside is still slightly pink
poached	[poutʃt]	cooked gently in boiling liquid; *a poached egg*
rare	[rɛ̱ər]	used for describing meat that is cooked very lightly so that the inside is still red
roast	[roust]	cooked in the oven or over a fire; *roast beef*
scrambled	[skræmbəld]	used to describe eggs that have been mixed together and heated in a pan
steamed	[sti̱md]	cooked in steam rather than water; *steamed vegetables*
well done	[wɛl dʌn]	if meat is well done, it has been cooked thoroughly

EXAMPLES
I'd like my steak well done.

countryside

agriculture	[ægrɪkʌltʃər]	the business or activity of taking care of crops and farm animals
barn	[bɑrn]	a building on a farm where animals and crops are kept
bulldozer	[bʊldoʊzər]	a large vehicle that is used for moving large amounts of earth
cave	[keɪv]	a large hole in the side of a hill or under the ground; *an underground cave*
cliff	[klɪf]	a high area of land with a very steep side next to water; *walk along the cliffs*
combine harvester	[kɒmbaɪn hɑrvɪstər]	a large machine that is used on farms to cut, sort, and clean grain
country	[kʌntri]	same as **countryside**
countryside	[kʌntrisaɪd]	land that is away from cities and towns; *We live in the country.*
crop	[krɒp]	a plant that people grow for food; *plant a crop*
ditch	[dɪtʃ]	a deep, long, narrow hole that carries water away from a road or a field
estate	[ɪsteɪt]	a large house in a large area of land in the country
farm	[fɑrm]	an area of land and buildings where people grow crops and keep animals
farmer	[fɑrmər]	a person who owns or works on a farm
farmyard	[fɑrmyɑrd]	an area near a farmhouse that is enclosed by walls or buildings; *farmyard animals*
fence	[fɛns]	a wooden or metal wall around a piece of land
field	[fild]	a piece of land where crops are grown, or where animals are kept

---

EXAMPLES

Lisa and Andrew live in the countryside.
Both of the boys work on the farm.
There is not enough good farm land here.
We drove past fields of sunflowers.

fishing	[fɪʃɪŋ]	the sport or business of catching fish
forest	[fɔrɪst]	a large area where trees grow close together
gate	[geɪt]	a structure like a door that you use to enter a field; *close the gate*
ground	[graʊnd]	the soil on the Earth's surface in which you can grow plants
harvest	[hɑrvɪst]	**1** the activity of collecting a crop, or the time when this is done **2** the amount of a crop that is collected; *a good/poor harvest*
hay	[heɪ]	grass that has been cut and dried so that it can be used for feeding animals
hedge	[hɛdʒ]	a row of small trees growing close together around a field
hike	[haɪk]	a long walk, especially in the countryside
hill	[hɪl]	an area of land that is higher than the land around it; *a steep hill*; *climb a hill*
hunt	[hʌnt]	an organized event when a group of people follow and kill wild animals as a sport; *go on a hunt*
hunter	[hʌntər]	a person who hunts wild animals for food or as a sport
lake	[leɪk]	a large area of water with land around it
land	[lænd]	an area of ground that is used for farming
market	[mɑrkɪt]	a place where people buy and sell products
marsh	[mɑrʃ]	a soft, wet area of land
meadow	[mɛdoʊ]	a field that has grass and flowers growing in it
moor	[mʊər]	an area of high open ground covered mainly with rough grass and heather
mountain	[maʊntᵊn]	a very high area of land with steep sides; *climb a mountain*

EXAMPLES

I walked through the gate and into the field.

The women prepare the ground for planting.

Mt. McKinley is the highest mountain in North America.

mud	[mʌd]	a sticky mixture of earth and water
path	[pæθ]	a long, narrow piece of ground that people walk along
picnic	[pɪknɪk]	an occasion when you eat a meal outdoors, usually in a park or a forest, or at the beach
plough	[plaʊ]	a large farming tool that is pulled across the soil to turn it over, usually before seeds are planted
pond	[pɒnd]	a small area of water
produce	[prɒdus]	food that you grow on a farm to sell
quarry	[kwɔri]	a place where stone or minerals are dug out of the ground
rain boots	[reɪn buts]	long rubber boots that you wear to keep your feet dry (*In British English, use* **wellingtons**)
river	[rɪvər]	a long line of water that flows into a sea; *a river bank*
rock	[rɒk]	**1** the hard substance that is in the ground and in mountains **2** a large piece of rock
ruins	[ruɪnz]	the parts of a building that remain after something destroys the rest
scarecrow	[skɛərkroʊ]	an object, in the shape of a person, that stands in a field where crops are growing in order to frighten birds away
scenery	[sinəri]	the land, water, or plants that you can see around you in a country area
soil	[sɔɪl]	the substance on the surface of the Earth in which plants grow

EXAMPLES

We went for a picnic.
The restaurant uses as much local produce as possible.
We tried to dig, but the ground was solid rock.
Maria sat on a rock and looked out across the sea.
The soil here is good for growing vegetables.

spring	[sprɪŋ]	a place where water comes up through the ground; *an underground spring*
stable	[steɪbᵊl]	a building in which horses are kept
stick	[stɪk]	a thin branch from a tree
stone	[stoʊn]	**1** a hard solid substance that is found in the ground and is often used for building **2** a small piece of rock that is found on the ground
stream	[striːm]	a small narrow river
track	[træk]	**1** a rough road or path; *a muddy track* **2** the marks that an animal leaves on the ground; *animal tracks*
tractor	[træktər]	a vehicle that a farmer uses to pull farm machinery; *drive a tractor*
valley	[væli]	a low area of land between hills; *a steep mountain valley*
view	[vyu]	everything that you can see from a place
village	[vɪlɪdʒ]	a very small town in the countryside
walk	[wɔk]	a trip that you make by walking, usually for pleasure; *go for a walk*
waterfall	[wɔtərfɔl]	a place where water flows over the edge of a steep part of hills or mountains, and falls into a pool below
well	[wɛl]	a deep hole in the ground from which people take water or oil
wellingtons *(BRIT)*		*see* **rain boots**
windmill	[wɪndmɪl]	a building with long, flat parts on the outside that turn as the wind blows to make machinery move inside
wood	[wʊd]	**1** the hard material that trees are made of **2** a large area of trees growing near each other; *in the woods*

EXAMPLES

She could feel cool, smooth stone beneath her feet.
Loose stones on the ground made walking difficult.
Zak found fresh bear tracks in the snow.
The view from the top of the hill was magnificent.

VERBS

climb	[klaɪm]	to move towards the top of something; *climb a hill*; *climb to the top*
go camping		to stay in a tent or a trailer for a short time
harvest	[hɑrvɪst]	to collect a farm crop; *harvest crops*
hike	[haɪk]	to go for a long walk
hunt	[hʌnt]	to chase and kill wild animals for food or as a sport
plough	[plaʊ]	to turn earth over, usually before seeds are planted

ADJECTIVES

peaceful	[piːsfəl]	quiet and calm
rural	[rʊərəl]	not near cities or large towns

PHRASE

in the open air	outside rather than in a building

EXAMPLES

The group hiked along a track in the forest.
The service is ideal for people who live in rural areas.
We eat our meals in the open air.

employment

NOUNS

annual leave (BRIT)   *see* **vacation**

application [æplɪkeɪʃⁿn] a document with questions that you must answer when you apply for a job; *fill in an application*

apprentice [əprɛntɪs] a young person who works for someone in order to learn their skill

benefits [bɛnɪfɪts] money or other advantages which come from your job, the government, or an insurance company such as a retirement plan; *a salaried position with benefits*

bonus [boʊnəs] an extra amount of money that you earn, usually because you have worked very hard; *a bonus payment*

boss [bɔs] the person who is in charge of you at the place where you work

career [kərɪər] a job that you do for a long time, or the years of your life that you spend working

colleague [kɒlig] a person someone works with

company [kʌmpəni] a business that sells goods or services

contract [kɒntrækt] an official agreement between two companies or two people

covering letter (BRIT)   *see* **cover letter**

cover letter [kʌvər lɛtər] a letter that you send with an application form in order to provide extra information (*In British English, use* **covering letter**)

co-worker [koʊwɜrkər] a person you work with

CV (BRIT)   *see* **résumé**

disability [dɪsəbɪlɪti] a permanent injury or condition that makes it difficult for you to work or live normally

---

EXAMPLES

Their son Dominic is an apprentice woodworker.

discrimination	[dɪskrɪm-ɪneɪʃᵊn]	the practice of treating one person or group unfairly, for example, by paying them less money than other people; *age discrimination*; *racial/sexual discrimination*
employee	[ɪmplɔɪi]	a person who is paid to work for another person or a company
employer	[ɪmplɔɪər]	the person or the company that you work for
employment	[ɪmplɔɪmənt]	work that you are paid for
equality	[ɪkwɒlɪti]	the fair treatment of all the people in a group
flexitime	[flɛksɪtaɪm]	a system that allows employees to start or finish work at different times, provided that they work an agreed number of hours in total
freelancer	[friːlænsər]	someone who is not employed by an organization, and does work for more than one company
HR		*see* **human resources**
human resources	[hyuːmən riːsɔrsɪz]	the department in a company that finds, trains, and looks after the staff
income	[ɪnkʌm]	the money that a person earns or receives
interview	[ɪntərvyu]	a formal meeting in which someone asks you questions to find out if you are the right person for a job; *ask someone for an interview*
job	[dʒɒb]	**1** the work that someone does to earn money; *get a good job* **2** a particular task; *do a good job*
layoffs	[leɪɔfz]	a situation in which you lose your job because it is no longer necessary or because the organization can no longer afford to pay you; *company-wide layoffs* (*In British English, use* **redundancy**)

EXAMPLES
When I went for my first interview for this job I arrived early.

maternity leave [mətɜrniti liv]		a period of time when a woman leaves her job to have a baby
minimum wage [mɪnɪməm weɪdʒ]		the lowest wage that an employer is allowed to pay an employee; *on the minimum wage*
notice [noʊtɪs]		the act of telling your employer that you are going to leave your job; *give in/hand in your notice*
occupation [ɒkyəpeɪʃᵊn]		someone's job; *What is your occupation?*
overtime [oʊvərtaɪm]		extra time that you spend doing your job
paternity leave [pətɜrniti liv]		a period of time when a man does not go to work because his child has just been born
pay [peɪ]		to give someone money for the work that they do
profession [prəfɛʃᵊn]		a type of job for which you need special education or training
promotion [prəmoʊʃᵊn]		a move to a more important job or rank in the organization that you work for; *get a promotion*
rate of pay [reɪt əv peɪ]		the money that workers can earn for a particular amount of work; *a higher/lower rate of pay*
recruitment [rɪkrutmənt]		the process of selecting people to work for an organization
redundancy (*BRIT*)		*see* **layoffs**
reference [rɛfərəns, rɛfrəns]		a statement from someone who knows you, describing your character and your abilities
résumé [rɛzʊmeɪ]		a document giving details of your education and work experience that you send to someone when you are trying to get a new job (*In British English, use* **CV**)

EXAMPLES

These workers are not even on the minimum wage.

You have to give one month's notice.

Could you write me a reference?

Please send your résumé and a cover letter to the following address.

retirement	[rɪtaɪərmənt]	the period in someone's life after they retire
rise	[raɪz]	an increase in the money that you earn; *get a rise*
salary	[sæləri]	the money that you earn from your employer
seasonal work	[sizənəl wɜrk]	work that is only available at particular times of the year
sick leave	[sɪk liv]	the time that a person spends away from work because of illness or injury
staff	[stæf]	the people who work for an organization
strike	[straɪk]	a period of time when workers refuse to work, usually in order to try to get more money; *go on strike*
temp	[tɛmp]	a temporary office worker
temping agency	[tɛmpɪŋ eɪdʒənsi]	a company that finds jobs for people who want to work in different offices for short periods of time
trade union	[treɪd yunyən]	an organization formed by workers in order to improve conditions for workers
training	[treɪnɪŋ]	the process of learning the skills that you need for a particular job; *a training course*
the unemployed	[ði ʌnɪmplɔɪd]	people who do not have a job
unemployment	[ʌnɪmplɔɪmənt]	a situation in which people cannot work because there are not enough jobs
vacation	[veɪkeɪʃən]	an amount of time in every year when you are paid, but you do not have to go to work; *take vacation*; *be on vacation* (*In British English, use* **annual leave**)
wages	[weɪdʒɪz]	money that is paid to someone for the work that they do; *get your wages*

EXAMPLES

Staff at the hospital went on strike yesterday.
We want to create jobs for the unemployed

| **work** | [wɜrk] | **1** a job that you do to earn money; *find work*
2 the place where you do your job; *go to work* |
| **working week** | [wɜrkɪŋ wik] | the total amount of time that you spend at work during the week; *a 35-hour working week* |

VERBS

apply for a job		to write a letter or write on a form in order to ask for a job
discriminate	[dɪskrɪmɪneɪt]	to treat a person or a group of people unfairly
dismiss	[dɪsmɪs]	to tell someone that they have to leave their job
earn	[ɜrn]	to receive money for work that you do; *earn money*
employ	[ɪmplɔɪ]	to pay someone to work for a person or a company
fire	[faɪər]	[INFORMAL] to tell someone that they have to leave their job; *She was fired from that job.*
hire	[haɪər]	to pay someone to do a job for you
interview	[ɪntərvyu]	to ask someone questions to find out if they are the right person for a particular job
lay off	[leɪ ɔf]	to be forced to leave your job or to force someone to leave a job; *get laid off*; *lay off someone*
pay	[peɪ]	to give someone money for the work that they do; *well/badly paid*
promote	[prəmoʊt]	to give someone a more important job in the same organization

---

EXAMPLES

I start work at 8:30 am and finish at 5 pm.
I'm lucky. I can walk to work.
Richard has just been promoted to general manager.

recruit	[rɪkru̱t]	to choose people to work in an organization
resign	[rɪza̱ɪn]	to tell your employer that you are leaving a job
retire	[rɪta̱ɪər]	to leave your job and stop working, usually because of your age
strike	[stra̱ɪk]	to refuse to work, usually to try to get more money
temp	[tɛmp]	to work as a temp
work	[wɜ̱rk]	to have a job and earn money for it

ADJECTIVES

absent	[æbsᵊnt]	not at work
blue-collar	[blu̱ kɒlər]	working in industry, doing physical work, rather than in offices
freelance	[fri̱læns]	working alone for different companies, rather than being employed by one company that pays you regularly
full-time	[fʊl ta̱ɪm]	working for the whole of each normal working week
laid off	[le̱ɪd ɔf]	without a job because there is not enough work or money to keep you (*In British English, use* **redundant**)
part-time	[pɑrt ta̱ɪm]	working for only part of each day or week
permanent	[pɜ̱rmənənt]	employed for an unlimited length of time
redundant *(BRIT)*		*see* **laid off**
temporary	[tɛmpəreri]	lasting or working for only a certain period of time; *a temporary job*; *temporary workers*
unemployed	[ʌnɪmplɔ̱ɪd]	able to work but without a job
white-collar	[wa̱ɪt kɒlər]	working in offices rather than doing physical work in industry

EXAMPLES
Workers have the right to strike.
Mrs Lee has been temping since losing her job.
Many people in the country are still working for less than the minimum wage.
Have you been unemployed for over six months?

PHRASE

**What do you do
(for a living)?**

you ask "What do you do (for a living)?"
when you want to know what someone's
job is

IDIOMS

get a foot in the door

to manage to enter an organization that
you hope to succeed in

a golden handshake

a large sum of money that a company may
give to an employee when he or she leaves

the rat race

a job or way of life in which people
compete aggressively with each other to
be successful; *get out of the rat race*

environment

NOUNS

bottle bank [bɒtᵊl bæŋk] a large container where you can put empty bottles so that the glass can be recycled

carbon dioxide [kɑrbən daɪɒksaɪd] a gas that is produced when animals and people breathe out, and by certain chemical processes

carbon monoxide [kɑrbən mənɒksaɪd] a harmful gas that is produced by the engines of vehicles

chemical [kɛmɪkᵊl] a substance that is made by changing or combining other substances

climate change [klaɪmɪt tʃeɪndʒ] changes in the Earth's climate (= normal weather) over a long period of time

conservation [kɒnsərveɪʃᵊn] the activity of taking care of the environment; *a conservation group*

crisis [kraɪsɪs] a situation that is very serious or (PL) **crises** [kraɪsiz] dangerous

damage [dæmɪdʒ] physical harm that happens to something

diesel [diːzᵊl] a type of oil that is used in the engines of some vehicles instead of gas

disaster [dɪzæstər] a very bad accident or event that may hurt many people

Earth [ɜrθ] the planet that we live on

electric car [ɪlɛktrɪk kɑr] a car that is powered by electricity

endangered species [ɪndeɪndʒərd spiʃiz] a type of animal or plant that may soon disappear from the world

energy [ɛnərdʒi] the power that makes machines work or that provides heat

the environment [ði ɪnvaɪrənmənt, -vaɪərn-] the natural world, consisting of land, the seas, the air, plants and animals

exhaust fumes [ɪgzɔst fyumz] gases that cars give out as waste

---

EXAMPLES

I'm going to take these bottles to the bottle bank.

Pandas are an endangered species.

You can save energy by switching off your computer when you are not using it.

These gases are harmful to the environment.

fuel	[fyuəl]	a substance such as coal or oil that is burned to provide heat or power
fumes	[fyumz]	the unpleasant and harmful gases that are produced by things such as chemicals and fuel
global warming	[gloubəl wɔrmɪŋ]	the slow rise in the Earth's temperature
greenhouse effect	[grinhaus ɪfɛkt]	the rise in the Earth's temperature caused by a build-up of gases around the Earth
habitat	[hæbɪtæt]	the place where an animal or a plant lives or grows
hydro-electric power	[haɪdrou ɪlɛktrɪk pauər]	electricity that is produced by water power
industrial waste	[ɪndʌstriəl weɪst]	waste produced by factories
landfill	[lændfɪl]	**1** a method of disposing of a lot of waste by burying it in a large deep hole; *the cost of landfill* **2** a large deep hole that waste is buried in; *a landfill site*
low-energy bulb	[lou ɛnərdʒi bʌlb]	a light bulb that uses less electricity than normal light bulbs
nature	[neɪtʃər]	all the animals and plants in the world, as well as the land and the sea
nuclear power	[nukliər pauər]	energy that is produced when the central part of an atom is split
nuclear waste	[nukliər weɪst]	harmful material from nuclear plants
oxygen	[ɒksɪdʒən]	a colorless gas that people, plants, and animals need to breathe in order to live
ozone layer	[ouzoun leɪər]	a part of the atmosphere that protects us from harmful rays from the sun; *a hole in the ozone layer*
planet	[plænɪt]	a large, round object in space that moves around a star. The Earth is a planet.

EXAMPLES

Scientists are trying to find a solution to global warming.
The pollution of rivers destroys the habitats of many fish.
Millions of plastic bags go to landfill every day.

pollution	[pəluʃən]	**1** the process of making water, air, or land dirty and dangerous; *the pollution of our oceans* **2** harmful substances that make water, air, or land dirty and dangerous; *high levels of pollution*
population	[pɒpyəleɪʃən]	all the people who live in a country or an area
rainforest	[reɪnfɔrɪst]	a thick forest of tall trees that grows in tropical areas where there is a lot of rain
recycling	[risaɪklɪŋ]	processing things such as paper and glass so that they can be used again
renewable energy	[rɪnuəbəl ɛnərdʒi]	power from wind, water, and sunlight, which are always available
sewage	[suɪdʒ]	waste material, especially from people's bodies, which flows away through underground pipes
solar panel	[soulər pænəl]	a piece of equipment on a roof that collects energy from sunlight in order to heat water and produce electricity
solar power	[soulər pauər]	energy from the sun that is used to heat water and produce electricity
solution	[səluʃən]	a way of dealing with a problem
unleaded gas	[ʌnlɛdɪd gæs]	gas that contains less lead than normal gas and causes less damage to the environment (*In British English, use* **unleaded petrol**)
unleaded petrol (*BRIT*)		*see* **unleaded gas**
wildlife	[waɪldlaɪf]	the animals and other living things that live in nature
wind power	[wɪnd pauər]	energy from the wind that can be used to make electricity

---

EXAMPLES

The government have plans to reduce air pollution.
The population of Bangladesh is rising every year.
We installed solar panels on our roof last year.
This car runs on unleaded gas.

world	[wɜrld]	the planet that we live on

VERBS

ban	[bæn]	to say officially that something must not be done, shown, or used; *ban the use of chemicals*
damage	[dæmɪdʒ]	to have a bad effect on something so that it is less strong or successful
destroy	[dɪstrɔɪ]	to cause so much damage to something that it cannot be used any longer, or does not exist any longer
dispose of something		to get rid of something; *dispose of waste*
dump	[dʌmp]	to leave something somewhere quickly and carelessly
harm	[hɑrm]	same as **damage**
pollute	[pəlut]	to make water, air, or land dirty
preserve	[prɪzɜrv]	to take action to save something or protect it; *preserve nature*
protect	[prətɛkt]	to keep someone or something safe from harm or damage; *protect wildlife*
recycle	[risaɪkəl]	to process things such as paper or bottles so that they can be used again
save	[seɪv]	**1** to protect something from harm; *save the rainforests* **2** to use less of something; *save paper*
use something up		to finish something so that none of it is left; *use up resources*

ADJECTIVES

biodegradable	[baɪoʊ-dɪgreɪdəbəl]	able to decay naturally without harming the environment; *biodegradable packaging*

EXAMPLES

This book was printed on recycled paper.

We should recycle our trash.

They are developing a new kind of biodegradable plastic.

eco-friendly	[ɛkoʊ frɛndli, ikoʊ]	same as **environmentally friendly**; *an eco-friendly product*
environ- mentally friendly	[ɪnvaɪrən- mɛntᵊli frɛndli, -vaɪərn-]	not harmful to the environment, or less harmful to the environment
extinct	[ɪkstɪŋkt]	not existing any more; *this species is extinct*
green	[grin]	relating to the protection of the environment; *green policies*
harmful	[hɑrmfəl]	having a bad effect on someone or something
organic	[ɔrgænɪk]	grown without using chemicals
sustainable	[səsteɪnəbᵊl]	using natural products in a way that does not damage the environment; *sustainable farming*; *sustainable development*

EXAMPLES

These houses were built using eco-friendly materials.
How can we make our company more environmentally friendly?
Many animals will soon be extinct.
We are trying to be greener by walking to work rather than driving.
This shop sells organic food.

feelings and personal qualities

anger	[æŋgər]	the strong emotion that you feel when you think that someone has behaved badly or has treated you unfairly
excitement	[ɪksaɪtmənt]	the feeling you have when you are excited
fear	[fɪər]	the unpleasant feeling you have when you think that you are in danger
feeling	[fiːlɪŋ]	a state in which you feel something such as anger or happiness
feelings	[fiːlɪŋz]	your emotions; *hurt someone's feelings*
guilt	[gɪlt]	an unhappy feeling that you have when you think that you have done something wrong
happiness	[hæpɪnɪs]	a feeling of being pleased and satisfied
honesty	[ɒnɪsti]	the quality of being honest
intelligence	[ɪntɛlɪdʒᵊns]	the ability to understand and learn things quickly and well
kindness	[kaɪndnɪs]	the quality of being friendly and helpful
mood	[muːd]	the way you are feeling at a particular time
nature	[neɪtʃər]	a person's character, which they show by the way they behave; *a friendly nature*
personality	[pɜrsənælɪti]	the qualities that make you different from other people

EXAMPLES

Everyone is in a state of great excitement.
My whole body was shaking with fear.
Sara has a fear of mice.
I have a feeling that everything will be all right.
They have strong feelings about politics.
She felt a lot of guilt about her children's unhappiness.
I am always in a good mood.
He is in a bad mood.
She is a very good-natured child.

pride	[praɪd]	**1** a feeling of satisfaction that you have because you have done something well; *a sense of pride* **2** a sense of dignity and self-respect
quality	[kwɒlɪti]	a particular characteristic that a person has
regret	[rɪgrɛt]	a feeling of sadness caused by something that you have done or not done; *express regret*
relief	[rɪliːf]	the feeling of happiness that you get when something unpleasant has not happened or is no longer happening
spite	[spaɪt]	a feeling that makes you do something to hurt or upset someone; *He did it out of spite.*
stupidity	[stupɪdɪti]	lack of intelligence or consideration
surprise	[sərpraɪz]	the feeling you have when something that you do not expect happens

ADJECTIVES

ambitious	[æmbɪʃəs]	having a strong feeling that you want to be successful, rich, or powerful
angry	[æŋgri]	feeling a strong emotion when someone has done something bad or has treated you unfairly
annoyed	[ənɔɪd]	angry about something
anxious	[æŋkʃəs]	nervous or worried
ashamed	[əʃeɪmd]	feeling embarrassed or guilty
bored	[bɔrd]	not interested in something, or having nothing to do; *get bored*

EXAMPLES

He takes great pride in his work.
His pride wouldn't allow him to ask for help.
She has lots of good qualities.
He had no regrets about leaving.
I breathed a sigh of relief.
To my surprise, I found I liked working hard.
I was ashamed of myself for getting so angry.

calm	[kɑm]	not worried, angry, or excited; *Try to keep calm.*
cheerful	[tʃɪərfəl]	happy
competent	[kɒmpɪtənt]	able to do something well
confident	[kɒnfɪdənt]	feeling sure about your own abilities and ideas
curious	[kyuəriəs]	wanting to know more about something
depressed	[dɪprɛst]	feeling very sad
dishonest	[dɪsɒnɪst]	not honest
dissatisfied	[dɪssætɪsfaɪd]	not happy about something; *dissatisfied customers*
embarrassed	[ɪmbærəst]	feeling shy, ashamed, or guilty about something
enthusiastic	[ɪnθuziæstɪk]	showing how much you like or enjoy something
envious	[ɛnviəs]	wanting something that someone else has
excited	[ɪksaɪtɪd]	very happy or enthusiastic
friendly	[frɛndli]	behaving in a pleasant, kind way; *Samir was friendly to me.*
frightened	[fraɪtᵊnd]	anxious or afraid
frustrated	[frʌstreɪtɪd]	upset or angry because there is nothing you can do about a problem
funny	[fʌni]	amusing and likely to make you smile or laugh
furious	[fyuəriəs]	extremely angry
glad	[glæd]	happy and pleased about something
grateful	[greɪtfəl]	wanting to thank someone for something that they have given you or done for you

EXAMPLES

She was very depressed after her husband died.
He looked a bit embarrassed when he noticed his mistake.
Tom was not very enthusiastic about the idea.
I have to admit I was a little envious
I was excited about playing football again.
She was frightened of making a mistake.
They seemed glad to see me.
She was grateful to him for being so helpful.

guilty	[gɪlti]	feeling unhappy because you think that you have done something wrong; *feel guilty*
happy	[hæpi]	feeling pleased and satisfied; *a happy child*
helpful	[hɛlpfʊl]	helping you by doing something useful for you
honest	[ɒnɪst]	always telling the truth and not stealing or cheating
hurt	[hɜrt]	upset because of something that someone has said or done
impatient	[ɪmpeɪʃⁿt]	**1** annoyed because you have to wait too long for something **2** becoming annoyed very quickly
independent	[ɪndɪpɛndənt]	able to take care of yourself without needing help or money from anyone else
insecure	[ɪnsɪkyʊər]	not confident
intelligent	[ɪntɛlɪdʒⁿnt]	able to understand and learn things quickly and well
jealous	[dʒɛləs]	**1** feeling angry because you think that another person is trying to take away someone or something that you love **2** feeling angry or unhappy because you do not have something that someone else has
kind	[kaɪnd]	friendly and helpful
lonely	[loʊnli]	unhappy because you are alone
loving	[lʌvɪŋ]	feeling or showing love for other people; *a loving husband*
mean	[min]	unkind or cruel

EXAMPLES

She was deeply hurt by Ali's remarks.
People are impatient for the war to be over.
Try not to be impatient with your kids.
Children become more independent as they grow.
Most people are a little insecure about their looks.
He got jealous and there was a fight.
She was jealous of her sister's success.
Don't be mean to your brother!

miserable	[mɪzərəbəl]	very unhappy
naughty	[nɔti]	badly behaved, and not doing what someone tells you to do; *a naughty boy*
nervous	[nɜrvəs]	frightened or worried
nice	[naɪs]	friendly and pleasant
optimistic	[ɒptɪmɪstɪk]	hopeful about the success of something
pessimistic	[pɛsɪmɪstɪk]	thinking that bad things are going to happen
pleased	[plizd]	happy about something or satisfied with something; *I am very pleased with your work.*
polite	[pəlaɪt]	behaving with respect towards other people
proud	[praʊd]	**1** pleased and satisfied about something good that you or other people close to you have done **2** thinking that you are better than other people
relaxed	[rɪlækst]	calm and not worried
relieved	[rɪlivd]	feeling happy because something unpleasant has not happened or is no longer happening
rude	[rud]	not polite
sad	[sæd]	unhappy
satisfied	[sætɪsfaɪd]	happy because you have what you wanted
scared	[skɛərd]	frightened; *I'm not scared of him.*
selfish	[sɛlfɪʃ]	caring only about yourself, and not about other people
sensitive	[sɛnsɪtɪv]	**1** showing that you understand other people's feelings **2** easily worried and offended about something when people talk about it

EXAMPLES

They were extremely nice to me.
His dad was very proud of him.
We are relieved to be back home.
The classroom teacher must be sensitive to a child's needs.
Young people can be sensitive about their appearance.

serious	[sɪərɪəs]	thinking a lot, and not smiling or laughing much
shocked	[ʃɒkt]	very upset because of something unpleasant that has happened
shy	[ʃaɪ]	nervous about talking to people that you do not know well
stupid	[stupɪd]	not intelligent, and not able to behave in a sensible way
surprised	[sərpraɪzd]	having the feeling you get when something happens that you did not expect
suspicious	[səspɪʃəs]	not trusting someone or something
thoughtful	[θɔtfəl]	thinking about other people's feelings
thoughtless	[θɔtlɪs]	not thinking about other people's feelings
uncomfortable	[ʌnkʌmftəbᵊl, -kʌmfərtə-]	slightly worried or embarrassed
unhappy	[ʌnhæpi]	**1** sad **2** not satisfied with something
upset	[ʌpsɛt]	unhappy because something bad has happened; *Marta looked upset.*
well-behaved	[wɛl bɪheɪvd]	behaving in a way that other people think is polite and correct; *well-behaved little boys*
worried	[wɜrid]	thinking about problems that you have or about unpleasant things that might happen

EXAMPLES
She was deeply shocked when she heard the news.
We were surprised by the play's success.
It was thoughtless of me to forget your birthday.
The request for money made them feel uncomfortable.
We were unhappy with the way we played on Friday.
When she did not come home, they got worried.

VERBS

become	[bɪkʌm]	to start to feel a particular way; *become anxious*
behave	[bɪheɪv]	to do and say things in a particular way; *behave strangely*
calm down		to become less upset or excited
enjoy	[ɪndʒɔɪ]	to like doing something
enjoy yourself		to get pleasure from an experience
feel	[fiːl]	to experience a particular emotion; *How do you feel?*
grow	[grou]	to begin to have a particular feeling; *Lisbet soon grew bored.*
hurt	[hɜrt]	to say or do something that makes someone unhappy
suffer	[sʌfər]	to feel pain, sadness or worry
upset	[ʌpsɛt]	to make you feel worried or unhappy

IDIOMS

down in the dumps	unhappy or depressed
get on someone's nerves	to annoy someone
hit the roof	to suddenly become very angry
over the moon	extremely happy and excited

EXAMPLES
I enjoyed playing basketball.
I'm really sorry if I hurt your feelings.
His behavior really upset me.

food and drink

NOUNS

food   [fu̠d]   the things that people and animals eat

MEAT AND FISH

bacon   [be̠ɪkən]   slices of salted or smoked meat that comes from a pig; *eggs and bacon for breakfast*

beef   [bi̠f]   meat from a cow

chicken   [tʃɪ̠kɪn]   **1** a bird that is kept on a farm for its eggs and meat
2 the meat of this bird; *chicken sandwiches*

fish   [fɪ̠ʃ]   an animal that lives and swims in water, that people eat as food
  (PL) **fish, fishes**

gravy   [gre̠ɪvi]   a sauce made from the juices that come from meat when it cooks

ground beef   [gra̠und bi̠f]   meat that has been cut into very small pieces using a machine (*In British English, use* **mince**))

ham   [hæ̠m]   meat from a pig that has been prepared with salt and spices; *ham sandwiches*

hamburger   [hæ̠mbɜrgər]   a type of food made from small pieces of meat that have been shaped into a flat circle. Hamburgers are fried or grilled and are often eaten in a round bread roll.

lamb   [læ̠m]   the flesh of a young sheep eaten as food

meat   [mi̠t]   the part of an animal that people cook and eat

mince *(BRIT)*   *see* **ground beef**

pork   [pɔ̠rk]   meat from a pig

sausage   [sɔ̠sɪdʒ]   a mixture of very small pieces of meat, spices and other foods, inside a long thin skin

---

EXAMPLES

We had roast beef for lunch.
I don't eat meat or fish.
Fry the ground beef in a frying pan.
For supper, she served lamb and vegetables.
They ate sausages for breakfast.

seafood	[sifud]	fish and other small animals from the sea that you can eat; *a seafood restaurant*
steak	[steɪk]	**1** a large flat piece of beef without much fat on it; *steak and fries* **2** a large piece of fish that does not contain many bones; *a salmon steak*

EGGS, CHEESE AND MILK PRODUCTS

butter	[bʌtər]	a soft yellow food made from cream that you spread on bread or use in cooking
cheese	[tʃiz]	a solid food that is usually white or yellow and is made from milk
cream	[krim]	a thick liquid that is made from milk; *whipped cream*
custard	[kʌstərd]	a sweet yellow sauce made of milk, eggs, and sugar
egg	[ɛg]	a hen's egg, that people eat as food in many countries; *a boiled egg*; *a hard-boiled egg*; *a poached egg*; *scrambled eggs*
ice cream	[aɪs krim]	**1** a frozen sweet food made from cream, sugar, and sometimes fruit or chocolate; *chocolate ice cream* **2** a portion of ice cream; *two ice creams*
margarine	[mɑrdʒərɪn]	a yellow substance that is made from vegetable oil, and is similar to butter; *a tub of margarine*
mayonnaise	[meɪəneɪz]	a cold, thick sauce made from eggs and oil
omelet	[ɒmlɪt, ɒməlɪt]	a type of food made by mixing eggs and cooking them in a frying pan; *a cheese omelet* (In British English, use **omelette**)
omelette (BRIT)		*see* **omelet**
yoghurt (BRIT)		*see* **yogurt**
yogurt	[yoʊgərt]	a thick liquid food that is made from milk (In British English, use **yoghurt**)

EXAMPLES

Jordi spread some butter on a roll.
We had apple pie and custard for dessert.
Break the eggs into a bowl.

BREAD, CAKES, AND BISCUITS

biscuit (BRIT)   *see* **cookie**

bread   [brɛd]   a food made mostly from flour and water and baked in an oven; *a slice of bread*

cake   [keɪk]   a sweet food that you make from flour, eggs, sugar, and butter; *a birthday cake*

cookie   [kʊki]   a type of hard, dry cake that is usually sweet and round in shape; *a chocolate biscuit* (*In British English, use* **biscuit**)

loaf   [loʊf]   bread that has been shaped and baked in one large piece; *a loaf of bread*

pancake   [pænkeɪk]   a thin, round food made from milk, flour, and eggs, cooked in a frying pan

roll   [roʊl]   bread in a small round or long shape

sandwich   [sænwɪtʃ,   two slices of bread with another food such
                   sænd-]   as cheese or meat between them; *a cheese sandwich*; *a toasted sandwich*

toast   [toʊst]   slices of bread that you have heated until they are hard and brown; *slices of toast*

OTHER FOOD

candy   [kændi]   small pieces of sweet food such as chocolates (*In British English, use* **sweets**)

cereal   [sɪəriəl]   **1** a food made from grain, that people eat with milk for breakfast; *a bowl of cereal*
                                   2 a plant that produces grain for food; *cereal grains such as corn and wheat*

chips   **1** very thin slices of potato that have been cooked in oil and are eaten as a snack; *a bag of potato chips* (*In British English, use* **crisps**)
                                   2 (BRIT) *see* **fries**

EXAMPLES

Patricia put two pieces of bread on a plate and buttered them.

I blew out the candles and Mom sliced the cake.

Raul ate a piece of chocolate cake.

He spread some butter on a roll.

Eat more fruit and vegetables and less candy.

chocolate	[tʃɔkəlɪt, tʃɔklɪt]	**1** a brown food eaten as a sweet; *a bar of chocolate* **2** a small sweet covered with chocolate; *a box of chocolates*
crisps (*BRIT*)		*see* **chips**
curry	[kɜri]	a dish, originally from Asia, that is cooked with hot spices; *vegetable curry*
dish	[dɪʃ]	food that is prepared in a particular way; *a chicken dish*
fast food	[fæst fud]	hot food, such as hamburgers, that is served quickly after you order it; *a fast food restaurant*
flour	[flaʊər]	a fine powder that is used for making bread, cakes, and pastry; *wholemeal flour*
fries	[fraɪz]	long thin pieces of potato, cooked in oil and eaten hot; *a burger and fries* (*In British English, use* **chips**)
honey	[hʌni]	a sweet, sticky food that is made by bees (= black-and-yellow insects); *a jar of honey*
jam	[dʒæm]	a sweet food containing soft fruit and sugar, that is usually spread on bread; *strawberry jam*
jello	[dʒɛloʊ]	a soft sweet food made from fruit juice and sugar that moves from side to side when you touch it; *jello and ice cream* (*In British English, use* **jelly**)
jelly	[dʒɛli]	**1** same as **jam**; *raspberry jelly* **2** (*BRIT*) *see* **jello**
lasagna	[ləzɑnyə]	a dish that consists of layers of pasta, sauce, and a filling such as meat or cheese, baked in an oven (*In British English, use* **lasagne**)
lasagne (*BRIT*)		*see* **lasagna**

EXAMPLES

Let's eat curry tonight.
My favorite dish is lasagna.

noodles	[nu̱dᵊlz]	long, thin strips of pasta, used especially in Chinese and Italian cooking; *a bowl of noodles*
oil	[ɔɪl]	a smooth, thick liquid made from plants, that is often used for cooking; *vegetable oil*
pasta	[pɑ̱stə]	a type of food made from a mixture of flour, eggs, and water that is made into different shapes and then boiled
pastry	[pe̱ɪstri]	a food made from flour, fat, and water that is often used for making pies
pâté	[pɑte̱ɪ]	a mixture of meat, fish, or vegetables that is mixed into a paste and eaten cold; *liver pâté*
pepper	[pɛ̱pər]	a brown or black spice with a hot taste that you put on food; *salt and pepper*
pie	[pa̱ɪ]	a dish consisting of fruit with a pastry crust
pizza	[pi̱tsə]	a flat, round piece of bread that is covered with tomatoes, cheese, and sometimes other foods, and then baked in an oven
rice	[ra̱ɪs]	white or brown grains from a plant that grows in warm, wet areas; *plain boiled rice*
salad	[sæ̱ləd]	a mixture of foods, especially vegetables, that you usually serve cold; *a green salad*; *a mixed salad*
salt	[sɔ̱lt]	a white substance that you use to improve the flavor of food
sauce	[sɔ̱s]	a thick liquid that you eat with other food; *pasta sauce*
snack	[snæ̱k]	a simple meal that is quick to prepare and eat; *have a snack*
soup	[su̱p]	a liquid food made by boiling meat, fish, or vegetables in water; *home-made soup*
spaghetti	[spəgɛ̱ti]	a type of pasta that looks like long pieces of string

EXAMPLES

The pasta is cooked in a garlic and tomato sauce.
Bruno ordered a thin-crust pizza.
The children have a snack when they come home from school.

stew	[stu]	a meal that you make by cooking meat and vegetables slowly in liquid
sugar	[ʃugər]	a sweet substance used for making food and drinks taste sweet; *a spoonful of sugar*
sweets (*BRIT*)		*see* **candy**
vinegar	[vɪnɪgər]	a sour, sharp-tasting liquid that is used in cooking

DRINKS

alcoholic drink	[ælkəhɔlɪk drɪŋk]	a drink that contains alcohol
beer	[bɪər]	an alcoholic drink made from grain
cider	[saɪdər]	an alcoholic drink made from apples
coffee	[kɔfi]	a drink made from boiling water and the beans of the coffee plant, made into a powder; *strong coffee; Two coffees, please.*
hot chocolate	[hɒt tʃɔkəlɪt, tʃɔklɪt]	a drink made by mixing chocolate powder with milk or water
ice cube	[aɪs kyub]	a small block of ice that you put into a drink to make it cold
juice	[dʒus]	the liquid that comes from a fruit or a vegetable; *orange/apple/lemon/fruit juice*
lemonade	[lɛməneɪd]	a drink that is made from lemons, sugar, and water
milk	[mɪlk]	the white liquid that cows and some other animals produce, which people drink
mineral water	[mɪnərəl wɔtər]	water that comes out of the ground naturally and is considered healthy to drink
soft drink	[sɔft drɪŋk]	a cold non-alcoholic drink such as ginger ale
tap water	[tæp wɔtər]	the water that comes out of a tap in a building such as a house or a hotel

EXAMPLES

She gave him a bowl of beef stew.
Do you take sugar in your coffee?
We ordered a couple of beers and asked for the menu.

tea	[ti]	a drink that you make by pouring boiling water on the dry leaves of a plant called the tea bush; *a pot of tea*
whisky	[wɪski]	a strong alcoholic drink made from grain
wine	[waɪn]	an alcoholic drink made from grapes (= small green or purple fruit); *red/white wine*; *a glass of wine*

ITEMS USED FOR EATING, DRINKING, AND SERVING MEALS

bottle	[bɒtˀl]	a glass or plastic container in which drinks and other liquids are kept
bowl	[boʊl]	a round container that is used for mixing and serving food
chopsticks	[tʃɒpstɪks]	a pair of thin sticks that people in East Asia use for eating food
cup	[kʌp]	a small round container that you drink from; *a cup of coffee*
dish	[dɪʃ]	a shallow container for cooking or serving food; *a serving dish*; *a dish of hot vegetables*
fork	[fɔrk]	a tool with long metal points, used for eating food; *knives and forks*
glass	[glæs]	a container made from glass, which you can drink from
jug	[dʒʌg]	a container with a handle, used for holding and pouring liquids; *a milk jug*
knife (PL) **knives**	[naɪf] [naɪvz]	a sharp flat piece of metal with a handle, used for cutting things; *a sharp/blunt knife*
mug	[mʌg]	a deep cup with straight sides; *a mug of coffee*
napkin	[næpkɪn]	a square of cloth or paper that you use when you are eating to protect your clothes, or to wipe your mouth or hands
plate	[pleɪt]	a flat dish that is used for holding food; *a plate of sandwiches*
saucer	[sɔsər]	a small curved plate that you put under a cup

EXAMPLES
Put the soup in a bowl.

spoon	[spun]	a long object with a round end that is used for eating, serving or mixing food; *a serving spoon*
straw	[strɔ]	a thin tube that you use to suck a drink into your mouth
teapot	[tipɒt]	a container that is used for making and serving tea
teaspoon	[tispun]	a small spoon that you use for putting sugar into tea or coffee

CAFÉS AND RESTAURANTS

à la carte	[ɑ lə kɑrt]	an à la carte menu in a restaurant is a list of dishes that each have a different price
bar	[bɑr]	a place where you can buy and drink alcoholic drinks
bill *(BRIT)*		*see* **check**
café	[kæfeɪ]	a place where you can buy drinks and small meals
check	[tʃɛk]	a document that shows how much money you must pay for something (*In British English, use* **bill**)
chef	[ʃɛf]	a person who prepares and cooks food in a restaurant
menu	[mɛnyu]	a list of the food and drink that you can have in a restaurant
order	[ɔrdər]	the food or drink that you ask for in a bar, café or restaurant
restaurant	[rɛstərənt, -tərɑnt, -trɑnt]	a place where you can buy and eat a meal
service	[sɜrvɪs]	the help that people in a restaurant or a shop give you; *give/get good/poor service*

EXAMPLES

Maisie was drinking juice with a straw.
Can we have the check please?

tip	[tɪp]	money that you give to a waiter or waitress to thank them for a job they have done for you
waiter	[weɪtər]	a man whose job is to serve food in a restaurant
waitress	[weɪtrɪs]	a woman whose job is to serve food in a restaurant
wine list	[waɪn lɪst]	a menu of wines that are available in a restaurant

EXPERIENCING FOOD

flavor	[fleɪvər]	the taste of a food or drink (*In British English, use* **flavour**)
flavour *(BRIT)*		*see* **flavor**
hunger	[hʌŋgər]	the feeling that you get when you need something to eat
smell	[smɛl]	the quality of something that you notice when you breathe in through your nose; *a lovely smell*
taste	[teɪst]	**1** the particular quality that something has when you put it in your mouth, for example whether it is sweet or salty; *the taste of chocolate*; *a horrible taste* **2** a small amount of food or drink that you try in order to see what the flavor is like; *Have a taste of this.*
thirst	[θɜrst]	the feeling that you get when you want to drink something

MEALS AND PARTS OF MEALS

appetizer	[æpɪtaɪzər]	a small amount of food that you eat as the first part of a meal
breakfast	[brɛkfəst]	the first meal of the day; *have breakfast*

EXAMPLES

I gave the waiter a tip.
The waitress brought our food and said, "Enjoy your meal!"
I added some pepper for extra flavor.
There was a horrible smell in the fridge.
I just love the smell of freshly baked bread.

course	[kɔrs]	one part of a meal; *a three-course meal*
dessert	[dɪzɜrt]	something sweet that you eat at the end of a meal
dinner	[dɪnər]	the main meal of the day, usually served in the evening; *have dinner*; *invite someone for dinner*
lunch	[lʌntʃ]	the meal that you have in the middle of the day; *have lunch*
main course	[meɪn kɔrs]	the most important course of a meal
meal	[mil]	**1** an occasion when people sit down and eat **2** the food that you eat during a meal
starter	[stɑrtər]	same as **appetizer**

VERBS

drink	[drɪŋk]	**1** to take liquid into your mouth and swallow it; *drink some water* **2** to drink alcohol; *I don't drink.*
eat	[it]	to put something into your mouth and swallow it
order	[ɔrdər]	to ask for food or drink in a bar, café or restaurant
serve	[sɜrv]	to give people food and drinks in a restaurant or bar; *A waiter served us.*
smell	[smɛl]	**1** to have a quality that you notice by breathing in through your nose; *That cake smells delicious.* **2** to notice something when you breathe in through your nose; *I can smell garlic.*
swallow	[swɒloʊ]	to make something go from your mouth down into your stomach

EXAMPLES

The meal consisted of chicken, rice, and vegetables.
Noah served me coffee and chocolate cake.
That smells good!
Polly took a bite of the apple and swallowed it.

taste	[teɪst]	**1** to have a particular flavor; *It tastes of lemons.*
		2 to eat or drink a small amount of food or drink in order to see what the flavor is like; *Taste the soup.*
		3 to be aware of the flavor of something that you are eating or drinking; *Can you taste the garlic?*

ADJECTIVES

bad	[bæd]	food that is bad tastes and smells unpleasant because it is no longer fresh enough to be eaten; *gone bad*
canned	[kænd]	canned food lasts a long time because it is in a strong metal container (called a can); *canned tomatoes* (In British English, use **tinned**)
carbonated	[kɑrbəneɪtɪd]	carbonated drinks contain small bubbles (In British English, use **fizzy**)
delicious	[dɪlɪʃəs]	very good to eat
disgusting	[dɪsgʌstɪŋ]	extremely unpleasant
fizzy *(BRIT)*		*see* **carbonated**
fresh	[frɛʃ]	picked or prepared recently; *fresh vegetables*
frozen	[froʊzᵊn]	used for describing food that has been stored at a very low temperature; *frozen vegetables*
hungry	[hʌngri]	wanting to eat
juicy	[dʒusi]	containing a lot of juice in a pleasant way
off *(BRIT)*		*see* **bad**
organic	[ɔrgænɪk]	grown without using chemicals
raw	[rɔ]	not cooked; *raw fish*

EXAMPLES
The water tasted of metal.
Don't add salt until you've tasted the food.
The pizza tastes delicious.

salty	[sɔlti]	containing salt or tasting of salt
savory	[seɪvəri]	having a salty flavor rather than a sweet one (*In British English, use* **savoury**)
savoury (*BRIT*)		*see* **savory**
sour	[sauər]	**1** with a sharp taste like the taste of a lemon **2** tasting bad; not fresh; *sour milk*
stale	[steɪl]	no longer fresh; *stale bread*
sweet	[swit]	containing a lot of sugar
thirsty	[θɜrsti]	wanting to drink something
tinned (*BRIT*)		*see* **canned**

[PHRASES]

Can I take your order?	used by a waiter to ask what you would like to eat
Cheers!	you say "Cheers!" to each other as you lift up your glasses to drink
Enjoy your meal!	you say "Enjoy your meal!" to someone just before they begin to eat
Is everything all right?	used by a waiter to ask if you are enjoying your food

friends and family

NOUNS

acquaintance	[əkwe͟ɪntəns]	someone you have met, but that you don't know well
adult	[ədʌ͟lt]	a fully grown person or animal
aunt	[æ͟nt, ɑ͟nt]	the sister of your mother or father, or the wife of your uncle
auntie	[æ͟nti, ɑ͟nti]	[INFORMAL] aunt
baby	[be͟ɪbi]	a very young child
baby boy	[be͟ɪbi bɔ͟ɪ]	a very young boy
baby girl	[be͟ɪbi gɜ͟rl]	a very young girl
bachelor	[bæ͟tʃələr]	a man who has never married
boy	[bɔ͟ɪ]	a male child
boyfriend	[bɔ͟ɪfrɛnd]	a man or a boy that someone is having a romantic relationship with
brother	[brʌ͟ðər]	a boy or a man who has the same parents as you
brother-in-law (PL) **brothers-in-law**	[brʌ͟ðər ɪn lɔ] [brʌ͟ðərz ɪn lɔ]	the brother of your husband or wife, or the man who is married to your sister.
child (PL) **children**	[tʃa͟ɪld] [tʃɪ͟ldrən]	a young boy or girl, someone's son or daughter
Christian name	[krɪ͟stʃən ne͟ɪm]	same as **first name**
couple	[kʌ͟pəl]	two people who are married or having a romantic relationship
cousin	[kʌ͟zən]	the child of your uncle or your aunt
dad	[dæ͟d]	[INFORMAL] **1** father; *This is my dad.* **2** a word you use when you are talking to your father; *Hi, Dad!*
daughter	[dɔ͟tər]	a person's female child

EXAMPLES
He was just a casual acquaintance.
I'm going to stay with my auntie for the holidays.
Hannah is going to have a baby.
Congratulations on the birth of your baby boy!
Do you have any brothers or sisters?
I have one brother and one sister.

daughter-in-law [dɔtər ɪn lɔ]   the wife of your son
(PL) **daughters-**
  in-law   [dɔtərz ɪn lɔ]

family   [fæmɪli,   a group of people who are related to each
      fæmli]   other, usually parents and their children

father   [fɑðər]   your male parent

father-in-law [fɑðər ɪn lɔ]   the father of your husband or wife
(PL) **fathers-in-law** [fɑðərz ɪn lɔ]

fiancé   [fiɑnseɪ,   the man that a woman is going to marry
     fiɑnseɪ]

fiancée   [fiɑnseɪ,   the woman that a man is going to marry
     fiɑnseɪ]

first name   [fɜrst neɪm]   the name that you were given when you
     were born

friend   [frɛnd]   someone who you like and know well

girl   [gɜrl]   a female child

girlfriend   [gɜrlfrɛnd]   a girl or woman who someone is having a
     romantic relationship with

grandchild   [græntʃaɪld]   the child of your son or daughter
(PL) **grandchildren** [græntʃɪldrən]

granddaughter [grændɔtər]   the daughter of your son or daughter

grandfather   [grænfɑðər]   the father of your father or mother

grandma   [grænmɑ]   [INFORMAL] **1** grandmother; *My grandma
     lives with us.*
     2 a word you use when you are talking to
     your grandmother; *Look, Grandma!*

grandmother   [grænmʌðər]   the mother of your father or mother

grandpa   [grænpɑ]   [INFORMAL] **1** grandfather; *My grandpa is
     nearly 70.*
     2 a word you use when you are talking to
     your grandfather; *Hello, Grandpa!*

EXAMPLES

May I introduce my fiancée, Cheryl Ferguson?
How many grandchildren have you got?
I visit my grandma every weekend.
My grandmother is dead.

grandparents	[grænd-pɛrənts, -pær-]	the parents of your mother or father
grandson	[grænsʌn]	the son of your son or daughter
grown-up	[groʊn ʌp]	a child's word for an adult
husband	[hʌzbənd]	the man that a woman is married to
last name	[læst neɪm]	the name that you share with other members of your family
maiden name	[meɪdən neɪm]	a woman's surname before she married
mom	[mɒm]	[INFORMAL] **1** mother; *This is my mom.* **2** a word you use when you are talking to your mother; *Can I go out, Mom?* (*In British English, use* **mum**)
mother	[mʌðər]	your female parent
mother-in-law (PL) **mothers-in-law**	[mʌðər ɪn lɔ] [mʌðərz ɪn lɔ]	the mother of your husband or wife
mum (*BRIT*)		*see* **mom**
name	[neɪm]	the word or words that you use to talk to a particular person, or to talk about them
neighbor	[neɪbər]	someone who lives near you (*In British English, use* **neighbour**)
neighbour (*BRIT*)		*see* **neighbor**
nephew	[nɛfyu]	the son of your sister or brother
nickname	[nɪkneɪm]	an informal name that people use for a particular person
niece	[nis]	the daughter of your sister or brother
old-age	[oʊld eɪdʒ]	the period of years towards the end of your life
only child (PL) **only children**	[oʊnli tʃaɪld] [oʊnli tʃɪldrən]	a child who does not have any brothers or sisters

---

EXAMPLES

"What is your last name?" — "Smith."
"What is your name?" — "Daniela."
His name is Paolo.
I am an only child.

orphan [ɔrfən] a child whose parents are dead

parents [pɛərənts, pær-] your mother and father

relative [rɛlətɪv] a member of your family

single man [sɪŋɡəl mæn] a man who is not married
  (PL) **single men** [sɪŋɡəl mɛn]

single parent [sɪŋɡəl pɛərənt, pær-] someone who looks after their children alone, because the other parent does not live with them

single woman [sɪŋɡəl wʊmən] a woman who is not married
  (PL) **single women** [sɪŋɡəl wɪmɪn]

sister [sɪstər] a girl or woman who has the same parents as you

sister-in-law [sɪstər ɪn lɔ] the sister of your husband or wife, or the woman who is married to your brother
  (PL) **sisters-in-law** [sɪstərz ɪn lɔ]

son [sʌn] your male child

son-in-law [sʌn ɪn lɔ] the husband of your daughter
  (PL) **sons-in-law** [sʌnz ɪn lɔ]

stepbrother [stɛpbrʌðər] the son of your stepfather or stepmother

stepdaughter [stɛpdɔtər] a daughter who was born to your husband or wife during a previous relationship

stepfather [stɛpfɑðər] the man who has married someone's mother but who is not their father

stepmother [stɛpmʌðər] the woman who has married someone's father but who is not their mother

stepsister [stɛpsɪstər] the daughter of your stepfather or stepmother

stepson [stɛpsʌn] a son who was born to your husband or wife during a previous relationship

surname [sɜrneɪm] same as **last name**

EXAMPLES
I get along with my parents.
I don't have any brothers or sisters.
My older sister is at college.
I have three stepsisters.

teenager	[tineɪdʒər]	someone who is between thirteen and nineteen years old
triplets	[trɪplɪts]	three children who were born at the same time to the same mother
twins	[twɪnz]	two children who were born at the same time to the same mother
uncle	[ʌŋkəl]	the brother of your mother or father, or the husband of your aunt
widow	[wɪdoʊ]	a woman whose husband has died
widower	[wɪdoʊər]	a man whose wife has died
wife	[waɪf]	the woman a man is married to
(PL) **wives**	[waɪvz]	

VERBS

adopt	[ədɒpt]	to take someone else's child into your own family and make them legally your son or daughter; *adopt a child*
be born		when a baby is born, it comes out of its mother's body at the beginning of its life
break up		**1** if two people break up, their relationship ends; *Marianne and Pierre broke up last year.* **2** if a marriage or relationship breaks up, it ends; *Their marriage broke up.* **3** if you break up with your boyfriend, girlfriend, husband, or wife, your relationship with that person ends; *I've broken up with Jamie.*
die	[daɪ]	to stop living
divorce	[dɪvɔrs]	if one person divorces another, their marriage is legally ended

EXAMPLES

My father is a widower.
I was born in 1990.
She died in 1995.

fall out		**1** if two people fall out, they have an argument; *We fell out.*
		2 if you fall out with someone, you have an argument and stop being friendly with them; *Chris fell out with Mike.*
foster	[fɔstər]	to take a child into your family for a period of time, without becoming its legal parent; *foster a child*
get divorced		if a man and woman get divorced, their marriage is legally ended
get married		**1** when two people get married they become husband and wife in a special ceremony; *John and Linda got married.*
		2 when you get married to someone, you become their husband or wife in a special ceremony; *John got married to Linda.*
live	[lɪv]	to stay alive until you are a particular age; *live to the age of 94*
marry	[mæri]	to legally become someone's husband or wife in a special ceremony
give birth		when a woman gives birth, she produces a baby from her body
go out with someone		to have a romantic or sexual relationship with someone
grow up		to gradually change from a child into an adult
make friends		**1** when two people make friends, they begin a friendship
		2 when you make friends with someone, you begin a friendship with them
make up		to become friends again after an argument
split up		same as **break up**

EXAMPLES

I fell out with my girlfriend last week, but we've made up now.
She married David Nichols in 2008.
"Are you going out with John?" — "No; we're just good friends."
I grew up in France.
I just split up with my boyfriend.

ADJECTIVES

dead	[dɛd]	not alive
divorced	[dɪvɔrst]	no longer legally married to your former husband or wife
engaged	[ɪngeɪdʒd]	if two people are engaged, they have agreed to marry each other
grown-up	[groʊn ʌp]	mature, and no longer dependent on your parents or another adult
married	[mærid]	having a husband or wife
pregnant	[prɛgnənt]	having a baby or babies developing in your body
separated	[sɛpəreɪtɪd]	living apart from your husband or wife, but not divorced
single	[sɪŋgəl]	not married

IDIOMS

go back a long way	if two people go back a long way, they have known each other for a long time
just good friends	used to say that two people are not having a romantic relationship
your nearest and dearest	your close relatives and friends
something runs in the family	used to say that a characteristic or medical condition is often found in members of a particular family
you would not give someone the time of day	used to say that you do not like someone at all

EXAMPLES
My parents are divorced.
Singing runs in the family.

fruit, nuts, and vegetables

NOUNS

FRUIT

apple	[æpᵊl]	a firm round fruit with green, red, or yellow skin; *apple pie*; *cooking apples*
apricot	[eɪprɪkɒt]	a small, soft, round fruit with yellow flesh and a large seed inside; *apricot jam*
avocado	[ævəkɑdoʊ]	a fruit that does not taste sweet, with dark green skin and a large seed in the middle
banana	[bənænə]	a long curved fruit with yellow skin; *a bunch of bananas*
berry	[bɛri]	a small, round fruit that grows on a bush or a tree
cherry	[tʃɛri]	a small, round fruit with red skin
coconut	[koʊkənʌt]	**1** a very large nut with a hairy shell and white flesh **2** the white flesh of a coconut
date	[deɪt]	a small, dark-brown, sticky fruit with a stone inside
fig	[fɪg]	a soft sweet fruit full of tiny seeds
fruit	[fruːt]	the part of a plant that contains seeds, covered with a substance that you can often eat; *a piece of fruit*; *fresh fruit and vegetables*
grapefruit (PL) **grapefruit,** **grapefruits**	[greɪpfruːt]	a large, round, yellow fruit that has a slightly sour taste
grapes	[greɪps]	small green or purple fruits that grow in bunches and are used to make wine; *a bunch of grapes*
lemon	[lɛmən]	a yellow fruit with a very sour taste
mango	[mæŋgoʊ]	a large, sweet, yellow or red fruit that grows on trees in hot countries; *a mango smoothie*

EXAMPLES

I always have a piece of fruit in my lunchbox.
He squeezed the lemon over his fish.
I like a slice of lemon in my tea.

melon	[mɛlən]	a large fruit with soft, sweet flesh and a hard green or yellow skin
nectarine	[nɛktərin]	a red and yellow fruit with a smooth skin
orange	[ɔrɪndʒ]	a round, juicy fruit with a thick, orange-colored skin
peach	[pitʃ]	a round fruit with a soft red and orange skin
pear	[pɛər]	a juicy fruit that is narrow at the top and wider at the bottom. Pears have white flesh and green, yellow, or brown skin.
peel	[pil]	the skin of a fruit such as a lemon or an apple, especially when it has been removed
pineapple	[paɪnæpᵊl]	a large fruit with sweet, yellow flesh and thick, rough, brown skin
pip (BRIT)		see **seed**
pit	[pɪt]	the large hard seed in the middle of a fruit such as a plum or a cherry; *a cherry pit* (In British English, use **stone**)
plum	[plʌm]	a small, sweet fruit with a smooth purple, red, or yellow skin and a large seed in the middle
raisin	[reɪzᵊn]	a dried grape
raspberry	[ræzbɛri]	a small, soft, red fruit that grows on bushes; *raspberry jam*
rhubarb	[rubɑrb]	a plant with large leaves and long red stems that are cooked with sugar to make jam or desserts
seed	[sid]	one of the small, hard pieces in a fruit such as an apple or an orange (In British English, use **pip**)
skin	[skɪn]	the outer part that covers a fruit
stone (BRIT)		see **pit**
strawberry	[strɔbɛri]	a small soft red fruit that has a lot of very small seeds on its skin; *strawberries and cream*

EXAMPLES

I'd like a pound of oranges, please.
It was a very sweet and juicy pear.
Can I have half a kilo of plums, please?

tomato	[təmeɪtoʊ]	a soft red fruit that you can eat raw in salads or cook like a vegetable; *sliced/chopped tomatoes*; *sun-dried tomatoes*; *tomato sauce/soup/juice*; *tomato puree/paste*

NUTS

brazil nut	[brəzɪl nʌt]	a curved nut with a hard dark-brown shell with three sides
cashew nut	[kæʃu nʌt, kæʃu]	a small curved nut that is often eaten salted
chestnut	[tʃɛsnʌt, -nət]	a reddish-brown nut with a shell that has points on it; *roasted chestnuts*
hazelnut	[heɪzᵊlnʌt]	a round nut with a hard shell
peanut	[pinʌt, -nət]	a small round nut often eaten roasted and salted; *a packet of salted peanuts*
walnut	[wɔlnʌt, -nət]	a nut that is hard and round, with a rough texture

VEGETABLES

aubergine *(BRIT)*		*see* **eggplant**
beans	[bins]	seeds or seed cases of a climbing plant, that are usually cooked before eating; *baked beans*; *green beans*; *broad beans*; *soy beans*
beet	[bit]	a dark red root, eaten as a vegetable and in salads; *pickled beet* (*In British English, use* **beetroot**)
beetroot *(BRIT)*		*see* **beet**
broccoli	[brɒkəli]	a vegetable with thick green stems and small green flowers on top
cabbage	[kæbɪdʒ]	a round vegetable with white, green, or purple leaves; *red cabbage*; *spring cabbages*
carrot	[kærət]	a long, thin, orange-colored vegetable; *grated carrot*; *raw carrot*; *carrot cake*
cauliflower	[kɔliflaʊər]	a large, round, white vegetable surrounded by green leaves; *steamed cauliflower*

EXAMPLES

Add the fruit and sprinkle with the chopped hazelnuts.

celery	[sɛləri]	a vegetable with long, pale-green sticks that you can cook or eat raw; *a stick of celery*; *celery sticks/stalks*
corn	[kɔrn]	a long round vegetable covered in small yellow seeds. The seeds are also called corn. (*In British English, use* **sweetcorn**)
courgette (*BRIT*)		*see* **zucchini**
cucumber	[kyuKʌmbər]	a long dark-green vegetable that you eat raw; *sliced cucumber*; *tomatoes and cucumber*; *cucumber sandwiches*
eggplant	[ɛgplænt]	a vegetable with a smooth, dark purple skin (*In British English, use* **aubergine**)
garlic	[gɑrlɪk]	a plant like a small onion with a strong flavor, that you use in cooking; *garlic bread*; *chopped/crushed garlic*
herb	[ɜrb]	a plant whose leaves are used in cooking to add flavor to food; *dried/fresh herbs*; *mixed herbs*
leek	[lik]	a long, thin vegetable that is white at one end and has long green leaves
lentils	[lɛntɪlz, -tᵊlz]	round flat seeds that are dried and then soaked and cooked before eating; *red/green lentils*; *lentil soup*
lettuce	[lɛtɪs]	a plant with large green leaves that is eaten mainly in salads; *lettuce leaves*
mushroom	[mʌʃrum]	a plant with a short stem and a round top that you can eat; *sliced mushrooms*; *wild mushrooms*; *button mushrooms*
olive	[ɒlɪv]	a small green or black fruit with a bitter taste; *olive oil*; *green/black olives*
onion	[ʌnyən]	a round vegetable with many layers, that has a strong, sharp smell and taste; *sliced/chopped onion*; *fried onion*; *red onions*; *pickled onions*

EXAMPLES

When the oil is hot, add the garlic.
Fry the mushrooms in a little olive oil and add the chopped herbs.

parsley	[pɑ̱rsli]	a herb with small green leaves that you use in cooking; *chopped parsley*
peas	[pi̱z]	very small round green seeds that grow in long narrow cases (called pods) and are cooked and eaten as a vegetable; *frozen green peas*
pepper	[pɛ̱pər]	a hollow green, red, or yellow vegetable with seeds inside it; *chopped/roasted peppers*; *sweet/chili peppers*
potato	[pəte̱ɪtoʊ]	a hard, round, white vegetable with brown or red skin, that grows under the ground; *roast potatoes*; *baked/jacket potatoes*; *mashed/boiled/fried potatoes*
pumpkin	[pʌ̱mpkɪn]	a large, round, orange vegetable with a thick skin; *pumpkin seeds*; *pumpkin pie*; *pumpkin soup*
spinach	[spɪ̱nɪtʃ]	a vegetable with large dark green leaves
squash	[skwɒ̱ʃ]	a large vegetable with thick skin and hard flesh
sweetcorn (BRIT)		*see* **corn**
turnip	[tɜ̱rnɪp]	a round white vegetable that grows under the ground
vegetable	[vɛ̱dʒtəbᵊl, vɛ̱dʒɪ-]	a plant that you can cook and eat; *roasted vegetables*; *fruit and vegetables*; *vegetable oil*
zucchini	[zuki̱ni]	a long, thin vegetable with a dark green skin (*In British English, use* **courgette**)

ADJECTIVES

ripe	[ra̱ɪp]	used for describing fruit that is ready to eat
vegetarian	[vɛ̱dʒɪtɛ̱əriən]	not containing meat or fish; *a vegetarian diet/dish/meal*

EXAMPLES

Thinly slice two red or green peppers.
Choose firm but ripe fruit.

health

accident	[æksɪdənt]	an occasion when something bad happens to a person by chance, causing injury or death
ache	[eɪk]	a steady pain in a part of your body
AIDS	[eɪdz]	a disease that destroys the body's ability to fight other diseases
ambulance	[æmbyələns]	a vehicle for taking people to the hospital; *call an ambulance*
appointment	[əpɔɪntmənt]	an arrangement to see someone such as a doctor at a particular time
aspirin	[æspərɪn, -prɪn]	a mild drug that reduces pain; *take an aspirin*
bandage	[bændɪdʒ]	a long piece of cloth that is wrapped around an injured part of your body to protect or support it
Band-aid	[bænd eɪd]	a piece of sticky material used for covering small cuts on your body (*In British English, use* **plaster**)
bruise	[bruːz]	a purple mark that appears on a part of your body when you injure it
cancer	[kænsər]	a serious disease that makes groups of cells in the body grow when they should not
chickenpox	[tʃɪkɪnpɒks]	a disease that gives you a high temperature and red spots that itch
cold	[koʊld]	an illness that makes liquid flow from your nose, and makes you cough
condom	[kɒndəm]	a rubber covering that a man wears on his penis during sex to stop a woman from becoming pregnant and to protect against disease; *use a condom*

EXAMPLES

The boy was injured in an accident at a swimming pool.

She made an appointment with her doctor.

How did you get that bruise on your arm?

I've got a cold.

cough	[kɔf]	an illness that makes you cough
crutch	[krʌtʃ]	a stick that you put under your arm to help you to walk if you have hurt your leg or your foot
dentist	[dɛntɪst]	a person whose job is to examine and treat people's teeth
the dentist's	[ðə dɛntɪsts]	the place where a dentist works
diarrhea	[daɪərɪə]	an illness that makes all the waste products come out of your body as liquid
diet	[daɪɪt]	the type of food that you regularly eat; *a balanced diet*; *a healthy diet*
doctor	[dɒktər]	a person whose job is to treat people who are sick or injured
the doctor's	[ðə dɒktərz]	the place where a doctor works
drug	[drʌg]	a chemical that is used as a medicine
earache	[ɪəreɪk]	a pain inside your ear
ER	[i ɑr]	short for "emergency room": the part of a hospital where people who have severe injuries or sudden illness go for emergency treatment
first aid kit	[fɜrst eɪd kɪt]	a collection of bandages and medicines for giving first aid when someone has an injury
flu	[flu]	short for "influenza": an illness that is like a very bad cold
germ	[dʒɜrm]	a very small living thing that can cause disease or illness
headache	[hɛdeɪk]	a pain in your head
health	[hɛlθ]	the condition of a person's body; *in good health*; *health problems*

EXAMPLES

I've got a bad cough.
I can walk without crutches now.
I'm going to the dentist's after work.
I went to the doctor's today.
This chemical is used for killing germs.
I have a headache.

heart attack	[hɑrt ətæk]	an occasion when someone's heart begins to beat irregularly or stops completely; *have a heart attack*
hospital	[hɒspɪtəl]	a place where doctors and nurses care for people who are sick or injured
illness	[ɪlnɪs]	**1** a particular disease or a period of bad health **2** the state of being sick
injection	[ɪndʒɛkʃən]	medicine that is put into your body using a special type of needle; *have an injection*
measles	[mizəlz]	an illness that gives you a high fever and red spots on your skin
medicine	[mɛdɪsɪn]	**1** the treatment of illness and injuries by doctors and nurses; *a career in medicine* **2** a substance that you use to treat or cure an illness; *take medicine*
nurse	[nɜrs]	a person whose job is to care for people who are sick or injured
ointment	[ɔɪntmənt]	a smooth, thick substance that you put on sore or damaged skin
operation	[ɒpəreɪʃən]	the process of cutting open a patient's body in order to remove, replace or repair a part
pain	[peɪn]	an unpleasant feeling that you have in a part of your body, because of illness or an injury; *chest/back pain*
patient	[peɪʃənt]	a person who receives medical treatment from a doctor
pharmacy	[fɑrməsi]	a place where you can get medicine
pill	[pɪl]	a small, solid, round piece of medicine that you swallow; *take a pill*
plaster (BRIT)		*see* **Band-aid**

EXAMPLES
She is recovering from a serious illness.
He was away from work because of illness.
The medicine saved his life.
Where do you feel the pain?

poison	[pɔɪzᵊn]	a substance that harms or kills people if they swallow or touch it
pregnancy	[prɛgnənsi]	the condition of having a baby or babies developing in your body
prescription	[prɪskrɪpʃᵊn]	a piece of paper on which a doctor writes an order for medicine
pulse	[pʌls]	the regular beat of your heart that you can feel when you touch your wrist
scar	[skɑr]	a mark that is left on the skin by an old wound
scratch	[skrætʃ]	a small cut made by a sharp object
sling	[slɪŋ]	a piece of cloth that you wear around your neck and arm, to hold up your arm when it is broken or injured
sore throat	[sɔr θroʊt]	a pain in your throat
splinter	[splɪntər]	a thin, sharp piece of wood or glass that has broken off from a larger piece
spoonful	[spunfʊl]	an amount of food that a spoon holds; *a spoonful of medicine*
stomachache	[stʌməkeɪk]	a pain in your stomach
stress	[strɛs]	an unpleasant feeling of worry caused by difficulties in life; *suffer from stress*
sunburn	[sʌnbɜrn]	pink sore skin caused by too much time in the sun; *suffer sunburn*
surgery	[sɜrdʒəri]	a process in which a doctor cuts open a patient's body in order to repair, remove or replace a diseased or damaged part; *knee surgery*; *heart surgery*

EXAMPLES

We keep a record of your weight gain during pregnancy.
Press very gently until you can feel the pulse.
She's got her arm in a sling.
I've got a sore throat.
I've got a splinter in my toe.
I have a stomachache.
It will need surgery.

tablet	[tæblɪt]	a small solid piece of medicine that you swallow; *take a sleeping tablet*
temperature	[tɛmprətʃər, -tʃʊər]	how hot someone's body is
thermometer	[θərmɒmɪtər]	an instrument that measures your body's temperature
wheelchair	[wiltʃɛər]	a chair with wheels that you use if you cannot walk very well
wound	[wund]	damage to part of your body caused by a gun or something sharp like a knife; *head wounds*
X-ray	[ɛks reɪ]	**1** a process in which a picture is taken of the bones or organs inside your body; *have an X-ray* **2** a picture of the bones or organs inside your body

VERBS

be ill *(BRIT)*		*see* **be sick**
be on a diet		to eat special types of food, or eat less food than usual
be sick		to not be in good health (*In British English, use* **be ill**)
bleed	[blid]	if a part of your body bleeds, you lose blood from it
break	[breɪk]	to make a bone in your body separate into pieces, by hitting it or falling on it
breathe	[brið]	to take air into your lungs and let it out again
bruise	[bruz]	to injure a part of your body so that a purple mark appears there

EXAMPLES

The baby's temperature continued to rise.
The wound is healing well.
I was too sick to go to work.
His nose was bleeding heavily.
He's broken his arm.

burn	[bɜrn]	if you burn a part of your body, you injure it with something hot
catch a cold		to become sick with a cold
cough	[kɔf]	to suddenly force air out of your throat with a noise
cure	[kyʊər]	to make someone become well again
cut	[kʌt]	if you cut a part of your body, you injure it with something sharp, such as a knife
die	[daɪ]	to stop living
faint	[feɪnt]	to become unconscious for a short time
feel better		to feel less sick than before
feel sick		to feel unwell
get better		to recover from an illness
have a temperature		to have a body temperature that is higher than it should be
hurt	[hɜrt]	to damage a part of your body, causing pain
itch	[ɪtʃ]	to have an unpleasant feeling on your skin that makes you want to scratch it
look after someone		to take care of someone who is sick
lose weight		to become thinner
pass out		to become unconscious for a short time
put on weight		to become fatter
rest	[rɛst]	to spend some time relaxing after doing something tiring
scratch	[skrætʃ]	to rub your fingernails against the skin on a part of your body

EXAMPLES

I've burnt myself.
Dry your hair so you don't catch a cold.
I cut my finger when I was slicing vegetables.
He is feeling much better today.
The thought of food made him feel sick.
Doctors have said that he may not get better.
I fell over and hurt myself.
Ouch! That hurts!
I put on a lot of weight and my symptoms got worse.

sneeze	[sniːz]	to suddenly take in your breath and then blow it down your nose noisily, for example, because you have a cold
take someone's temperature		to use a thermometer to measure the temperature of someone's body
treat	[triːt]	to try to make a patient well again
twist	[twɪst]	to injure a part of your body by turning it too suddenly
vomit	[vɒmɪt]	if you vomit, food and drink comes up from your stomach and out through your mouth

ADJECTIVES

bleeding	[bliːdɪŋ]	losing blood as a result of injury or illness; *bleeding gums*
cold	[koʊld]	feeling uncomfortable because you are not warm enough
feverish	[fiːvərɪʃ]	feeling ill and very hot
fit	[fɪt]	healthy and strong; *keep fit*
healthy	[hɛlθi]	1 well, and not often sick 2 good for your health
ill	[ɪl]	not in good health
in a cast	[ɪn ə kæst]	with a hard white cover around your leg or arm to protect a broken bone
injured	[ɪndʒərd]	if you are injured, part of your body is damaged
in plaster (BRIT)		*see* **in a cast**
off sick (BRIT)		*see* **out sick**

EXAMPLES
Doctors treated the boy for a minor head wound.
He twisted an ankle playing football.
The headache was accompanied by vomiting.
People need to exercise to be healthy.
Try to eat a healthy diet.
I had my arm in a cast for two months.
No one was seriously injured.

out sick	[aʊt sɪk]	not at work because you are unwell (*In British English, use* **off sick**)
painful	[peɪnfəl]	causing pain; *painful joints*
pregnant	[prɛgnənt]	having a baby or babies developing in your body
sick	[sɪk]	unwell; *a sick child*
sore	[sɔr]	painful and uncomfortable
sweaty	[swɛti]	covered with sweat (= liquid that forms on your body when you are hot)
tired	[taɪərd]	feeling that you want to rest or sleep
uncomfortable	[ʌnkʌmftəbəl, -kʌmfərtə-]	feeling slight pain or discomfort
unconscious	[ʌnkɒnʃəs]	not awake and not aware of what is happening around you because of illness or a serious injury
wounded	[wundɪd]	injured by an attack

IDIOMS

(as) right as rain	completely well or healthy again after an illness
off-color	slightly unwell; *feel off-color* (*In British English, use* **off-colour**)
off-colour (*BRIT*)	*see* **off-color**
under the weather	feeling slightly unwell

EXAMPLES

I sometimes feel uncomfortable after eating in the evening.
I was still feeling a bit under the weather.

hotels

NOUNS

alarm call (*BRIT*) — *see* **wake-up call**

baggage [bægɪdʒ] — same as **luggage**

bar [bɑr] — a place where you can buy and drink alcoholic drinks; *the hotel bar*

bath (*BRIT*) — *see* **bathtub**

bathroom [bæθrum] — a room that contains a toilet

bathtub [bæθtʌb] — a long container that you fill with water and sit or lie in to wash your body (*In British English, use* **bath**)

bed and breakfast [bɛd ənd brɛkfəst] —
1 a small hotel offering rooms and breakfast, but not lunch or dinner
2 if the price at a hotel includes bed and breakfast, it includes breakfast, but not lunch or dinner

bellhop [bɛlhɒp] — a person whose job is to carry people's luggage (*In British English, use* **porter**)

bill [bɪl] — a document that shows how much money you must pay for something

breakfast [brɛkfəst] — the first meal of the day

chambermaid [tʃeɪmbərmeɪd] — a woman who cleans the bedrooms in a hotel

complaint [kəmpleɪnt] — when you say that you are not satisfied; *make a complaint*

deposit [dɪpɒzɪt] — a part of the full price of something that you pay when you agree to buy it

double room [dʌbəl rum] — a bedroom for two people

EXAMPLES

I'd like a room with a bathtub.
Double rooms cost $180 per night for bed and breakfast.
We stayed in a small bed and breakfast by the sea.
They paid the bill and left the hotel.
What time is breakfast served?
The chambermaid came to clean the room.
No booking will be accepted unless the deposit is paid.
Would you like a single or a double room?

elevator	[ɛlɪveɪtər]	a machine that carries people or things up and down inside tall buildings; *take/use the lift* (*In British English, use **lift***)
en-suite bathroom	[ɒn swit bæθrum]	a bathroom that is joined to a bedroom and can only be reached by a door in the bedroom
entrance	[ɛntrəns]	the door or gate that you use to go into a place; *the main entrance*; *the hotel entrance*
facilities	[fəsɪlɪtiz]	something such as rooms, buildings, or pieces of equipment that are used for a particular purpose
fire escape	[faɪər ɪskeɪp]	a metal staircase on the outside of a building, which can be used to escape from the building if there is a fire
floor	[flɔr]	one of the levels of a building; *the ground/first/second/third floor*
foyer	[fɔɪər, fɔɪeɪ, fwɑyeɪ]	the large area inside the doors of a hotel where people meet or wait
guest	[gɛst]	someone who is staying in a hotel; *hotel guests*
guest house	[gɛst haʊs]	a small hotel; *stay in a guest house*
hotel	[hoʊtɛl]	a building where people pay to sleep and eat meals
key	[ki]	a specially shaped piece of metal that opens or closes a lock
key card	[ki kɑrd]	a small plastic card that you can use instead of a key to open a door in some hotels
lift (*BRIT*)		*see* **elevator**
luggage	[lʌgɪdʒ]	the bags that you take with you when you travel

EXAMPLES

Every room has an en-suite bathroom.
The hotel has excellent sports facilities.
All rooms have tea and coffee-making facilities.
Our hotel room was on the third floor.
Ali stayed the night in a small hotel near the harbor.
Do you have any luggage?

manager	[mænɪdʒər]	a person who controls all or part of a business or organization; *a hotel manager*
minibar	[mɪnibɑr]	a small fridge containing drinks in a hotel room
passport	[pæspɔrt]	an official document that you have to show when you enter or leave a country
porter *(BRIT)*		*see* **bellhop**
price	[praɪs]	the amount of money that you have to pay for something
rate	[reɪt]	the amount of money that goods or services cost
reception	[rɪsɛpʃən]	the desk in a hotel that you go to when you first arrive
receptionist	[rɪsɛpʃənɪst]	in a hotel, a person whose job is to answer the telephone and deal with guests
restaurant	[rɛstərənt, -tərɑnt, -trɑnt]	a place where you can buy and eat a meal; *the hotel restaurant*
room	[rum]	a separate area inside a building that has its own walls
room number	[rum nʌmbər]	the number given to a bedroom in a hotel
room service	[rum sɜrvɪs]	in a hotel, a service that provides meals or drinks for guests in their room; *order room service*
safe	[seɪf]	a strong metal box with a lock, where you keep money or other valuable things
shower	[ʃaʊər]	a piece of equipment that covers you with water when you stand under it to wash yourself
single room	[sɪŋgəl rum]	a room for one person

EXAMPLES
Does that price include breakfast?
The hotel offers a special weekend rate.
I checked in at reception.
I'd prefer a room overlooking the sea.
You are advised to deposit valuables in the hotel safe.

stay	[steɪ]	a period of living in a place for a short time
suitcase	[sutkeɪs]	a case for carrying your clothes when you are traveling
swimming pool	[swɪmɪŋ pul]	a large hole filled with water that people can swim in; *the hotel swimming pool*
tip	[tɪp]	money that you give someone to thank them for a job they have done for you
view	[vyu]	everything that you can see from a place
youth hostel	[yuθ hɒstəl]	a cheap place where people can stay when they are traveling
wake-up call	[weɪkʌp kɔl]	a telephone call that is intended to wake you up (*In British English, use* **alarm call**)

VERBS

book	[bʊk]	to arrange to stay in a hotel room
make a reservation		to make an arrangement for a room in a hotel to be kept for you
stay	[steɪ]	to live somewhere for a short time
tip	[tɪp]	to give someone some money to thank them for a job they have done for you

ADJECTIVES

| **accessible** | [æksɛsɪbəl] | easy for people to reach or enter |
| **luxury** | [lʌkʃəri, lʌgʒə-] | comfortable, beautiful, and expensive; *a luxury hotel* |

EXAMPLES

Please contact the hotel reception if you have any problems during your stay.

He handed the bellhop a tip.

From our hotel room we had a spectacular view of the sea.

Could I have a wake-up call at 5:30 tomorrow morning, please?

I'd like to book a room.

Samir made a reservation for two rooms at the hotel.

Wolfgang stayed at The Park Hotel, Milan.

Anna tipped the chambermaid.

The hotel is wheelchair accessible.

| three-/four-/five- etc. star | used for talking about the quality of a hotel, which is indicated by a number of star-shaped symbols |

[PHRASES]

| "Do not disturb" | if a sign on a hotel room door says "Do not disturb," it means that the person inside does not want to be interrupted |
| "Vacancies" | if a sign outside a hotel says "Vacancies," it means that there are some rooms available |

EXAMPLES
They own a three-star hotel.

houses and homes

NOUNS

accommodation (BRIT)		see **housing**
address	[əˈdrɛs]	the number of the building, the name of the street, and the town or city where you live or work; postal address
apartment	[əpɑrtmənt]	a set of rooms for living in, usually on one floor and part of a larger building (In British English, use **flat**)
attic	[ætɪk]	a room at the top of a house, just under the roof
balcony	[bælkəni]	a place where you can stand or sit on the outside of a building, above the ground
basement	[beɪsmənt]	a part of a building below ground level; a basement apartment
bathroom	[bæθrum]	a room that contains a toilet
bedroom	[bɛdrum]	a room that is used for sleeping in
building	[bɪldɪŋ]	a structure that has a roof and walls; an office building
ceiling	[silɪŋ]	the top inside part of a room; low/high ceilings
cellar	[sɛlər]	a room under a building; a wine cellar
chimney	[tʃɪmni]	a pipe above a fire that lets the smoke travel up and out of the building
conservatory	[kənsɜrvətɔri]	a glass room built onto a house
cottage	[kɒtɪdʒ]	a small house, usually in the country
detached house	[dɪtætʃt haʊs]	a house that is not joined to any other building
dining room	[daɪnɪŋ rum]	the room in a house where people have their meals
door	[dɔr]	a piece of wood, glass, or metal that fills an entrance

EXAMPLES

Please give your full name and address.

"What's your address?" — "It's 24 Cherry Road, Chicago, IL 60657."

They are renting a two-bedroom apartment.

I knocked at the front door, but there was no answer.

doorbell	[dɔrbɛl]	a button next to a door that makes a noise when you press it to tell the people inside that you are there
doorstep	[dɔrstɛp]	a step in front of a door outside a building
driveway	[draɪvweɪ]	a small road that leads from the street to the front of a building
elevator	[ɛlɪveɪtər]	a machine that carries people or things up and down inside tall buildings (*In British English, use* **lift**)
entrance	[ɛntrəns]	the door or gate where you go into a place
estate agent (*BRIT*)		*see* **realtor**
flat (*BRIT*)		*see* **apartment**
floor	[flɔr]	**1** the part of a room that you walk on **2** all the rooms that are on a particular level of a building; *the ground/first/second floor*
front door	[frʌnt dɔr]	the main door of a house or other building, that is usually in the wall that faces a street
garage	[gərɑʒ]	a building where you keep a car
garden (*BRIT*)		*see* **yard**
gate	[geɪt]	a type of door that you use to enter the area around a building
hall	[hɔl]	the area inside the main door of a house that leads to other rooms
home	[hoʊm]	the house or apartment where someone lives
house	[haʊs]	a building where people live
housing	[haʊzɪŋ]	buildings or rooms where people live or stay; *rented housing* (*In British English, use* **accommodation**)
kitchen	[kɪtʃən]	a room that is used for cooking

EXAMPLES

The doorbell rang.
I went and sat on the doorstep.
There were no seats, so we sat on the floor.
The bathroom was on the second floor.
They have a lovely home in the country.
I live in a three-bedroom house.
I'm having a party at my house tomorrow night.

landing	[lændɪŋ]	the flat area at the top of the stairs in a house
landlady	[lændleɪdi]	a woman who owns a building and allows people to live there in return for rent
landlord	[lændlɔrd]	a man who owns a building and allows people to live there in return for rent
lift (BRIT)		see **elevator**
living room	[lɪvɪŋ rum]	a room where people sit together and talk or watch television
owner	[ounər]	the person that something belongs to; property owners
patio	[pætiou]	a flat area next to a house, where people can sit and relax or eat
porch	[pɔrtʃ]	a covered area with a roof and sometimes walls at the entrance to a building
property	[prɒpərti]	a building and the land around it; buy/sell property; private property
realtor	[riəltər, -tɔr]	someone who works for a company selling houses and land (In British English, use **estate agent**)
rent	[rɛnt]	money that you pay to live in a house or apartment that is owned by someone else
roof	[ruf]	the top surface that covers a building
room	[rum]	a separate area inside a building that has its own walls
row house	[rou haus]	one of a row of houses that are joined together by both of their side walls (In British English, use **terraced house**)
semi-detached house	[sɛmidɪtætʃt, sɛmaɪ-]	a house that is joined to another house on one side by a shared wall
shutters	[ʃʌtərz]	wooden or metal covers fitted on the outside of a window; open/close the shutters
sitting room	[sɪtɪŋ rum]	same as **living room**
spare room	[spɛər rum]	a bedroom that is kept especially for visitors to sleep in

EXAMPLES

We have meals on the patio in the summer.
She worked hard to pay the rent on the apartment.

stairs	[stɛərz]	a set of steps inside a building that go from one level to another; *climb the stairs*
step	[stɛp]	a raised flat surface that you put your feet on in order to walk up or down to a different level; *go up/down the steps*
storey (BRIT)		*see* **story**
story (PL) **stories**	[stɔri]	one of the different levels of a building; *the top story* (In British English, use **storey**)
study	[stʌdi]	a room in a house that is used for reading, writing, and studying
tenant	[tɛnənt]	someone who pays money to use a house
terraced house (BRIT)		*see* **row house**
wall	[wɔl]	one of the sides of a building or a room
window	[wɪndoʊ]	a space in the wall of a building that has glass in it
yard	[yɑrd]	the part of the land by your house where you grow flowers and vegetables; *the front/ back yard* (In British English, use **garden**)

VERBS

decorate	[dɛkəreɪt]	to put paint or paper on the walls of a room
live	[lɪv]	to have your home in a particular place
move		to change the place where you live (In British English, use **move house**)
move house (BRIT)		*see* **move**
own	[oʊn]	to have something that belongs to you
rent	[rɛnt]	to pay the owner of a house or apartment in order to be able to live in it yourself

EXAMPLES

Houses must not be more than two stories high.
They were decorating Claude's bedroom.
Where do you live?
When Dad got a new job, we had to move.
He owns an apartment in Paris.
She rents a house with three other women.

ADJECTIVES

downstairs	[daʊnstɛərz]	on a lower floor of a building; *a downstairs toilet*
furnished	[fɜrnɪʃt]	containing furniture; *a furnished apartment*; *elegantly furnished rooms*
homeless	[hoʊmlɪs]	having nowhere to live; *homeless people*
residential	[rɛzɪdɛnʃəl]	containing houses rather than offices or shops; *a residential area*
upstairs	[ʌpstɛərz]	on a higher floor of a building; *an upstairs window*

ADVERBS

at home	[æt hoʊm]	in the place where you live
downstairs	[daʊnstɛərz]	on or to a lower floor of a building
home	[hoʊm]	in or to the house or apartment where you live
next door	[nɛkst dɔr]	in the next room or building
upstairs	[ʌpstɛərz]	on or to a higher floor of a building

PHRASES

"Make yourself at home"	used for telling someone that you want them to relax and feel comfortable in your home
"There's no place like home."	used for saying that your home is the place where you feel happiest and most comfortable

EXAMPLES

At least 100,000 people were left homeless by the earthquake.
She wasn't at home.
Nobody lives downstairs.
She went downstairs to the kitchen.
She wasn't feeling well and she wanted to go home.
Hi Mom! I'm home!
Who lives next door?
The children are upstairs.
He went upstairs and changed his clothes.

in the home

FURNITURE

armchair	[ɑrmtʃɛər]	a big comfortable chair that supports your arms
bed	[bɛd]	a piece of furniture that you lie on when you sleep; *a double/single bed*
bookcase	[bʊkkeɪs]	a piece of furniture with shelves that you keep books on
chair	[tʃɛər]	a piece of furniture for one person to sit on, with a back and four legs
chest of drawers	[tʃɛst əv drɔrz]	a piece of furniture with drawers in which you keep clothes
cot (BRIT)		*see* **crib**
crib	[krɪb]	a bed for a baby; *a baby crib* (In British English, use **cot**)
cupboard	[kʌbərd]	a piece of furniture with doors and shelves for storing things like food or dishes; *a kitchen cupboard*
desk	[dɛsk]	a table that you sit at to write or work
drawer	[drɔr]	the part of a desk, for example, that you can pull out and put things in; *open/close a drawer; a kitchen drawer; a desk drawer*
fireplace	[faɪərpleɪs]	the place in a room where you can light a fire
furniture	[fɜrnɪtʃər]	large objects in a room such as tables, chairs, or beds; *a piece of furniture*
lampshade	[læmpʃeɪd]	a covering that is fitted round an electric light bulb
mattress	[mætrɪs]	the thick, soft part of a bed that you lie on
shelf	[ʃɛlf]	a long flat piece of wood on a wall or in a cupboard that you can keep things on

---

EXAMPLES
We went to bed at about 10 p.m.
Ana was already in bed.
Francine rearranged all the furniture.

sofa	[soʊfə]	a long, comfortable seat with a back, that two or three people can sit on
stool	[stul]	a seat with legs and no support for your arms or back
table	[teɪbəl]	a piece of furniture with a flat top that you put things on; *a wooden table*; *a kitchen table*; *a dining table*
wardrobe	[wɔrdroʊb]	a cupboard where you hang your clothes

APPLIANCES

appliance	[əplaɪəns]	a machine that you use to do a job in your home; *a kitchen appliance*
computer	[kəmpyutər]	an electronic machine that can store and deal with large amounts of information; *computer software*
cooker	[kʊkər]	a piece of kitchen equipment that is used for cooking food; *an electric cooker*; *a gas cooker*
dishwasher	[dɪʃwɒʃər]	a machine that washes and dries dishes; *load/unload the dishwasher*
freezer	[frizər]	a large container used for freezing food
fridge	[frɪdʒ]	a large container that is used for keeping food cool and fresh
hairdryer	[hɛərdraɪr]	a machine that you use to dry your hair
heater	[hitər]	a piece of equipment that is used for making a room warm; *an electric heater*; *a gas heater*
iron	[aɪərn]	a piece of electrical equipment with a flat metal base that you heat and move over clothes to make them smooth
ironing board	[aɪərnɪŋ bɔrd]	a long board covered with cloth on which you iron clothes
kettle	[kɛtəl]	a metal container with a lid and a handle, that you use for boiling water; *put the kettle on*

EXAMPLES

He shut the dishwasher and switched it on.
James put the kettle on for a cup of tea.

lamp	[læmp]	a light that works using electricity or by burning oil or gas; *a bedside lamp*
microwave oven	[maɪkrouweɪv ʌvən]	an oven that cooks food very quickly using electric waves
oven	[ʌvən]	a piece of equipment for cooking that is like a large metal box with a door
phone	[foun]	same as **telephone**; *The phone rang.*; *make a phone call*; *a phone number*
radio	[reɪdiou]	a piece of equipment that you use in order to listen to radio programs; *listen to the radio*; *a radio program*
stereo	[stɛriou, stɪər-]	a machine that plays music, with two parts (= speakers) that the sound comes from
telephone	[tɛlɪfoun]	a piece of equipment that you use for speaking to someone who is in another place
television	[tɛlɪvɪʒən, -vɪʒ-]	a piece of electrical equipment with a screen on which you watch moving pictures with sound; *a television program*; *a television show*
tumble-dryer	[tʌmbəl draɪər]	a machine that uses hot air to dry clothes
vacuum cleaner	[vækyum klinər, -yuəm]	an electric machine that sucks up dust and dirt from carpets
washing machine	[wɒʃɪŋ məʃin]	a machine that you use for washing clothes

OTHER THINGS IN THE HOME

bath (*BRIT*)		*see* **bathtub**
bathtub	[bæθtʌb]	a long container that you fill with water and sit or lie in to wash your body; *drain the bathtub* (*In British English, use* **bath**)

EXAMPLES

He switched on the lamp.
Put the potatoes in the oven for thirty minutes.
He never answers his phone.
Can I use your phone?
She's always on the phone.
What's on television tonight?

bin *(BRIT)*		*see* **garbage can**
blanket	[blæŋkɪt]	a large, thick piece of cloth that you put on a bed to keep you warm
blinds	[blaɪndz]	pieces of cloth or other material that you can pull down over a window to cover it; *close/open the blinds*
brush	[brʌʃ]	an object with a lot of bristles or hairs attached to it that you use for cleaning things
bucket	[bʌkɪt]	a round metal or plastic container with a handle, used for holding water; *a plastic bucket*
carpet	[kɑrpɪt]	a thick, soft covering for the floor; *a patterned carpet*
central heating	[sɛntrəl hitɪŋ]	a heating system in which water or air is heated and passed round a building through pipes and radiators; *gas central heating*
clock	[klɒk]	an object that shows you what time it is
curtain	[kɜrtᵊn]	a piece of material that hangs from the top of a window to cover it at night; *open/close the curtains*
cushion	[kuʃᵊn]	a bag of soft material that you put on a seat to make it more comfortable
dish soap	[dɪʃ soup]	liquid soap for cleaning dirty dishes (*In British English, use* **washing-up liquid**)
dust	[dʌst]	a fine powder of dry earth or dirt
duster	[dʌstər]	a cloth that you use for removing dust from furniture
duvet	[duveɪ]	a thick warm cover for a bed
garbage can	[gɑrbɪdʒ kæn]	a container that you put trash in (*In British English, use* **bin**)

EXAMPLES

The blinds were drawn to shut out the sun.

He filled the bucket with water.

She could hear the hall clock ticking.

She closed her bedroom curtains.

I took the letter and threw it in the garbage can.

key	[kiː]	a specially shaped piece of metal that opens or closes a lock; *a door key*
laundry	[lɔːndri]	**1** clothes and other things that you are going to wash; *dirty laundry* **2** clothes and other things that you have just washed; *clean laundry*
laundry liquid	[lɔːndri lɪkwɪd]	liquid soap for washing laundry
light	[laɪt]	something such as an electric lamp that produces light; *switch on/off the light*
light bulb	[laɪt bʌlb]	the round glass part of an electric light that light shines from
lock	[lɒk]	the part of a door or a container that you use to make sure that no-one can open it. You can open a lock with a key.
mirror	[mɪrər]	a flat piece of special glass that you can see yourself in; *look in the mirror*; *a full-length mirror*
ornament	[ɔːrnəmənt]	an attractive object that you use to decorate your home
pillow	[pɪloʊ]	a soft object that you rest your head on when you are in bed
plug	[plʌg]	**1** the plastic object with metal pins that connects a piece of electrical equipment to the electricity supply **2** a round object that you use to block the hole in a bath or a sink
radiator	[reɪdieɪtər]	a metal object that is full of hot water or steam, and is used for heating a room
rubbish *(BRIT)*		*see* **trash**
rug	[rʌg]	a piece of thick cloth that you put on a small area of a floor
sheet	[ʃiːt]	a large piece of cloth that you sleep on or cover yourself with in bed

---

EXAMPLES
Fold the laundry neatly after washing and drying it.
She turned on all the lights and drew the curtains.
I turned the key in the lock.
She put the plug in and turned on the taps.

shower	[ʃaʊər]	a piece of equipment that covers you with water when you stand under it to wash yourself
sink	[sɪŋk]	a large fixed container in a kitchen or a bathroom that you can fill with water; *a kitchen sink; a bathroom sink*
soap	[soʊp]	a substance that you use with water for washing yourself or for washing clothes; *Wash with soap and water.*
socket	[sɒkɪt]	a small hole in a wall where you can connect electrical equipment to the power supply
switch	[swɪtʃ]	a small control for turning electricity on or off
tablecloth	[teɪbəlklɔθ]	a cloth that you use to cover a table
tap	[tæp]	an object that controls the flow of a liquid or a gas from a pipe; *turn on/off a tap*
tea towel	[ti taʊəl]	a cloth that you use to dry dishes after they have been washed
toilet	[tɔɪlɪt]	a large bowl with a seat that you use when you want to get rid of waste from your body; *go to the toilet*
toothpaste	[tuθpeɪst]	a thick substance that you put on a toothbrush and use for cleaning your teeth
toy	[tɔɪ]	an object that children play with
trash	[træʃ]	things you do not want any more (*In British English, use* **rubbish**)
tray	[treɪ]	a flat piece of wood, plastic, or metal that is used for carrying and serving food and drinks
vase	[veɪs, vɑz]	a container that is used for holding flowers
wallpaper	[wɔlpeɪpər]	colored or patterned paper that is used for decorating the walls of rooms
washing-up liquid (*BRIT*)		*see* **dish soap**

EXAMPLES

I turned the bathtub taps on.

(VERBS)

clean	[klin]	to remove the dirt from something; *clean the windows*
do housework		to do work in your home such as cleaning, washing, and ironing
do the laundry		to wash dirty clothes, towels, etc.
draw the curtains		to pull the curtains across a window in order to open or close them
dust	[dʌst]	to remove dust from furniture with a cloth
iron	[aɪərn]	to make clothes smooth using an iron; *an ironed shirt*
lock	[lɒk]	to close a door or a container with a key
plug something in		to connect a piece of electrical equipment to the electricity supply
put things away		to organize a place by putting things in their proper places (*In British English*, use **tidy things away**)
sweep	[swip]	to push dirt away from an area using a brush with a long handle; *sweep the floor*
switch something off		to stop electrical equipment from working by operating a switch
switch something on		to make electrical equipment start working by operating a switch
take a bath		to sit or lie in a bath filled with water to wash your body
take a shower		to wash yourself by standing under the water that comes from a shower

---

EXAMPLES

He brought soapy water and brushes to clean the floor.
Men are doing more housework nowadays.
She got out of bed and drew the curtains.
They had forgotten to lock the front door.
She plugged in the telephone.
It's time for the children to put away their toys.
She switched off the television.
He switched on the TV.

throw something in

see **throw something in the garbage the bin** (*BRIT*)

throw something in the garbage

to get rid of something that you do not want by putting it in the garbage (*In British English, use* **throw something in the bin**)

tidy things away (*BRIT*)

see **put things away**

vacuum [vækyum, -yuəm]

to clean a room or a surface using a piece of electrical equipment that sucks up dirt (called a vacuum cleaner)

industry

NOUNS

assembly line	[əsɛmbli laɪn]	an arrangement of workers and machines in a factory where a product passes from one worker to another until it is finished
banking	[bæŋkɪŋ]	the business activity of banks and similar institutions
call center	[kɔl sɛntər]	an office where people work answering or making telephone calls for a company
catering	[keɪtərɪŋ]	the activity or business of providing food for people; *a catering business*
clothing industry	[kloʊðɪŋ ɪndəstri]	an industry that makes and sells clothes
construction	[kənstrʌkʃ°n]	the business of building things such as houses, roads, and bridges
engineering	[ɛndʒɪnɪərɪŋ]	the business of designing and constructing machines or structures such as roads and bridges
export	[ɛkspɔrt]	a product that one country sells to another country
factory	[fæktəri, -tri]	a large building where people use machines to make goods
farming	[fɑrmɪŋ]	the business of growing crops or raising animals on a farm
film industry	[fɪlm ɪndəstri]	an industry that produces and sells films
fishing	[fɪʃɪŋ]	the business of catching fish
forestry	[fɔrɪstri]	the science of growing trees in forests
goods	[gʊdz]	things that you can buy or sell
heavy industry	[hɛvi ɪndəstri]	industry that uses large machines to produce raw materials or to make large objects

EXAMPLES

He works on an assembly line.

She wants a career in banking.

Italy's clothing industry is one of the most successful in the world.

Jason was an engineer with a large construction company.

Ghana's main export is cocoa.

They invested $1 million in the British film industry.

Money can be exchanged for goods or services.

hospitality industry	[hɒspɪtælɪti ɪndəstri]	an industry that provides food, drink, and entertainment
import	[ɪmpɔrt]	a product bought from another country for use in your own country
industrial sector	[ɪndʌstriəl sɛktər]	the part of a country's economy that produces things from raw materials
industry	[ɪndəstri]	**1** the work of making things in factories; *Industry is growing.* **2** all the people and activities involved in making a particular product or providing a particular service; *the Scottish tourist industry*
insurance industry	[ɪnʃʊərəns ɪndəstri]	an industry that provides insurance (= money given to someone if something bad happens to them, in return for regular payments)
invention	[ɪnvɛnʃ°n]	**1** something that someone has invented; *a new invention* **2** an occasion when something is invented; *the invention of the telephone*
leisure industry	[liʒər ɪndəstri, lɛʒ-]	an industry that provides activities for people to do when they are not working
light industry	[laɪt ɪndəstri]	industry in which only small items are made, for example household goods and clothes
machinery	[məʃinəri]	large pieces of electrical equipment that do a particular job
manufacturer	[mænyə-fæktʃərər]	a company that makes large amounts of things
manufacturing	[mænyə-fæktʃərɪŋ]	the business of making things in factories

EXAMPLES

John works in the hospitality industry.
Antigua has a small industrial sector producing clothing and electronic equipment.
The insurance industry lost billions of dollars because of the floods.
He works for the world's largest doll manufacturer.
During the 1980s, 300,000 workers in the manufacturing industry lost their jobs.

mass production	[mæs prədʌkʃən]	the production of something in large quantities, usually using machinery
mining	[maɪnɪŋ]	the business of getting valuable substances such as coal and gold from the ground; *coal mining*
oil drilling	[ɔɪl drɪlɪŋ]	the business of getting oil by making deep holes in the ground
output	[aʊtpʊt]	the amount that a person or a thing produces
plant	[plænt]	**1** a factory; *a clothes manufacturing plant* **2** a place where power is produced; *a nuclear power plant*
private sector	[praɪvɪt sɛktər]	the part of a country's economy that the government does not control or own
processing	[prɒsɛsɪŋ]	the business of preparing raw materials before they are sold
product	[prɒdʌkt]	something that you make or grow in order to sell it
production	[prədʌkʃən]	**1** the process of making or growing something in large amounts; *the production of oil* **2** the quantity of goods that you make or grow; *the volume of production*
production line	[prədʌkʃən laɪn]	an arrangement of machines in a factory where the products pass from one machine to another until they are finished
public sector	[pʌblɪk sɛktər]	the part of a country's economy that the government controls or gives money to
raw materials	[rɔ mətɪərɪəlz]	substances that have not been processed
research and development	[rɪsɜrtʃ ənd dɪvɛləpmənt]	the activity of improving products and making new products
retailing	[riteɪlɪŋ]	the activity of selling goods directly to the public

EXAMPLES

This equipment allows the mass production of baby food.
Industry output has decreased.
We import raw materials and export industrial products.

service	[sɜrvɪs]	something that the public needs, such as transportation, hospitals, or energy supplies
service sector	[sɜrvɪs sɛktər]	the part of a country's economy that provide services
shipping	[ʃɪpɪŋ]	the business of transporting goods, especially by ship; *the international shipping industry*
supplier	[səplaɪər]	a company that sells something such as goods or equipment to customers
textile industry	[tɛkstaɪl ɪndəstri]	an industry that makes cloth
tourism	[tʊərɪzəm]	the business of providing hotels, restaurants, and activities for people who are on vacation
trade	[treɪd]	the activity of buying and selling goods
transportation	[trænspərteɪʃ°n]	the activity of taking goods or people somewhere in a vehicle

(VERBS)

assemble	[əsɛmb°l]	to fit the different parts of something together
deliver	[dɪlɪvər]	to take something to a particular place
export	[ɪkspɔrt]	to sell products to another country
import	[ɪmpɔrt]	to buy goods from another country for use in your own country
invent	[ɪnvɛnt]	to be the first person to think of something or to make it
manufacture	[mænyəfæktʃər]	to make something in a factory

EXAMPLES

We are campaigning for better day care and school services.

They are one of the biggest food suppliers in the U.S.

Another 75,000 jobs will be lost in the textile industry.

Tourism is very important for the Spanish economy.

Workers were assembling airplanes.

The U.S. imports over half of its oil.

produce	[prədu͟s]	to make or grow something
provide	[prəva͟ɪd]	to make available something that people need or want
ship	[ʃɪp]	to send goods somewhere
subcontract	[sʌbkəntræ͟kt]	to pay another company to do part of the work that you have been employed to do; *subcontract work to someone*
supply	[səpla͟ɪ]	to give someone an amount of something

(ADJECTIVES)

corporate	[kɔ͟ːrpərɪt, -prɪt]	relating to large companies; *the corporate sector*
domestic	[dəme͟stɪk]	happening or existing within one particular country
economic	[ɛ͟kənɒ͟mɪk, i͟k-]	relating to the organization of the money and industry of a country
financial	[faɪnæ͟nʃəl, fɪn-]	relating to money
foreign	[fɔ͟rɪn]	coming from a country that is not your own; *a foreign import*
industrial	[ɪndʌ͟striəl]	**1** relating to industry; *industrial machinery* **2** used to describe a city or a country in which industry is very important; *an industrial country*
international	[ɪntərnæ͟ʃənəl]	involving different countries; *international trade*
modern	[mɒ͟dərn]	new, or relating to the present time
private	[pra͟ɪvɪt]	not owned by the government; *a private company*
public	[pʌ͟blɪk]	owned or controlled by the government; *a public company*

EXAMPLES
The company produces about 2.3 billion tons of steel a year.
We provide a wide range of products and services.
They supply many cities with gas.
We need to increase domestic oil production.

jobs and careers

accountant	[əkaʊntənt]	someone whose job is to keep financial records
architect	[ɑrkɪtɛkt]	someone whose job is to design buildings
attorney	[ətɜrni]	mainly in the U.S., a lawyer
builder	[bɪldər]	someone whose job is to build or repair houses and other buildings
businessman (PL) **businessmen**	[bɪznɪsmæn] [bɪznɪsmɛn]	a man who works in a business
businesswoman (PL) **business-woman**	[bɪznɪswʊmən] [bɪznɪswɪmɪn]	a woman who works in a business
carer (BRIT)		see **caretaker**
caretaker	[kɛərteɪkər]	someone whose job is to look after another person (In British English, use **carer**)
carpenter	[kɑrpɪntər]	someone whose job is to make and repair wooden things
cashier	[kæʃɪər]	someone whose job is to take customers' money in stores or banks
chef	[ʃɛf]	someone whose job is to cook in a restaurant
cleaner	[klinər]	someone whose job is to clean the rooms and furniture inside a building
clerk	[klɜrk]	**1** someone whose job is to work with numbers or documents in an office **2** someone who works in a store selling things to customers
cook	[kʊk]	someone who prepares and cooks food
decorator	[dɛkəreɪtər]	someone whose job is to paint houses and put wallpaper on walls
dentist	[dɛntɪst]	someone whose job is to examine and treat people's teeth

---

EXAMPLES
She's a successful businesswoman who manages her own company.
Henry Harris is the head chef at The Fifth Floor Restaurant in London.

doctor	[dɒktər]	someone whose job is to treat people who are ill or injured
editor	[ɛdɪtər]	someone whose job is to check and correct texts
electrician	[ɪlɛktrɪʃⁿn, ilɛk-]	someone whose job is to repair electrical equipment
engineer	[ɛndʒɪnɪər]	someone who designs, builds, and repairs machines, or structures such as roads, railroads, and bridges
factory worker	[fæktəri wɜrkər, -tri]	someone who works in a factory (= a large building where machines are used to make things)
farmer	[fɑrmər]	someone who owns or works on a farm
firefighter	[faɪərfaɪtər]	someone whose job is to put out fires
hairdresser	[hɛərdrɛsər]	someone whose job is to cut and style people's hair
housewife (PL) **housewives**	[haʊswaɪf] [haʊswaɪvz]	a woman who does not have a paid job, but spends most of her time looking after her house and family
journalist	[dʒɜrnəlɪst]	someone whose job is to write about news stories for newspapers, magazines, television, or radio
judge	[dʒʌdʒ]	the person in a court of law who decides how criminals should be punished
lawyer	[lɔɪər, lɔyər]	someone whose job is to advise people about the law and to represent them in court
librarian	[laɪbrɛəriən]	someone who works in a library (= a place where people can borrow books)
mailman (PL) **mailmen**	[meɪlmæn] [meɪlmɛn]	a man who collects and delivers letters and packages (*In British English, use* **postman**)
manager	[mænɪdʒər]	someone who controls all or part of a business or organization
mechanic	[mɪkænɪk]	someone whose job is to repair machines and engines, especially car engines

EXAMPLES
She is a doctor.

miner	[maɪnər]	someone whose job is to work underground to obtain materials such as coal
monk	[mʌŋk]	a member of a group of religious men who live together in a special building
musician	[myuzɪʃᵊn]	someone who plays a musical instrument
nanny	[næni]	someone whose job is to look after children in the children's own home
nun	[nʌn]	a member of a group of religious women who often live together in a special building
nurse	[nɜrs]	someone whose job is to care for people who are ill or injured
optician	[ɒptɪʃᵊn]	someone whose job is to make and sell glasses
painter	[peɪntər]	**1** someone whose job is to paint walls, doors, or other parts of buildings **2** an artist who paints pictures
pilot	[paɪlət]	someone whose job is to control an aircraft
plumber	[plʌmər]	someone whose job is to put in and repair things like water and gas pipes, toilets, and bathtubs
police officer	[pəlis ɔfɪsər]	a member of the police force
porter	[pɔrtər]	someone whose job is to carry things, for example, people's luggage
postman (BRIT)		see **mailman**
priest	[prist]	someone who has religious duties in a place where people worship
programmer	[proʊɡræmər]	someone whose job is to write programs for computers
professor	[prəfɛsər]	a teacher at a college or university, especially a teacher of the highest rank
publisher	[pʌblɪʃər]	someone whose job is to prepare and print copies of books, newspapers, or magazines
rabbi	[ræbaɪ]	a Jewish religious leader

receptionist	[rɪsɛpʃənɪst]	someone in a hotel or a large building whose job is to answer the telephone and greet visitors
sales clerk	[seɪlz klɜrk]	someone who works in a store selling things to customers (*In British English, use* **shop assistant**)
sales representative	[seɪlz rɛprɪzɛntətɪv]	someone whose job is to travel around an area and sell the goods of a particular company
salesman (PL) **salesmen**	[seɪlzmən] [seɪlzmən]	a man whose job is to sell things
saleswoman (PL) **saleswomen**	[seɪlzwumən] [seɪlzwɪmɪn]	a woman whose job is to sell things
secretary	[sɛkrɪtɛri]	someone whose job is to type letters, answer the telephone, and do other office work
shop assistant (*BRIT*)		*see* **sales clerk**
social worker	[souʃ°l wɜrkər]	someone whose job is to give help and advice to people who have serious family problems or financial problems
soldier	[souldʒər]	a member of an army
surgeon	[sɜrdʒ°n]	a doctor who is specially trained to perform operations
surveyor	[sərveɪər]	someone whose job is to examine the condition of a house, usually in order to give information to people who want to buy the house
teacher	[titʃər]	someone whose job is to teach (= give lessons on a subject), usually in a school
technician	[tɛknɪʃ°n]	someone who works with scientific or medical equipment or machines
vet	[vɛt]	someone whose job is to treat ill or injured animals
waiter	[weɪtər]	a man whose job is to serve food in a restaurant

EXAMPLES

I was a teacher for 20 years.

waitress   [weɪtrɪs]   a woman whose job is to serve food in a restaurant

writer   [raɪtər]   someone whose job is to write books, stories, or articles

law

NOUNS

accident	[ǽksɪdənt]	an occasion when something bad happens to a person by chance, sometimes causing injury or death
assault	[əsɔ́lt]	a physical attack on a person
attorney	[ətɜ́rni]	mainly in the U.S., a lawyer
burglar	[bɜ́rglər]	someone who enters a building by force in order to steal things
burglary	[bɜ́rgləri]	the crime of entering a building by force and stealing things
charge	[tʃɑ́rdʒ]	a formal accusation that someone has committed a crime
corpse	[kɔ́rps]	a dead body
court	[kɔ́rt]	**1** a place where a judge and a jury decide if someone has done something wrong **2** (BRIT) see **courthouse**
courthouse	[kɔ́rthaʊs]	the building in which a court of law meets (*In British English, use* **court**)
crime	[kráɪm]	an illegal act; *commit a crime*
criminal	[krɪmɪnəl]	someone who does something illegal
drug	[drʌ́g]	a type of illegal substance that some people take because they enjoy its effects
drug dealer	[drʌ́g dilər]	someone who sells illegal drugs
evidence	[ɛ́vɪdəns]	information that is used in a court in order to try to show that something really happened
fault	[fɔ́lt]	if something bad is your fault, you made it happen

EXAMPLES

The police say the man's death was an accident.
At the police station, he was charged with assault.
They faced charges of murder.
She will appear in court later this month.
There is no evidence that he stole the money.
It's not my fault.

fine	[faɪn]	money that someone has to pay because they have done something wrong; *pay a fine*
fraud	[frɔd]	the crime of getting money by not telling the truth
gang	[gæŋ]	an organized group of criminals
gun	[gʌn]	a weapon that shoots bullets
homicide	[hɒmɪsaɪd, houmɪ-]	the crime of deliberately killing a person
hostage	[hɒstɪdʒ]	someone who is kept as a prisoner by someone who refuses to let them go until they get what they want
identity	[aɪdɛntɪti]	who you are
jail	[dʒeɪl]	same as **prison**
judge	[dʒʌdʒ]	the person in a court who decides how criminals should be punished
jury	[dʒʊəri]	the group of people in a court who listen to the facts about a crime and decide if a person is guilty or not
law	[lɔ]	**1** a system of rules that a society or government develops to deal with things like crime; *break the law* **2** one of the rules in a system of law; *a new law*
lawyer	[lɔɪər, lɔyər]	someone whose job is to advise people about the law and to represent them in court
murder	[mɜrdər]	the crime of deliberately killing a person
murderer	[mɜrdərər]	someone who deliberately kills a person
passport	[pæspɔrt]	an official document that you have to show when you enter or leave a country

EXAMPLES

He got a fine for speeding.
She got a 100-dollar fine.
He used a different name to hide his identity.
Driving too fast is against the law.

police	[pəlis]	**1** the organization that is responsible for making sure that people obey the law **2** men and women who are members of the police
police officer	[pəlis ɔfisər]	a member of the police force
police station	[pəlis steɪʃᵊn]	the local office of a police force in a particular area
prison	[prɪzᵊn]	a building where criminals are kept as punishment; *send someone to prison*
prisoner	[prɪzənər]	someone who is in prison
proof	[pruf]	something that shows that something else is true
reward	[rɪwɔrd]	something that someone gives you because you have done something good
robbery	[rɒbəri]	the crime of stealing money or property from a place
sentence	[sɛntəns]	the punishment that a person receives in a law court
shoplifter	[ʃɒplɪftər]	someone who steals money from a store
spy	[spaɪ]	someone whose job is to find out secret information about another country or organization
statement	[steɪtmənt]	something that you say or write that gives information in a formal way; *make a statement*
suspect	[sʌspɛkt]	someone who the police think may be guilty of a crime
terrorism	[tɛrərɪzəm]	the use of violence to force a government to do something
terrorist	[tɛrərɪst]	someone who uses violence to achieve their aims

EXAMPLES

The police are looking for the stolen car.
There wasn't enough proof to charge them.
The firm offered a $10,000 reward for information about the killer.
He was given a four-year sentence.
Three suspects were arrested in connection with the assault.

theft	[θɛft]	the crime of stealing
thief	[θif]	someone who steals something from
(PL) **thieves**	[θivz]	another person
trial	[traɪəl]	a formal meeting in a court, at which people decide whether someone is guilty of a crime
vandal	[vændəl]	someone who deliberately damages property
victim	[vɪktəm]	someone who has been hurt or killed
will	[wɪl]	a legal document that says who will receive someone's money when they die
witness	[wɪtnɪs]	someone who appears in a court to say what they know about a crime or other event

VERBS

arrest	[ərɛst]	to take someone to a police station, because they may have broken the law
assault	[əsɔlt]	to attack a person physically
break the law		to do something illegal
burglarize	[bɜrgləraɪz]	to enter a building by force and steal things (*In British English, use* **burgle**)
burgle (BRIT)		*see* **burglarize**
charge	[tʃɑrdʒ]	to formally tell someone that they have done something wrong
commit	[kəmɪt]	to do something illegal; *commit a crime*; *commit murder*
confess	[kənfɛs]	to admit that you have done something wrong

EXAMPLES

He is on trial for murder.
The driver apologized to the victim's family.
Police arrested five young men in connection with the robbery.
Our house was burglarized last year.
Police charged Mr. Bell with murder.
He confessed to seventeen murders.

convict	[kənvɪkt]	to find someone guilty of a crime in a court
escape	[ɪskeɪp]	to manage to get away from a place; *escape from prison*
fine	[faɪn]	to order someone to pay a sum of money because they have done something illegal
forge	[fɔrdʒ]	to make illegal copies of paper money, a document, or a painting in order to cheat people
hold something up		to point a gun at someone in a place such as a bank or a shop, in order to get their money; *hold up a bank*
kidnap	[kɪdnæp]	to take someone away by force and keep them as a prisoner, often until their friends or family pay a ransom (= a large amount of money)
mug	[mʌg]	to attack someone and steal their money
murder	[mɜrdər]	to kill someone deliberately
prove	[pruv]	to show that something is true
rape	[reɪp]	to force someone to have sex when they do not want to
rob	[rɒb]	to steal money or property from someone
sentence	[sɛntəns]	to say in court what a person's punishment will be
solve	[sɒlv]	to find out who committed a crime; *solve a crime*
steal	[stil]	to take something from someone without their permission
suspect	[səspɛkt]	to believe that someone probably did something wrong
vandalize	[vænd³laɪz]	to damage something on purpose

EXAMPLES

He was convicted of manslaughter.
She was fined $300.
She was sentenced to nine years in prison.
Someone stole my wallet!
Police suspect him of fraud.

witness	[wɪtnɪs]	to see something happen

ADJECTIVES

criminal	[krɪmɪnəl]	connected with a crime; *criminal charges*
guilty	[gɪlti]	having committed a crime or an offense
illegal	[ɪliɡəl]	not allowed by law
innocent	[ɪnəsənt]	not guilty of a crime
legal	[liɡəl]	**1** used for describing things that relate to the law; *the legal system* **2** allowed by law
violent	[vaɪələnt]	using physical force to hurt or kill other people

EXAMPLES
Anyone who witnessed the attack should call the police.
He was found guilty.
He was proved innocent.
Is this legal?

materials

acrylic   [ækrɪlɪk]   a soft artificial material that feels like wool

aluminium (*BRIT*)   *see* **aluminum**

aluminum   [əlu_mɪnəm]   a light metal used for making things such as cooking equipment and cans for food and drink (*In British English, use* **aluminium**)

brass   [bræs]   a yellow-colored metal

brick   [brɪk]   a rectangular block used in the building of walls; *a brick wall*

bronze   [brɒnz]   a yellowish-brown metal that is a mixture of copper and tin

canvas   [kænvəs]   a strong, heavy material that is used for making tents and bags

cardboard   [kɑrdbɔrd]   thick, stiff paper that is used for making boxes; *a cardboard box*

cement   [sɪmɛnt]   a gray powder that is mixed with sand and water in order to make concrete

china   [tʃaɪnə]   a hard white substance that is used for making expensive cups and plates

clay   [kleɪ]   a type of earth that is soft when it is wet and hard when it is dry. Clay is used for making things such as pots and bricks; *a clay pot*

coal   [koʊl]   a hard black substance that comes from under the ground and is burned to give heat

concrete   [kɒŋkrit]   a hard substance made by mixing cement with sand and water. Concrete is used for building.

EXAMPLES
We ate from small bowls made of china.
He put some more coal on the fire.

copper	[kɒpər]	a soft reddish-brown metal
cotton	[kɒtⁿn]	cloth or thread that is made from the soft fibers of a plant called a cotton plant
crystal	[krɪstⁿl]	**1** a small, hard piece of a natural substance; *ice crystals* **2** a clear rock used in jewelry; *a crystal necklace* **3** high-quality glass; *a crystal vase*
denim	[dɛnɪm]	a thick cotton cloth, usually blue, that is used for making clothes; *a denim jacket*
elastic	[ɪlæstɪk]	a rubber material that stretches when you pull it, and then returns to its original size and shape
fabric	[fæbrɪk]	cloth that you use for making things like clothes and bags
fur	[fɜr]	the thick hair that grows on the bodies of many animals; *a fur coat*
glass	[glæs]	a hard, transparent substance that is used for making things such as windows and bottles
glue	[glu]	a sticky substance that is used for joining things together
gold	[goʊld]	a valuable, yellow-colored metal that is used for making jewelry, ornaments, and coins
iron	[aɪərn]	a hard, dark gray metal; *an iron gate*
lace	[leɪs]	a delicate cloth with a design made of fine threads; *lace curtains*
lead	[lɛd]	a soft, gray, heavy metal; *a lead pipe*
leather	[lɛðər]	animal skin that is used for making shoes, clothes, bags, and furniture
linen	[lɪnɪn]	a type of strong cloth

EXAMPLES

The documents were rolled up and held together with elastic.
We sell our tablecloths in plain or printed fabric.
This ring is made of solid gold.
He was wearing a white linen suit.

liquid	[lɪkwɪd]	a substance, for example water or oil, that flows and can be poured
marble	[mɑrbᵊl]	a type of very hard rock that people use to make parts of buildings or statues (= models of people)
material	[mətɪəriəl]	1 any solid substance 2 cloth 3 the things that you need for a particular activity; *building materials*
metal	[mɛtᵊl]	a hard, usually shiny substance such as iron, steel, or gold
nylon	[naɪlɒn]	a strong, artificial substance that is used for making cloth and plastic
paper	[peɪpər]	a material that you write on or wrap things with; *a piece of paper*
plaster	[plæstər]	a substance that is used for making a smooth surface on the inside of walls and ceilings
plastic	[plæstɪk]	a light but strong material that is produced by a chemical process; *a plastic bag*
pottery	[pɒtəri]	pots, dishes, and other objects made from clay
rubber	[rʌbər]	a strong substance that is used for making tires, boots, and other products
satin	[sætᵊn]	a smooth, shiny cloth that is made of silk or other materials
silk	[sɪlk]	a smooth, shiny cloth that is made from very thin threads from an insect called a silkworm
silver	[sɪlvər]	a valuable pale gray metal that is used for making jewelry
steel	[stil]	a very strong metal that is made mainly from iron

EXAMPLES

The thick material of her skirt was too warm for summer.

stone	[stoʊn]	**1** a hard solid substance that is found in the ground and is often used for building; *a stone wall* **2** a piece of beautiful and valuable rock that is used in making jewelry; *a precious stone*
straw	[strɔ]	the dried, yellow stems of crops; *a straw hat*
string	[strɪŋ]	very thin rope that is made of twisted threads
textile	[tɛkstaɪl]	any type of cloth
thread	[θrɛd]	a long, very thin piece of cotton, nylon, or silk that you use for sewing
timber	[tɪmbər]	wood that is used for building and making things
tin	[tɪn]	a type of soft metal
velvet	[vɛlvɪt]	soft cloth that is thick on one side; *velvet curtains*
wax	[wæks]	a solid, slightly shiny substance that is used for making candles (= sticks that you burn for light) and polish for furniture
wire	[waɪər]	a long, thin piece of metal; *a wire fence*
wood	[wʊd]	the hard material that trees are made of
wool	[wʊl]	a material made from the hair that grows on sheep and on some other animals

ADJECTIVES

hard	[hɑrd]	not easily bent, cut, or broken
man-made	[mæn meɪd]	created by people, rather than occurring naturally; *man-made fibers*
natural	[nætʃərəl, nætʃrəl]	existing in nature and not created by people
raw	[rɔ]	used for describing materials or substances that are in their natural state; *raw materials*

EXAMPLES
She works in the textile industry.

rough	[rʌf]	not smooth or even
smooth	[smuð]	flat, with no rough parts, lumps or holes
soft	[sɔft]	1 pleasant to touch, and not rough or hard 2 changing shape easily when pressed
solid	[sɒlɪd]	1 hard; not like liquid or gas 2 with no holes or space inside; *solid rock*
synthetic	[sɪnθɛtɪk]	made from chemicals or artificial substances rather than from natural ones
transparent	[trænspɛərənt, -pær-]	used for describing an object or a substance that you can see through
wooden	[wʊdᵊn]	made of wood; *a wooden chair*
woolen	[wʊlən]	made from wool; *a woolen sweater*

EXAMPLES

Shoes made from synthetic materials can be washed easily.
He fell on the hard wooden floor.

math

NOUNS

addition [ədɪʃⁱn] the process of calculating the total of two or more numbers

algebra [ældʒɪbrə] a type of math in which letters and signs are used to represent numbers

angle [æŋgⁱl] the space between two lines or surfaces that meet in one place; *a 30° angle*

area [ɛəriə] the amount of flat space that a surface covers, measured in square units

arithmetic [ərɪθmɪtɪk] the basic calculation of numbers, for example adding or multiplying

average [ævərɪdʒ, ævrɪdʒ] the result that you get when you add two or more amounts together and divide the total by the number of amounts you added together; *The average of 1, 2, and 6 is 3.*

axis [æksɪs]
(PL) **axes** [æksiz] one of the two lines on a graph on which you mark points to show measurements or amounts

bar chart *(BRIT)* *see* **bar graph**

bar graph [bɑr græf] a chart that shows amounts as thick lines of different heights (*In British English, use* **bar chart**)

calculator [kælkyəleɪtər] a small electronic machine that you use to calculate numbers

chart [tʃɑrt] a diagram or graph that shows information

circle [sɜrkⁱl] a round shape

circumference [sərkʌmfrəns] the distance around the edge of a circle

column [kɒləm] a section in a table that you read from top to bottom

compass [kʌmpəs] a piece of equipment that you use for drawing circles

---

EXAMPLES

She can count to 100 and do simple addition problems.

What's the area of this triangle?

We can label the axes: time is on the vertical axis and money is on the horizontal one.

cone	[koʊn]	a solid shape with one flat, round end and one pointed end
cube	[kyub]	**1** a solid object with six square surfaces **2** the number that you get if you multiply a number by itself twice
cylinder	[sɪlɪndər]	a shape with circular ends and long straight sides
decimal	[dɛsɪməl]	a part of a whole number that is written in the form of a period followed by one or more numbers, for example 0.25 or 10.6
decimal point	[dɛsɪməl pɔɪnt]	the period in front of a decimal
degree	[dɪgri]	**1** a unit for measuring temperature that is often written as °; *180° Celsius* **2** a unit for measuring angles that is often written as °; *a 45° angle*
diameter	[daɪæmɪtər]	the length of a straight line that can be drawn across a round object, passing through the middle of it
digit	[dɪdʒɪt]	a written symbol for any of the ten numbers from 0 to 9
division	[dɪvɪʒ°n]	the process of dividing one number by another number
figure	[fɪgyər]	**1** one of the symbols from 0 to 9 that you use to write numbers **2** an amount or a price expressed as a number
formula (PL) **formulas,** **formulae**	[fɔrmyələ] [fɔrmyəli]	a group of letters, numbers, or other symbols that represents a scientific rule
fraction	[frækʃ°n]	a part of a whole number, such as ½ or ⅓

EXAMPLES

The cube of 2 is 8.

The waiter forgot to put a decimal point in their $45.00 bill and they were charged $4500.

They put the figures in the wrong column.

The mathematical formula describes the distances of the planets from the Sun.

geometry	[dʒiɒmɪtri]	a type of math relating to lines, angles, curves, and shapes
graph	[græf]	a picture that shows information about sets of numbers or measurements
half	[hæf]	one of two equal parts of a number,
(PL) **halves**	[hævz]	an amount, or an object
height	[haɪt]	the amount that something measures from the bottom to the top
hexagon	[hɛksəgɒn]	a shape with six straight sides
length	[lɛŋθ]	the amount that something measures from one end to the other, along the longest side
math	[mæθ]	the study of numbers, quantities, or shapes (*In British English, use* **maths**)
mathematics	[mæθəmætɪks]	same as **math**
maths (*BRIT*)		*see* **math**
multiplication	[mʌltɪplɪkeɪʃən]	the process of calculating the total of one number multiplied by another
number	[nʌmbər]	a word such as "two," "nine," or "twelve" or a symbol such as 1, 3, or 47 that is used in counting
numeral	[numərəl]	a written symbol that represents a number; *The Roman numeral for 7 is VII.*
oblong	[ɒblɒŋ]	a shape that has two long sides and two short sides
pentagon	[pɛntəgɑn]	a shape with five straight sides
percent	[pərsɛnt]	used for talking about an amount as part of 100, often written as %
percentage	[pərsɛntɪdʒ]	an amount of something, considered as part of 100

EXAMPLES

The graph shows that prices went up about 20 percent last year.

More than half of all U.S. houses are heated with gas.

The table is about one yard in length.

Only ten percent of our customers live in this city.

A large percentage of the population speaks English.

perimeter	[pərɪmɪtər]	the total distance around the edge of a flat shape
pie chart	[paɪ tʃɑrt]	a circle that is divided into sections to show something divided into different amounts
pyramid	[pɪrəmɪd]	a solid shape with a flat base and flat sides that form a point where they meet at the top
quarter	[kwɔrtər]	one of four equal parts of something
radius (PL) **radiuses,** **radii**	[reɪdiəs] [reɪdiaɪ]	the distance from the center of a circle to its outside edge
ratio	[reɪʃoʊ, -ʃioʊ]	a relationship between two things when it is expressed in numbers or amounts
rectangle	[rɛktæŋɡəl]	a shape with four straight sides and four 90° angles
right angle	[raɪt æŋɡəl]	an angle of 90°
row	[roʊ]	a section in a table that you read from one side to the other
ruler	[rulər]	a long, flat object that you use for measuring things and for drawing straight lines
scale	[skeɪl]	a set of levels or numbers that you use to measure things
semicircle	[sɛmisɜrkəl, sɛmaɪ-]	one half of a circle
shape	[ʃeɪp]	something such as a circle, a square, or a triangle
sphere	[sfɪər]	an object that is completely round, like a ball

---

EXAMPLES

To work out the perimeter of a rectangle, you need to know its length and width.

A quarter of them are over 55 years old.

The adult to child ratio is one to six.

The earthquake measured 5.5 on the Richter scale.

square	[skwɛər]	**1** a shape with four straight sides that are all the same length **2** the number that you get if you multiply a number by itself
square root	[skwɛər rut]	a number that you multiply by itself to produce another number; *The square root of 36 is 6.*
subtraction	[səbtrækʃən]	the process of taking one number away from another number
sum	[sʌm]	the number that you get when you add two or more numbers together; *Fourteen is the sum of six and eight.*
table	[teɪbəl]	a set of numbers that you arrange in neat rows and columns
triangle	[traɪæŋgəl]	a shape with three straight sides
unit	[yunɪt]	a fixed measurement such as a liter or an inch
volume	[vɒlyum]	the amount of space that an object contains
width	[wɪdθ, wɪtθ]	the amount that something measures from one side to the other

VERBS

add	[æd]	to calculate the total of various numbers or amounts
calculate	[kælkyəleɪt]	to find out an amount by using numbers
count	[kaʊnt]	**1** to say all the numbers in order up to a particular amount; *count to 20* **2** to see how many there are in a group; *count the money*
divide	[dɪvaɪd]	to find out how many times one number can fit into another bigger number

EXAMPLES

The cube of 2 is 4.

What is the volume of a cube with sides 3cm long?

Add all the numbers together, and divide by three.

Have you calculated the cost of your trip?

Measure the floor area and divide it by six.

equal	[i̱kwəl]	to be the same as a particular number or amount; *Nine minus two equals seven.*
multiply	[mʌ̱ltɪplaɪ]	to add a number to itself a certain number of times; *If you multiply 3 by 4, you get 12.*
subtract	[səbtræ̱kt]	to take one number away from another number; *If you subtract 3 from 5, you get 2.*
take something away		same as **subtract**
work something out		same as **calculate**

ADJECTIVES

circular	[sɜ̱rkyələr]	shaped like a circle
diagonal	[daɪæ̱gənᵊl, -æ̱gnᵊl]	going from one corner of a square across to the opposite corner
even	[i̱vᵊn]	used for describing numbers that can be divided exactly by two, for example 4, 8, and 24
mathematical	[mæ̱θə-mæ̱tɪkᵊl]	involving numbers and calculating; *a mathematical formula*
negative	[nɛ̱gətɪv]	less than zero; *a negative number*
odd	[ɒ̱d]	used for describing numbers such as 3 and 17, that cannot be divided exactly by two
parallel	[pæ̱rəlɛl]	used for describing two lines that are the same distance apart along their whole length; *parallel lines*
positive	[pɒ̱zɪtɪv]	higher than zero; *a positive number*
rectangular	[rɛktæ̱ŋgyələr]	shaped like a rectangle
square	[skwɛ̱ər]	**1** used for describing a shape that has four straight sides that are all the same length; *a square table* **2** used for talking about the area of something; *30 square feet*
triangular	[traɪæ̱ŋgyələr]	shaped like a triangle

EXAMPLES
Add up the bills for each month. Take this away from the income.
It took me some time to work out the answer to the question.
The screen showed a pattern of diagonal lines.

PREPOSITIONS

minus   [maɪnəs]   used when you are taking one number away from another number; *Ten minus two is eight*.

plus   [plʌs]   used for showing that one number is being added to another; *Three plus four equals seven*.

times   [taɪmz]   used when you are multiplying one number by another; *Five times two is ten*.

money

allowance [əlaʊəns] money that is given regularly to someone (*In British English, use* **pocket money**)

ATM [eɪ ti ɛm] a machine, usually outside a bank, from which you can get money using a special plastic card (*In British English, use* **cash machine**)

balance [bæləns] the amount of money you have in your bank account; *check your balance*

bank [bæŋk] a place where people can keep their money

bank account [bæŋk əkaʊnt] an arrangement with a bank where they look after your money for you; *open/close a bank account*

bill [bɪl] a document that shows how much money you must pay for something; *pay the bill*

billfold [bɪlfoʊld] a small case that you can keep money and cards in (*In British English, use* **wallet**

breadwinner [brɛdwɪnər] the person in a family who earns the money that the family needs

budget [bʌdʒɪt] the amount of money that you have available to spend; *a low-budget film*

bureau de change (*BRIT*) *see* **currency exchange**

cash [kæʃ] money in the form of bills and coins; *two thousand dollars in cash*

cashier [kæʃɪər] a person whose job is to take your money in a store or a bank

cash machine (*mainly BRIT*) *see* **ATM**

change [tʃeɪndʒ] **1** the money that you get back when you pay with more money than something costs
2 coins; *change for the parking meter*

change purse [tʃeɪndʒ pɜrs] a very small bag used for carrying money, especially by women (*In British English, use* **purse**)

EXAMPLES

They couldn't afford to pay their bills.

I've always paid the bills and been the breadwinner.

charge	[tʃɑrdʒ]	an amount of money that you have to pay for a service; *a small charge*
checking account	[tʃɛkɪŋ əkaʊnt]	a bank account that you can take money out of at any time (*In British English, use* **current account**)
check	[tʃɛk]	a printed piece of paper from a bank that you write an amount of money on and use to pay for things; *pay by check* (*In British English, use* **cheque**)
checkbook	[tʃɛkbʊk]	a book containing checks
cheque (*BRIT*)		*see* **check**
coin	[kɔɪn]	a small round piece of metal money
cost	[kɔst]	the amount of money you need in order to buy, do, or make something; *the high cost of housing*
credit	[krɛdɪt]	an arrangement that allows someone to buy something and pay for it later; *They bought it on credit.*
credit card	[krɛdɪt kɑrd]	a plastic card that you use to buy goods on credit; *pay by credit card*
currency	[kɜrənsi]	the money that is used in a particular country; *pay in a different currency*
currency exchange	[kɜrənsi ɪkstʃeɪndʒ]	an office where you can buy and sell different currencies (*In British English, use* **bureau de change**)
current account (*BRIT*)		*see* **checking account**
debit card	[dɛbɪt kɑrd]	a bank card that you can use to pay for things; *pay by debit card*
debt	[dɛt]	an amount of money that you owe someone; *get into debt*

EXAMPLES

He gave me a check for $1500.
He counted out the coins into her hand.
The cost of a loaf of bread has gone up.
There will be an increase in the cost of posting a letter.
He is trying to pay off his debts.

deposit	[dɪpɒzɪt]	**1** a sum of money that is part of the full price of something, and that you pay when you agree to buy it; *a 10% deposit* **2** an amount of money that you put into a bank account; *make a deposit*
direct debit (*BRIT*)		*see* **direct deposit**
direct deposit	[dɪrɛkt dɪpɒzɪt, daɪ-]	an arrangement that you make with a company, allowing them to take money that you owe them from or put money that they owe you into your bank account every month (*In British English, use* **direct deposit**)
economy	[ɪkɒnəmi]	the system for organizing the money and industry of the world, a country, or local government
expenses	[ɪkspɛnsɪz]	money that you spend on things
income	[ɪnkʌm]	the money that a person earns or receives
inheritance	[ɪnhɛrɪtᵊns]	money or property that you receive from someone who has died
insurance	[ɪnʃʊərəns]	an agreement that you make with a company in which you pay money to them regularly, and they pay you if something bad happens to you or your property; *travel insurance*
interest	[ɪntrɪst, -tərɪst]	the extra money that you pay if you have borrowed money, or the extra money that you receive if you have money in some types of bank accounts
loan	[loʊn]	an amount of money that you borrow
money	[mʌni]	the coins or bills that you use to buy things
mortgage	[mɔrgɪdʒ]	a loan of money that you get from a bank in order to buy a house

---

EXAMPLES

The Indian economy is changing fast.
Her hotel expenses were paid by the company.
She used her inheritance to buy a house.
How much interest do you have to pay on the loan?
Do you earn much interest on that account?
I had to sell my home because I couldn't afford the mortgage payments.

payment	[peɪmənt]	**1** an amount of money that is paid to someone; *weekly payments* **2** the act of paying money or of being paid; *immediate payment*
pension	[pɛnʃən]	money that you regularly receive from a business or the government after you stop working because of your age
PIN	[pɪn]	short for "Personal Identification Number:" a secret number that you can use, for example, with a bank card to get money from a cash machine; *enter in your PIN*
pocket money	[pɒkɪt mʌni]	**1** a small amount of money **2** *(BRIT) see* **allowance**
poverty	[pɒvərti]	the state of being very poor; *living in poverty*
price	[praɪs]	the amount of money that you have to pay in order to buy something
profit	[prɒfɪt]	the amount of money that you gain when you sell something for more than you paid for it
purse	[pɜrs]	**1** a small bag used for carrying money and other items, especially by women **2** *(BRIT) see* **change purse**
rent	[rɛnt]	money that you pay to someone so that you can use something that belongs to them; *pay the rent*
salary	[sæləri]	the money that you earn from your employer
sales tax	[seɪlz tæks]	a tax that is added to the price of goods or services
savings	[seɪvɪŋz]	all the money that you have saved, especially in a bank
savings account	[seɪvɪŋz əkaʊnt]	a bank account that gives you interest on your money

EXAMPLES

To use the service you'll need a PIN number.
We have seen huge changes in the price of gas.
They expect house prices to rise.
The lawyer was paid a huge salary.

savings and loan	[seɪvɪŋz ənd loʊn]	a business that lends people money to buy houses and that provides savings accounts; *savings and loan association*
share	[ʃɛər]	one of the equal parts that the value of a company is divided into, which people can buy so that they own a part of the company and have a part of its profit
statement	[steɪtmənt]	a document showing how much money you have put into and taken out of your bank account
tax	[tæks]	an amount of money that you have to pay to the government so that it can pay for public services such as roads and schools; *raise/lower taxes*
wages	[weɪdʒɪz]	the amount of money that is paid to someone for the work that they do
wallet *(BRIT)*		*see* **billfold**

VERBS

borrow	[bɒroʊ]	to get money from someone and agree to pay it back some time in the future
buy	[baɪ]	to get something by paying money for it
charge	[tʃɑrdʒ]	to ask someone to pay money for something
cost	[kɔst]	to have as a price; *cost a lot*
deposit	[dɪpɒzɪt]	to put an amount of money into a bank account
donate	[doʊneɪt]	to give something to an organization

EXAMPLES

I bought shares in my brother's new company.
His wages have gone up.
I lost my wallet.
He could not afford to buy a house.
Lizzie bought herself a bike.
The driver charged us only $2 each.
How much do you charge for printing photos?
He has no children to inherit his house.

earn	[ɜrn]	to receive money for work that you do
inherit	[ɪnhɛrɪt]	to receive money or property from someone who has died
invest	[ɪnvɛst]	to put money into a business or a bank, in order to try to make a profit from it
lend	[lɛnd]	to give someone money that they must give back after a certain amount of time
make money		to get money for doing something
owe	[oʊ]	to have to pay money to someone
pay	[peɪ]	**1** to give someone an amount of money for something that you are buying; *pay for the food* **2** to give someone an amount of money for something such as a bill or a debt; *pay the bill* **3** to give someone money for the work that they do; *We can pay you every week.* **4** to give someone the money that you owe them; *I haven't paid him back yet.*
pay something in		to put money into a bank account
pay up		to give someone the money that you owe them, even though you would prefer not to
save	[seɪv]	to gradually collect money by spending less than you get
sign	[saɪn]	to write your name on a document; *sign a check*
spend	[spɛnd]	to pay money for things that you want or need; *spend money*
withdraw	[wɪðdrɔ, wɪθ-]	to take money out of a bank account

EXAMPLES

He made a lot of money from his first book.
The company owes money to more than 60 banks.
Blake owed him $50.
Tim and Barbara are saving for a house.
I was saving money to go to college.

ADJECTIVES

bankrupt	[bæŋkrʌpt]	without enough money to pay your debts
cheap	[tʃip]	**1** costing little money, or less than you expected **2** not willing to spend much money
expensive	[ɪkspɛnsɪv]	costing a lot of money
generous	[dʒɛnərəs]	giving you more than you expect of something; *a generous gift*
poor	[pʊər]	having very little money and few possessions
rich	[rɪtʃ]	having a lot of money or valuable possessions
thrifty	[θrɪfti]	saving money, not buying unnecessary things, and not wasting things
valuable	[vælyuəbəl]	worth a lot of money
wealthy	[wɛlθi]	having a large amount of money, property, or valuable possessions

IDIOMS

be rolling in it	[INFORMAL] to have a lot of money
in the red	[INFORMAL] owing money to a bank
make ends meet	to manage to live on your income
money doesn't grow on trees	used for saying that money is not freely available
save something for a rainy day	to keep money to use if an unexpected need arises
tighten your belt	to spend less money than you usually do

EXAMPLES

I want to rent a cheap room near the university.

She was always dressed in the most expensive silk and cashmere.

My mother taught me to be thrifty.

Do not leave any valuable items in your hotel room.

The company is $5 million in the red.

music

music	[myuzɪk]	**1** the pleasant sound that you make when you sing or play instruments; *listen to music* **2** the symbols that you write on paper to tell people what to sing or play; *read music*

TYPES OF MUSIC

classical music	[klæsɪkᵊl myuzɪk]	a traditional type of music, written in a standard form
country music	[kʌntri myuzɪk]	a type of music in the style of the traditional music of the southern and western U.S.
folk music	[fouk myuzɪk]	music that is traditional or typical of a particular group of people or country
jazz	[dʒæz]	a style of music that has strong rhythms. It was invented by African-American musicians in the early part of the twentieth century.
pop music	[pɒp myuzɪk]	modern popular music, usually with a strong rhythm and simple tunes
rap	[ræp]	a type of modern music in which the words are spoken
rock and roll	[rɒk ənd roʊl]	a type of pop music developed in the 1950s which has a strong beat for dancing

MUSICAL INSTRUMENTS

cello	[tʃɛloʊ]	a musical instrument that is like a large violin. You sit behind it and rest it on the floor.
clarinet	[klærɪnɛt]	a musical instrument that you blow. It is a long black wooden tube with keys on it that you press and a single reed (= small flat part that moves and makes a sound when you blow).

EXAMPLES

This is a collection of traditional folk music from nearly 30 countries.
The club plays live jazz on Sundays.
Elvis Presley was known as the King of Rock and Roll.

drum [drʌm] a simple musical instrument that you hit with sticks or with your hands

flute [flut] a musical instrument that you play by blowing. You hold it sideways to your mouth.

guitar [gɪtɑr] a musical instrument that has six strings and a long neck

harp [hɑrp] a large musical instrument that has strings stretched from the top to the bottom of a frame. You play the harp with your fingers.

horn [hɔrn] a musical instrument with a long metal tube that you play by blowing into it

keyboard [kibɔrd] **1** the set of black and white keys that you press when you play a piano
2 an electronic musical instrument that has a keyboard

musical instrument [myuzɪkᵊl ɪnstrəmənt] an object such as a piano, guitar, or violin that you use for playing music

oboe [oʊboʊ] a musical instrument that you blow. It is a long black wooden tube with keys on it that you press and a double reed (= small flat part that moves and makes a sound when you blow).

organ [ɔrgən] a large musical instrument that is like a piano

piano [piænoʊ, pyænoʊ] a large musical instrument that you play by pressing black and white bars (= keys)

recorder [rɪkɔrdər] a wooden or plastic musical instrument in the shape of a pipe. You play it by blowing down one end and covering holes with your fingers.

saxophone [sæksəfoʊn] a musical instrument made of metal that you play by blowing into it

sitar [sɪtɑr] an Indian musical instrument with two layers of strings, a long neck, and a round body

---

EXAMPLES
Sam is a great guitar player.

tambourine	[tæmbərɪn]	a round musical instrument that has small bells around its edge. You shake it or hit it with your hand.
trumpet	[trʌmpɪt]	a metal musical instrument that you blow
violin	[vaɪəlɪn]	a musical instrument made of wood with four strings. You hold it under your chin, and play it by moving a long stick (= a bow) across the strings
xylophone	[zaɪləfoʊn]	a musical instrument with a row of wooden bars of different lengths that you play with special hammers

PEOPLE

band	[bænd]	a group of people who play music together; *play in a band*
choir	[kwaɪər]	a group of people who sing together
composer	[kəmpoʊzər]	a person who writes music
conductor	[kəndʌktər]	a person who stands in front of a group of musicians and directs their performance
drummer	[drʌmər]	a person who plays a drum or a drum kit
guitarist	[gɪtɑrɪst]	a person who plays the guitar
musician	[myuzɪʃᵊn]	a person who plays a musical instrument as their job or hobby
orchestra	[ɔrkɪstrə]	a large group of musicians who play different instruments together
pianist	[piænɪst, piənɪst]	a person who plays the piano
singer	[sɪŋər]	a person who sings, especially as a job

PIECES AND PARTS OF MUSIC

chord	[kɔrd]	a number of musical notes played or sung at the same time; *a chord of G major*
chorus	[kɔrəs]	a part of a song that you repeat several times
duet	[duɛt]	a piece of music performed by two people; *a duet for two guitarists*

EXAMPLES

He sang in his church choir for ten years.

harmony	[hɑrməni]	the pleasant combination of different notes of music played at the same time; *play in harmony*
key	[ki]	a particular scale of musical notes; *the key of C*
lyrics	[lɪrɪks]	the words of a song
melody	[mɛlədi]	a group of musical notes that make a tune
note	[nout]	1 one particular musical sound; *a wrong note* 2 a symbol that represents this sound
octave	[ɒktɪv]	a series of eight notes in music, or the difference between the first and last notes in the series
piece of music	[pis əv myuzɪk]	a complete musical work; *an orchestral piece*
rhythm	[rɪðəm]	a regular pattern of sounds or movements
scale	[skeɪl]	a set of musical notes that are played in a fixed order
solo	[soulou]	a piece of music performed by one person
song	[sɔŋ]	words and music sung together
verse	[vɜrs]	one of the groups of lines in a poem or song

RECORDING, PERFORMING, AND LISTENING TO MUSIC

album	[ælbəm]	a collection of songs on a CD
CD	[si di]	short for "compact disc:" a disc for storing music
concert	[kɒnsərt]	a performance of music
iPod™	[aɪpɒd]	a small piece of electronic equipment that stores music, photos, and movies
karaoke	[kæriouki]	a form of entertainment in which a machine plays songs, and you sing the words

EXAMPLES

She has a deep voice so she can't sing high notes.
He raised his sticks and beat out the rhythm of the song.
The band released their new album on July 1.
The weekend began with an outdoor rock concert.

MP3 player	[ɛm pi θri pleɪər]	a small piece of electronic equipment that stores and plays music
microphone	[maɪkrəfoʊn]	a piece of electronic equipment that you use to make sounds louder or to record them onto a machine
record	[rɛkərd]	a round, flat piece of black plastic on which sound, especially music, is stored. A record can be played on a record player.

VERBS

compose	[kəmpoʊz]	to write a piece of music
conduct	[kəndʌkt]	to stand in front of musicians and direct their performance
perform	[pərfɔrm]	to play a piece of music in front of an audience
play	[pleɪ]	1 to produce music from a musical instrument 2 to put a CD into a machine and listen to it
practice	[præktɪs]	to do something regularly in order to do it better (*In British English, use* **practise**)
practise (*BRIT*)		*see* **practice**
record	[rɪkɔrd]	to store something such as a speech or a performance in a computer file or on a disk so that it can be heard or seen again later
sing	[sɪŋ]	to make music with your voice
tune	[tun]	to adjust a musical instrument so that it produces the right notes

EXAMPLES

the Orchestra of Welsh National Opera conducted by Carlo Rizzi
They will be performing works by Bach and Scarlatti.
Nina was playing the piano.
She played her CDs too loudly.
My brother and I used to sing this song.

ADJECTIVES

acoustic	[əkustɪk]	an acoustic musical instrument is one which is not electric; *an acoustic guitar*
classical	[klæsɪkəl]	traditional in form, style, or content; *classical music*
flat	[flæt]	used for describing a note that is slightly lower than another note
major	[meɪdʒər]	used for talking about a scale with half steps in sound between the third and fourth and the seventh and eighth notes; *a scale of G major*
minor	[maɪnər]	used in music for talking about a scale in which the third note is one half step lower that the related major scale
musical	[myuzɪkəl]	1 relating to playing or studying music; *musical training* 2 having a natural ability and interest in music; *musical children*
sharp	[ʃɑrp]	used for describing a note that is slightly higher than another note

ADVERBS

in tune	[ɪn tun]	singing or playing the correct musical notes; *sing in tune*
loudly	[laʊdli]	easily heard because the level of sound is very high; *playing loudly*
out of tune	[aʊt əv ʌv tun]	not singing or playing the correct musical notes; *sing out of tune*
softly	[sɔftli]	quietly or gently; *singing softly*

the office

binder [baɪndər] a cover for holding loose sheets of paper together

briefcase [brifkeɪs] a small suitcase for carrying business papers in; *a leather briefcase*

bulletin board [bulɪtɪn bɔrd] a board on a wall for notices giving information (*In British English, use* **noticeboard**)

business card [bɪznɪs kɑrd] a small card printed with your name, job, business address, and other contact information; *give someone your business card*

calculator [kælkyəleɪtər] a small electronic machine that you use to calculate numbers

conference room [kɒnfərəns rum, -frəns] a room in an office building where people have meetings

department [dɪpɑrtmənt] one of the sections in an organization

desk [dɛsk] a table that you sit at to write or work

fax machine [fæks məʃin] a special machine that you use to send and receive documents electronically

file [faɪl] **1** a box or a type of envelope that you keep papers in
2 a collection of information that you keep on your computer; *open a file*; *a computer file*

filing cabinet [faɪlɪŋ kæbɪnɪt] a tall piece of office furniture with deep drawers for documents

folder [foʊldər] **1** a folded piece of cardboard or plastic that you keep papers in; *a work folder*
2 a group of files that are stored together on a computer

highlighter [haɪlaɪtər] a brightly colored pen that is used for marking important parts of a document

---

EXAMPLES

Her telephone number was pinned to the bulletin board.
She works in the accounting department.
The file contained letters and reports.

ink cartridge	[ɪŋk kɑrtrɪdʒ]	a small container filled with ink that you put into a printer
notepad	[noʊtpæd]	**1** a pad of paper for writing notes on **2** a pocket-sized personal computer
noticeboard (*BRIT*)		*see* **bulletin board**
office	[ɔfɪs]	a place where people work sitting at a desk; *work in an office*
overhead projector	[oʊvərhɛd prədʒɛktər]	a piece of equipment that you use to make an image on a plastic sheet appear large on a screen
scissors	[sɪzərz]	a small tool for cutting, with two sharp parts that are joined together
paperclip	[peɪpərklɪp]	a small metal clip used for holding sheets of paper together
pen	[pɛn]	a long thin object that you use for writing with ink (= colored liquid)
pencil	[pɛnsəl]	a thin piece of wood with a black or colored substance through the middle that you use to write or draw with
photocopier	[foʊtəkɒpiər]	a machine that copies documents by photographing them
photocopy	[foʊtəkɒpi]	a copy of a document that you make using a photocopier; *make a photocopy*
printer	[prɪntər]	a machine for printing copies of computer documents on paper
reception	[rɪsɛpʃən]	the desk in an office building that you go to when you first arrive
receptionist	[rɪsɛpʃənɪst]	a person who deals with people on the phone or in person at a reception desk
safe	[seɪf]	a strong metal box with a lock, where you keep money or other valuable things
Scotch tape™	[skɒtʃ teɪp]	clear plastic sticky tape that is used for sticking things together; *a roll of Scotch tape* (In British English, use **sellotape**)
sellotape (*BRIT*)		*see* **Scotch tape™**
stapler	[steɪplər]	a small piece of equipment that is used for attaching sheets of paper together with staples

staples	[steɪpᵊlz]	pieces of thin wire that attach sheets of paper together
toner	[toʊnər]	a black or colored powder used as ink in a printer or a photocopier
vending machine	[vɛndɪŋ məʃin]	a machine that you can buy small articles from, such as food, drinks, or cigarettes

VERBS

photocopy	[foʊtəkɒpi]	to make a copy of a document using a photocopier; *photocopy a document*
scan	[skæn]	to make an electronic copy of a picture or a document using a special piece of equipment (called a scanner)
type	[taɪp]	to write something using a machine like a computer

personal items

NOUNS

billfold	[bɪlfoʊld]	a small case in which you keep money and cards (*In British English, use* **wallet**)
bracelet	[breɪslɪt]	a piece of jewelry that you wear around your wrist; *a silver bracelet*
brush	[brʌʃ]	an object with a lot of hairs attached to it that you use for making your hair tidy
change purse	[tʃeɪndʒ pɜrs]	a very small bag used for carrying money, especially by women (*In British English, use* **purse**)
comb	[koʊm]	a thin piece of plastic or metal with narrow, pointed parts (called teeth). You use a comb to make your hair tidy.
cotton ball	[kɒtᵊn bɔl]	soft, fluffy cotton, often used for applying creams to your skin (*In British English, use* **cotton wool**)
cotton wool (BRIT)		*see* **cotton ball**
dental floss	[dɛntᵊl flɔs]	a type of thread that is used to clean between your teeth
deodorant	[dioʊdərənt]	a substance that you can put on your skin to hide or prevent bad smells
diamond	[daɪmənd, daɪə-]	a hard, clear stone that is very expensive, and is used for making jewelry; *diamond earrings*
earring	[ɪərɪŋ]	a piece of jewelry that you wear on your ear
face cream	[feɪs krim]	a thick substance that you can rub into your face to keep it soft
face powder	[feɪs paʊdər]	a very fine soft powder that you can put on your face to make it look smoother
flannel (BRIT)		*see* **washcloth**
gel	[dʒɛl]	a thick substance like jelly, used for keeping your hair in a particular style or for washing your body; *shower gel*
hairdryer	[hɛərdraɪr]	a machine that you use to dry your hair
hairspray	[hɛərspreɪ]	a sticky substance that you spray out of a can onto your hair in order to hold it in place

handbag (BRIT)		*see* **purse**
handkerchief	[hǽŋkərtʃɪf]	a small square piece of cloth that you use for blowing your nose
jewelry	[dʒúəlri]	decorations that you wear on your body, such as a ring that you wear on your finger; *a jewelry box* (*In British English, use* **jewellery**)
jewellery (BRIT)		*see* **jewelry**
key ring	[kí rɪŋ]	a metal ring that you use to keep your keys together
lipstick	[lɪpstɪk]	a colored substance that women sometimes put on their lips
makeup	[méɪkʌp]	the creams and powders that you can put on your face to make yourself look more attractive; *put on makeup*; *take off makeup*
mirror	[mɪrər]	a flat piece of special glass that you can see yourself in
mouthwash	[máʊθwɒʃ]	a liquid that you put in your mouth to clean it and make your breath smell pleasant
nail file	[néɪl faɪl]	a small rough strip that you rub across the ends of your nails to shorten them or shape them
nail varnish	[néɪl vɑrnɪʃ]	a thick liquid that you can paint on your nails
necklace	[nɛkləs]	a piece of jewelry that you wear around your neck
perfume	[pɜrfyum, pərfyúm]	a liquid with a pleasant smell that you put on your skin
purse	[pɜrs]	**1** a small bag that a woman uses for carrying things such as money and keys (*In British English, use* **handbag**) **2** (BRIT) *see* **change purse**

EXAMPLES

Eva was wearing red lipstick.
Anna doesn't usually wear much makeup.
Dan looked at himself in the mirror.
The hall smelled of her mother's perfume.

razor	[reɪzər]	a tool that people use for shaving
ring	[rɪŋ]	a small circle of metal that you wear on your finger; *a wedding ring*
shampoo	[ʃæmpu]	liquid soap that you use for washing your hair
soap	[soʊp]	a substance that you use with water for washing yourself; *a bar of soap*
sponge	[spʌndʒ]	a piece of a very light soft material with a lot of small holes in it, that you use for washing yourself
suncream (*BRIT*)		*see* **sunscreen**
sunscreen	[sʌnskrin]	a cream that you can put on your skin to protect it from the sun (*In British English, use* **suncream**)
tissue	[tɪʃu]	a piece of thin, soft paper that you use to wipe your nose; *a packet of tissues*
toilet paper	[tɔɪlɪt peɪpər]	paper that you use to clean yourself after using the toilet
toiletries	[tɔɪlətriz]	the things that you use when you are washing or taking care of your body, such as soap and toothpaste
toothbrush	[tuθbrʌʃ]	a small brush that you use for cleaning your teeth
toothpaste	[tuθpeɪst]	a thick substance that you put on a toothbrush for cleaning your teeth
towel	[taʊəl]	a piece of thick soft cloth that you use to dry yourself; *a bath towel*
wallet (*BRIT*)		*see* **billfold**
washcloth	[wɒʃklɔθ]	a small cloth that you use for washing yourself (*In British English, use* **flannel**)
watch	[wɒtʃ]	a small clock that you wear on your wrist

[VERBS]

brush	[brʌʃ]	to tidy something using a brush; *brush your hair*
carry	[kæri]	1 to hold something in your hand and take it with you; *carry a handbag* 2 to always have something with you; *carry a passport*
comb	[koʊm]	to use a comb to make your hair tidy; *comb your hair*
put something on		to place clothing or makeup on your body in order to wear it
take something off		to remove clothing or makeup
wear	[wɛər]	to have something such as clothes, shoes, or jewelry on your body

EXAMPLES
She put on her makeup.
Rosalinda was wearing gold earrings.

plants, trees, and gardens

NOUNS

ash	[æʃ]	a tree that has smooth gray bark and loses its leaves in the winter
bark	[bɑrk]	the rough surface of a tree
beech	[bitʃ]	a tree with a smooth gray trunk
birch	[bɜrtʃ]	a tall tree with thin branches
bird feeder	[bɜrd fidər]	a container that you fill with food for birds
blossom	[blɒsəm]	the flowers that appear on a fruit tree; *cherry blossom*
border	[bɔrdər]	a long area of ground along the edge of a garden that is planted with flowers; *border plants*
branch	[bræntʃ]	one of the parts of a tree that have leaves, flowers, and fruit
bud	[bʌd]	a new growth on a tree or plant that develops into a leaf or flower
bush	[bʊʃ]	a plant with leaves and branches that is smaller than a tree; *a rose bush*
buttercup	[bʌtərkʌp]	a small wild plant with bright yellow flowers
compost	[kɒmpoʊst]	a mixture of dead plants and vegetables that is used to improve soil
daffodil	[dæfədɪl]	a yellow flower with a long stem that appears in spring
daisy	[deɪzi]	a small wildflower with a yellow center and white petals
dandelion	[dændɪlaɪən]	a wild plant with yellow flowers that turn into balls of soft white seeds
elm	[ɛlm]	a tree with broad leaves that it loses in the fall
fence	[fɛns]	a wooden or metal wall around a piece of land
fern	[fɜrn]	a plant that has long stems with leaves that look like feathers

EXAMPLES

We picked apples from the upper branches of a tree.

Small pink buds were beginning to form on the bushes.

fertilizer	[fɜrtᵊlaɪzər]	a substance that you put on soil to make plants grow well
fir tree	[fɜr tri̱]	a tall evergreen tree that has thin needle-like leaves
flower	[flaʊər]	the brightly colored part of a plant; *a bunch of flowers*; *a flower bed*; *a flower pot*
forest	[fɔrɪst]	a large area where trees grow close together; *a forest fire*
forget-me-not	[fərgɛt mi nɒt]	a small plant with very small blue flowers
garden	[gɑrdᵊn]	**1** the part of the land by your house where you grow flowers and vegetables **2** places with plants, trees, and grass, that people can visit
garden bench	[gɑrdᵊn bɛntʃ]	a long seat of wood or metal that two or more people can sit on in a garden
garden center	[gɑrdᵊn sɛntər]	a store, usually with an outdoor area, where you can buy plants and tools for your garden
gardener	[gɑrdənər]	a person who works in a garden
gardening	[gɑrdᵊnɪŋ]	the activity of working in a garden
grass	[græs]	a plant with thin, green leaves that cover the surface of the ground; *cut the grass*
greenhouse	[gri̱nhaʊs]	a glass building where you grow plants to protect them from bad weather
ground	[graʊnd]	the soil on the Earth's surface in which you can grow plants
grounds	[graʊndz]	the garden or area of land around a large or important building
hedge	[hɛdʒ]	a row of small trees growing close together around a garden or a field

EXAMPLES

She has a beautiful garden.
The gardens are open from 10:30 a.m. until 5:00 p.m.
Mrs. Daly employs a gardener.
My favorite hobby is gardening.
We walked around the palace grounds.

hoe	[hoʊ]	a tool with a long handle and a small square blade that you use to break up the surface of the soil
holly	[hɒli]	a plant that has hard, shiny leaves with sharp points, and red berries in the winter
hose	[hoʊz]	a long rubber or plastic pipe that you use to put water on plants; *a garden hose*
ivy	[aɪvi]	a dark-green plant that grows up walls or along the ground
jasmine	[dʒæzmɪn]	a climbing plant which has small white or yellow flowers with a pleasant smell
lawn	[lɔn]	an area of short grass around a house or other building
lawnmower	[lɔnmoʊər]	a machine for cutting grass
leaf (PL) **leaves**	[lif] [livz]	the parts of a tree or plant that are flat, thin, and usually green; *an oak leaf*
lily	[lɪli]	a plant with large sweet-smelling flowers
oak	[oʊk]	a type of large tree
orchard	[ɔrtʃərd]	an area of land where fruit trees grow; *a cherry orchard*
orchid	[ɔrkɪd]	a plant with brightly colored, unusually shaped flowers
palm tree	[pɑm tri]	a straight tree with a lot of long leaves at the top, which grows in tropical countries
path	[pæθ]	a long, narrow piece of ground that people walk along
patio	[pætioʊ]	a flat area next to a house, where people can sit and relax or eat; *patio furniture*
petal	[pɛtəl]	the thin colored parts of a plant that form the flower; *rose petals*
pine	[paɪn]	a tall tree with long, thin leaves that it keeps all year

EXAMPLES
We had lunch on the lawn.
We followed the path through the grounds.

plant	[plænt]	a living thing that grows in the earth and has a stem, leaves, and roots
poppy	[pɒpi]	a plant with large, delicate, red flowers
primrose	[prɪmroʊz]	a wild plant with pale yellow flowers
rainforest	[reɪnfɔrɪst]	a thick forest of tall trees that grows in tropical areas where there is a lot of rain
rake	[reɪk]	a tool with a long handle, used for collecting loose grass or leaves
root	[rut]	the part of a plant that grows under the ground
rose	[roʊz]	a flower with a pleasant smell and sharp points (called thorns) on its stems
seed	[sid]	the small, hard part of a plant from which a new plant grows
shade	[ʃeɪd]	an area where direct sunlight does not reach; *in the shade*
shed	[ʃɛd]	a small building where you store things
shrub	[ʃrʌb]	a small bush
soil	[sɔɪl]	the substance on the surface of the Earth in which plants grow
sprinkler	[sprɪŋklər]	a machine that spreads drops of water over an area of grass
stalk	[stɔk]	the thin part of a flower, leaf, or fruit that joins it to the plant or tree
stem	[stɛm]	the long, thin part of a plant that the flowers and leaves grow on
sunflower	[sʌnflaʊər]	a very tall plant with large yellow flowers
thorn	[θɔrn]	a sharp point on some plants and trees

EXAMPLES

Water each plant daily.

Plant the seeds in small plastic pots.

They grow well in sun or partial shade.

This book tells you how to choose shrubs for your garden.

The soil here is good for growing vegetables.

A single flower grows on each long stalk.

He cut the stem and gave her the flower.

He removed a thorn from his foot.

tree	[triː]	a tall plant that lives for a long time. It has a trunk, branches, and leaves; *apple trees*
trunk	[trʌŋk]	the large main stem of a tree from which the branches grow
tulip	[tuːlɪp]	a flower that grows in the spring and is shaped like a cup
vase	[veɪs, vɑz]	a container that is used for holding flowers
violet	[vaɪəlɪt]	a small plant that has purple or white flowers in the spring
watering can	[wɔtərɪŋ kæn]	a container with a handle that is used to water plants
weed	[wiːd]	a plant that grows where you do not want it
weedkiller	[wiːdkɪlər]	a substance that you put on your garden to kill weeds
weeping willow	[wiːpɪŋ wɪloʊ]	a type of tree with long thin branches that hang down to the ground
wheelbarrow	[wiːlbæroʊ]	an open container with one wheel and two handles, that is used for moving things such as earth or plants
window box	[wɪndoʊ bɒks]	a long narrow container on a shelf at the bottom of a window that is used for growing plants
woods	[wʊdz]	a large area of trees growing near each other
yew	[yuː]	an evergreen tree with sharp leaves that are broad and flat, and red berries

VERBS

blossom	[blɒsəm]	to produce flowers
cultivate	[kʌltɪveɪt]	to grow plants on a piece of land
flower	[flaʊər]	to produce flowers

EXAMPLES

There was a small vase of flowers on the table.
The garden was full of weeds.
Rain begins to fall, and peach trees blossom.
These plants will flower soon.

grow	[grou]	**1** to gradually become bigger **2** used for saying that a plant or a tree lives in a particular place **3** to put seeds or young plants in the ground and take care of them
mow	[mou]	to cut an area of grass using a machine (called a mower); *mow the lawn*
pick	[pɪk]	to take flowers, fruit, or leaves from a plant or tree
plant	[plænt]	to put something into the ground so that it will grow
prune	[prun]	to cut out parts of a bush or tree in order to make it grow thicker and better
tend	[tɛnd]	to look after your garden and the plants in it
water	[wɔtər]	to pour water over plants in order to help them to grow
weed	[wid]	to remove the weeds from an area

[ADJECTIVES]

deciduous	[dɪsɪdʒuəs]	a deciduous tree loses its leaves in the fall every year
evergreen	[ɛvərgrin]	an evergreen tree has green leaves all year
indoor	[ɪndɔr]	done or used inside a building; *indoor plants*
leafy	[lifi]	**1** having a lot of leaves; *leafy trees* **2** you say that a place is leafy when there are a lot of trees and plants there
mature	[mətyuər, -tuər, -tʃuər]	fully grown; *mature fruit trees*
outdoor	[autdɔr]	happening outside and not in a building
overgrown	[ouvərgroun]	thickly covered with plants that have not been looked after

EXAMPLES

There were roses growing by the side of the door.
He plans to plant fruit trees.
Try not to walk on the flower beds while you are weeding.

shady [ˈʃeɪdi] not in direct sunlight

PHRASE

"Stay off the grass" used on signs to tell people not to walk on the grass

IDIOMS

have a green thumb to be good at making plants grow
(*In British English, use* **have green fingers**)

have green fingers *(BRIT)* *see* **have a green thumb**

reading and writing

alphabet	[ælfəbɛt, -bɪt]	a set of letters that is used for writing words
article	[ɑrtɪkəl]	a piece of writing in a newspaper or magazine; *a newspaper article*
author	[ɔθər]	the person who wrote a book or a document
ballpoint pen	[bɔlpɔɪnt pɛn]	a pen with a small metal ball at the tip (*In British English, use* **Biro**)
Biro (*BRIT*)		*see* **ballpoint pen**
book	[bʊk]	a number of pieces of paper, usually with words printed on them, that are fastened together and bound inside a cover
capitals	[kæpɪtəlz]	letters in the form that is used at the beginning of sentences or names, for example "T," "B," and "F," rather than "t," "b," and "f."
chapter	[tʃæptər]	a part of a book; *See chapter 4.*
character	[kærɪktər]	one of the people in a story
colon	[koʊlən]	the punctuation mark (:) that you can use to join parts of a sentence
comic book	[kɒmɪk bʊk]	a magazine that contains stories told in pictures
comma	[kɒmə]	the punctuation mark (,) that you use to separate parts of a sentence or items in a list
conclusion	[kənkluʒən]	the ending of a story
correction fluid	[kərɛkʃən fluɪd]	a white liquid that you use to cover written mistakes
cover	[kʌvər]	the outside part of a book or a magazine

EXAMPLES

The Russian alphabet has 31 letters.
Jill Phillips is the author of "Give Your Child Music."
Please write your name and address in capitals.
The main character in "Great Expectations" is Pip.
Her photograph was on the front cover of "Zoo" magazine.

diary	[da̱ɪəri]	a book in which you record what happens in your life
dictionary	[dɪkʃənɛri]	a book in which the words and phrases of a language are listed, together with their meanings
document	[dɒkyəmənt]	an official piece of paper with important information on it
draft	[dræft]	a piece of writing that you have not finished working on; *a first draft*
e-book	[i̱ bʊk]	short for "electronic book:" a book that you can read on a computer screen
editor	[ɛdɪtər]	someone whose job is to check and correct texts
encyclopedia	[ɪnsa̱ɪkləpi̱diə]	a book or a CD-ROM containing facts about many different subjects
eraser	[ɪre̱ɪsər]	a small object that you use for removing marks you have made with a pencil (*In British English, use* **rubber**)
essay	[ɛseɪ]	a short piece of writing on a subject
exclamation mark (*BRIT*)		*see* **exclamation point**
exclamation point	[ɛkskləme̱ɪʃ°n pɔɪnt]	the punctuation mark (!) that you use at the end of a sentence to show excitement or anger (*In British English, use* **exclamation mark**)
fairy tale	[fɛ̱əri teɪl]	a story for children about magic and fairies
fiction	[fɪkʃ°n]	books and stories about people and events that are not real
full stop (*BRIT*)		*see* **period**
handwriting	[hændraɪtɪŋ]	your style of writing with a pen or a pencil
headline	[hɛdlaɪn]	the title of a newspaper story, printed in large letters
hero	[hɪ̱əroʊ]	the main male character of a story

EXAMPLES

I have kept a diary since I was eleven.
She writes romantic fiction.
The address was in Anna's handwriting.
The headline read "Government plans to build new hospitals."

heroine	[hɛroʊɪn]	the main female character of a story
hyphen	[haɪfᵊn]	the punctuation sign (-) that you use to join two words together, as in "left-handed"
index	[ɪndɛks]	a list at the back of a book that tells you what is in the book and on which pages you can find each item
ink	[ɪŋk]	the colored liquid that you use for writing or printing
introduction	[ɪntrədʌkʃᵊn]	the part at the beginning of a book that tells you what the book is about
journal	[dʒɜrnᵊl]	**1** a magazine or a newspaper that deals with a special subject; *an academic journal* **2** same as **diary**
journalist	[dʒɜrnəlɪst]	someone whose job is to collect news stories and write about them for newspapers, magazines, television, or radio
language	[læŋgwɪdʒ]	**1** a system of sounds and written symbols that people of a particular country or region use in talking or writing; *the English language* **2** the use of a system of communication that has a set of sounds or written symbols; *improve your language skills*
legend	[lɛdʒᵊnd]	a very old and popular story
letter	[lɛtər]	**1** a message that you write or type on paper and send to someone; *send someone a letter* **2** a written symbol that represents a sound in a language; *the letters of the alphabet*
library	[laɪbrɛri]	a place where books, newspapers, DVDs, and music are kept for people to use or borrow

EXAMPLES
The letter was written in blue ink.

literature	[lɪtərətʃər, -tʃʊr]	books, plays, and poetry that most people consider to be of high quality
magazine	[mægəzin, -zin]	a thin book with stories and pictures that you can buy every week or every month
myth	[mɪθ]	an ancient story about gods and magic; *a Greek myth*
narrator	[næreɪtər]	the person who tells the story in a book
newspaper	[nuzpeɪpər, nus-]	a number of large sheets of folded paper, with news, advertisements, and other information printed on them
nonfiction	[nɒnfɪkʃən]	writing that is about real people and events rather than imaginary ones
novel	[nɒvəl]	a long written story about imaginary people and events
novelist	[nɒvəlɪst]	someone who writes novels
page	[peɪdʒ]	one side of a piece of paper in a book, a magazine, or a newspaper; *Turn to page 7.*
paper	[peɪpər]	**1** a material that you write on; *a piece of paper* **2** a newspaper
paperback	[peɪpərbæk]	a book with a thin cardboard or paper cover
paragraph	[pærəgræf]	a section of a piece of writing that begins on a new line and contains more than one sentence
pen	[pɛn]	a long thin object that you use for writing with ink
pencil	[pɛnsəl]	a long thin piece of wood with a black substance through the middle that you use for writing

EXAMPLES

Ayumi is studying English literature at Leeds University.
I read about the fire in the newspaper.
The library contains both fiction and nonfiction.
My favorite novel is *War and Peace*.
I'm going to the store to buy a paper.
I'll buy the book when it comes out in paperback.

period	[pɪəriəd]	the punctuation mark (.) that you use at the end of a sentence (*In British English, use* **full stop**)
play	[pleɪ]	a piece of writing performed in a theatre, on the radio, or on television
plot	[plɒt]	a series of events that make up the story of a book
poem	[poʊəm]	a piece of writing in which the words are chosen for their beauty and sound, and are arranged in short lines
poet	[poʊɪt]	someone who writes poems
poetry	[poʊɪtri]	the form of literature that consists of poems
punctuation	[pʌŋktʃueɪʃən]	signs such as ( ), !, or ? that you use to divide writing into sentences and phrases
question mark	[kwɛstʃən mark]	the punctuation mark (?) that is used in writing at the end of a question
quotation	[kwoʊteɪʃən]	a sentence or a phrase from a book, a poem, a speech, or a play
quotation marks	[kwoʊteɪʃən marks]	the punctuation marks (" ") or (' ') that are used in writing to show where speech or a quotation begins and ends
report	[rɪpɔrt]	**1** a newspaper article that gives information about something that happened; *a newspaper report* **2** a piece of work that a student writes on a particular subject; *a book report*
rubber (BRIT)		*see* **eraser**
scene	[sin]	a part of a play or a book in which all the events happen in the same place
script	[skrɪpt]	the written words that actors speak in a play

EXAMPLES

Hamlet is my favorite play.
He told me the plot of his new novel.
We studied French poetry last term.
Check your spelling and punctuation.
The opening scene shows a mother and daughter having an argument.

semicolon	[sɛmikoʊlən]	the mark (;) that you use in writing to separate different parts of a sentence
sentence	[sɛntəns]	a group of words that tells you something or asks a question
story	[stɔri]	a description of imaginary people and events, that is intended to entertain people
summary	[sʌməri]	a short description of something that gives the main points but not the details
table of contents	[teɪbᵊl əv kɒntɛnts]	a list of chapters that is shown at the beginning of a book
thesaurus (PL) **thesauruses, thesauri**	[θɪsɔrəs] [θɪsɔraɪ]	a reference book in which words with similar meanings are grouped together
thriller	[θrɪlər]	an exciting book or play about a crime
title	[taɪtᵊl]	the name of something such as a book or a play
translation	[trænzleɪʃᵊn]	a piece of writing or speech that has been put into a different language
vocabulary	[voʊkæbyələɛri]	**1** all the words that someone knows in a particular language; *She has a large vocabulary.* **2** all the words in a language; *a new word in the English vocabulary* **3** the words that you use when you are talking about a particular subject; *technical vocabulary*
word	[wɜrd]	a unit of language with meaning
writer	[raɪtər]	someone whose job is to write books, stories, or articles

EXAMPLES

Here is a short summary of the news.
The title of the novel is *Jane Eyre*.
The Italian word for "love" is "amore."

writing	[raɪtɪŋ]	**1** something that has been written or printed **2** any piece of written work; *a piece of writing* **3** the activity of writing, especially of writing books for money

VERBS

copy	[kɒpi]	to write something that is exactly like another thing
delete	[dɪliːt]	to put a line through something that has been written down
look something up		to try to find something in a book such as a dictionary
print	[prɪnt]	**1** to use a machine to put words or pictures on paper; *print copies of a novel* **2** to write letters that are not joined together; *print your name*
publish	[pʌblɪʃ]	to prepare and print copies of a book, a magazine, or a newspaper
read	[riːd]	**1** to look at written words and understand them; *read a book* **2** to say words that you can see; *read someone a story*
rhyme	[raɪm]	to end with a very similar sound to another word; *"June" rhymes with "moon."*
set	[sɛt]	if a story is set in a particular place or time, the events in it take place in that place or time
skim	[skɪm]	to read something quickly

EXAMPLES

Lydia tried to read the writing on the next page.

Elizabeth Johnston teaches creative writing at Concordia University.

I didn't know what "subscribe" meant, so I looked it up in the dictionary.

HarperCollins will publish his new novel in March.

The novel is set in China in 1900.

He skimmed the pages quickly, then read them again more carefully.

spell	[spɛl]	**1** to write or speak each letter of a word in the correct order; *How do you spell "potato"?* **2** to have a good knowledge of the correct order of letters in words; *Many students cannot spell.*
translate	[trænzleɪt]	to say or write something again in a different language
type	[taɪp]	to write something using a machine such as a computer
write	[raɪt]	**1** to use a pen or a pencil to produce words, letters, or numbers **2** to create something such as a book or a poem **3** to give someone information, ask them something, or express your feelings in a letter or an email; *write to someone*

EXAMPLES

Martin Luther translated the Bible into German.

Please write your name and address on the back of the photo.

She writes articles for French newspapers.

routines

NOUNS

chore	[tʃɔr]	a job that you have to do, for example, cleaning the house; *household chores*; *do the chores*
day off	[deɪ ɔf]	a day when you do not go to work; *have a day off*
free time	[fri taɪm]	time when you are not working or studying, when you can do things that you enjoy; *in your free time*
habit	[hæbɪt]	something that you do often or regularly; *a bad habit*; *an old habit*
hobby	[hɒbi]	an activity that you enjoy doing in your free time
housework	[haʊswɜrk]	the work that you do to keep a house clean and tidy; *do housework*
lifestyle	[laɪfstaɪl]	the way someone has chosen to live and behave; *a healthy lifestyle*
lunch break	[lʌntʃ breɪk]	the period in the middle of the day when you stop work in order to have a meal; *have your lunch break*
routine	[rutin]	the usual activities that you do every day; *your daily routine*
rush hour	[rʌʃ aʊər]	one of the periods of the day when most people are traveling to or from work; *rush-hour traffic*
time off	[taɪm ɔf]	a period of time when you do not work; *take time off*; *give someone time off*

VERBS

commute	[kəmyut]	to travel to work or school
shave	[ʃeɪv]	to remove hair from your face or body

EXAMPLES

She's always busy and has lots of hobbies.
Skiing is an expensive hobby.
I had to drive eight miles during rush hour.
Many women shave their legs.
He always shaves before breakfast.

do the shopping	to go to stores to buy things
drop someone off	to take someone to a place in a car and leave them there
get dressed	to put clothes on yourself
get ready	to completely prepare yourself for something
get up	to get out of bed
go home	to return to the place where you live
go to bed	to lie down in your bed to sleep
go to sleep	to fall asleep
go to work	to go to the place where you do your job
take a bath	to sit or lie down in a bath filled with water to wash your body
take a shower	to wash yourself by standing under the water that comes from a shower
have breakfast	to eat the first meal of the day
have dinner	to eat the main meal of the day, which is usually served in the evening
have lunch	to eat the meal that you have in the middle of the day
make dinner	to prepare the main meal of the day, which is usually served in the evening
pick someone up	to collect someone from a place, often in a car
set your alarm	to adjust an alarm clock so that it will wake you at a particular time
sleep in	to sleep until after the time you usually get up in the morning

EXAMPLES

Dad dropped me off at school on his way to work.
It takes her a long time to get ready for school.
They have to get up early in the morning.
We went to bed at about 10 p.m.
It was time to go to work.
Would you like to stay and have dinner?
I pick the children up from school at three o'clock.
Dad set the alarm for eight the next day.

tidy up	to organize a place by putting things in their usual places
wake up	to stop sleeping

ADVERBS

during the week	on any day from Monday to Friday
every day	on each day without exception
every week	at least one time each week
in the afternoon	during the part of the day that begins at lunchtime and ends at about six o'clock
in the evening	during the part of the day between the end of the afternoon and midnight
in the morning	during the part of the day between the time that people usually wake up and noon
on weekends	on Saturdays and Sundays

IDIOMS

burn the candle at both ends	to stay up very late at night and get up very early in the morning
go out like a light	to fall asleep very quickly
on the go	always busy and active

EXAMPLES

It was cold and dark when I woke up at 6:30.
He never goes out during the week.
They got up every day before dawn.
He calls his mother every week.
He's arriving in the afternoon.
We usually have dinner at seven in the evening.
The first thing people do in the morning is open the curtains.
She was never at home on weekends.
I've been on the go all day.

school

NOUNS

assembly [əsɛmbli] a meeting of all the teachers and students at the beginning of a school day; *a school assembly*

attendance [ətɛndəns] an official list of when students attend a class; *take attendance* (*In British English, use* **register**)

blackboard [blækbɔrd] a chalkboard

box lunch [bɒks lʌntʃ] food that you take to school and eat as your lunch; *take/have a box lunch* (*In British English, use* **packed lunch**)

break (*BRIT*) *see* **recess**

bully [bʊli] someone who uses their strength or power to frighten other people; *school bullies*

cafeteria [kæfɪtɪəriə] a place in a school where students can buy and eat lunch; *the school cafeteria* (*In British English, use* **canteen**)

canteen (*BRIT*) *see* **cafeteria**

caretaker (*BRIT*) *see* **janitor**

chalkboard [tʃɔkbɔrd] a big, dark-colored board for writing on in a classroom

class [klæs] **1** a group of students who learn at school together
2 a time when you learn something at school

classroom [klæsrum] a room in a school where lessons take place

desk [dɛsk] a table that you sit at to write or work

education [ɛdʒʊkeɪʃən] teaching and learning; *secondary/ elementary education*; *higher/continuing education*; *sex/health education*

EXAMPLES
We have an assembly on Tuesday and Friday mornings.
He spent six months in a class with younger students.
Classes start at 9 o'clock.
We do lots of reading in class.

elementary school	[ɛlɪmɛntəri skul, -tri]	a school for children between the ages of five and 11 (*In British English, use* **primary school**)
essay	[ɛseɪ]	a short piece of writing on a subject; *write an essay*
exam	[ɪgzæm]	a formal test that you take to show your knowledge of a subject; *take/sit an exam*; *pass/fail an exam*; *exam results*
examination	[ɪgzæmɪneɪʃən]	[FORMAL] exam
exercise	[ɛksərsaɪz]	an activity that you do in order to practice a skill; *a writing exercise*; *an exercise book*
grade	[greɪd]	**1** the mark that a teacher gives you to show how good your work is (*In British English, use* **mark**) **2** a group of classes taken by children who are of a similar age
gym	[dʒɪm]	a large room with equipment for doing physical exercises
holiday (*BRIT*)		*see* **vacation**
homework	[hoʊmwɜrk]	school work that teachers give to students to do at home in the evening or during the weekend; *do your homework*
janitor	[dʒænɪtər]	someone who looks after a school building and the area around it; *a school janitor* (*In British English, use* **caretaker**)
lesson	[lɛsən]	a time when you learn about a particular subject; *a history lesson*
lunchbox	[lʌntʃbɒks]	a small container for taking lunch to school
mark	[mɑrk]	a number or letter on a student's work to show how good it is
mistake	[mɪsteɪk]	something that is not correct

EXAMPLES

She always got the highest grades.
He stayed there until the fifth grade, when he was about eleven.
I have homework every day.
Tony made three spelling mistakes in this essay.

packed lunch *(BRIT)*		*see* **box lunch**
PE	[pi i]	short for "physical education:" a class in which students do physical exercises or sports
period	[pɪəriəd]	one of the parts of the school day when lessons take place; *a free period*
playground	[pleɪgraʊnd]	a piece of land where children can play at school; *the school playground*
preschool	[priskul]	a school for children between the ages of two and five or six
primary school *(BRIT)*		*see* **elementary school**
principal	[prɪnsɪpəl]	a teacher who is in charge of a public school
private school	[praɪvɪt skul]	a school that parents have to pay for their children to go to
public school	[pʌblɪk skul]	**1** in the USA, Australia, and some other countries, a school that usually provides free education **2** in the UK, a private school that provides secondary education which parents have to pay for
pupil	[pyupɪl]	one of the children who go to a school
recess	[rɪsɛs, risɛs]	a period of time between classes at school when students can play or eat (*In British English, use* **break**)
register *(BRIT)*		*see* **attendance**
result	[rɪzʌlt]	facts such as a score that you get at the end of a competition or a test; *test results*
schedule	[skɛdʒul, -uəl]	a list that shows the times in the week when particular subjects are taught; *an exam schedule*
school	[skul]	a place where people go to learn; *a school bus*; *school lunch*

EXAMPLES

He goes to a private school.
After the first two lessons, we have recess.

school rules	[skul rulz]	a list of things that students must do or must not do when they are at school; *obey school rules*
school uniform	[skul yunifɔrm]	the special clothes that some students wear at school; *wear/have a school uniform*
schoolchildren	[skultʃɪldrən]	children who go to school
secondary school	[sɛkəndɛri skul]	the same as **high school**
semester	[sɪmɛstər]	one of the periods of time that a school year is divided into; *this/last semester*
smart board™	[smɑrt bɔrd]	a large electronic board that can be used for teaching and learning
special education	[spɛʃəl ɛdʒʊkeɪʃən]	teaching for students who need extra help with their studies
state school	[steɪt skul]	a government school that children can attend without having to pay; *go to a state school*
student	[studənt]	a person who is studying at a school
subject	[sʌbdʒɪkt]	an area of knowledge that you study in school
teacher	[titʃər]	a person whose job is to give lessons in a subject at a school; *an English teacher*; *a science teacher*; *a elementary/high school school teacher*
term	[tɜrm]	a semester
test	[tɛst]	a series of questions that students must answer to show how much they know about a subject; *pass/fail a test*
textbook	[tɛkstbʊk]	a book containing facts about a particular subject
tutor	[tutər]	someone who gives private lessons to one student or a very small group of students; *a private tutor*; *an English tutor*

EXAMPLES

The school's principal will retire at the end of the semester.

Math is my favorite subject.

vacation	[veɪkeɪʃⁿn]	the time when children do not have to go to school; *summer vacation* (In British English, use **holiday**)
whiteboard	[waɪtbɔrd]	a shiny, white board that teachers draw or write on, using special pens

VERBS

ask	[ɑsk, æsk]	to say something in the form of a question; *ask a question*
answer	[ænsər]	to write or say what you think is the correct answer to a question; *answer a question*
bully	[buli]	to use your strength or power to frighten other people
cheat	[tʃit]	to do something that is not honest or fair, often because you want to get something
correct	[kərɛkt]	to look at a piece of writing and mark the mistakes in it; *correct students' work*; *correct mistakes*
expel	[ɪkspɛl]	to officially tell a student to leave a school permanently
fail	[feɪl]	not to pass an exam or a test; *fail an exam*
grade	[greɪd]	to judge the quality of a test or essay using with a letter or number; *grade a student's paper*
learn	[lɜrn]	to get knowledge or a skill by studying
let out		to start summer vacation
mark	[mɑrk]	to write a number or letter on a student's work to show how good it is; *mark an essay*
pass	[pæs]	to succeed in an exam; *pass an exam*
punish	[pʌnɪʃ]	to make someone suffer in some way because they have done something wrong

EXAMPLES

I think they were bullied in school.
Students sometimes cheated in order to get into top schools.
She was expelled for cheating on an exam.
The schools let out this weekend.

put up your hand		to raise your hand in the air in order to show that you want to answer a question
read	[rid]	to look at written words and understand them; *learn to read and write*
repeat	[rɪpit]	to say or write the same thing that someone else has said or written
review	[rɪvyu]	to study something again in order to prepare for an exam (*In British English, use* **revise**)
revise *(BRIT)*		*see* **review**
study	[stʌdi]	to spend time learning about a particular subject; *study history*
teach	[titʃ]	to give lessons in a subject at a school
write	[raɪt]	to use a pen or a pencil to produce words, letters, or numbers

ADJECTIVES

absent	[æbsᵊnt]	not at school
correct	[kərɛkt]	right or true; *a correct answer*
difficult	[dɪfɪkʌlt, -kəlt]	requiring a lot of effort; *a difficult question*
easy	[izi]	not difficult; *an easy task*
present	[prɛzᵊnt]	at school; *be present*

ADVERB

| off by heart | | using only your memory |

EXAMPLES

I have to review for my math exam.
Christine teaches biology at Piper High.
"Was he at school yesterday?" — "No, he was absent."
She's learnt the whole speech off by heart.

science

NOUNS

acid	[æsɪd]	a chemical, usually a liquid, that can burn your skin and cause damage to other substances; *citric acid*
astronaut	[æstrənɔt]	a person who is trained to travel in space
astronomy	[əstrɒnəmi]	the scientific study of the stars, planets, and other natural objects in space
atom	[ætəm]	the very smallest part of a substance
axis (PL) **axes**	[æksɪs] [æksiz]	**1** an imaginary line through the middle of something; *the Earth's axis* **2** one of the two lines of a graph on which you mark points to show amounts; *the vertical/horizontal axis*
botany	[bɒtəni]	the scientific study of plants
cell	[sɛl]	the smallest part of an animal or plant; *brain cells*
charge	[tʃɑrdʒ]	the amount or type of electrical force that something has; *an electrical charge*
chemical	[kɛmɪkəl]	a substance that is used in a chemical process or made by a chemical process
chemist	[kɛmɪst]	a scientist who studies chemistry
chemistry	[kɛmɪstri]	the science of the structure of gases, liquids, and solids, and how they change
circuit	[sɜrkɪt]	a complete path that electricity can flow around; *an electrical circuit*
compound	[kɒmpaʊnd]	a substance that is made from two or more elements, for example, carbon dioxide
current	[kɜrənt]	a steady flow of water, air, or energy
electricity	[ɪlɛktrɪsɪti, ilɛk-]	energy that is used for producing heat and light, and to provide power for machines
element	[ɛlɪmənt]	a basic chemical substance such as gold, oxygen, or carbon
energy	[ɛnərdʒi]	the power from electricity or the sun, for example, that makes machines work or provides heat

EXAMPLES

The device converts energy from the sun into electrical energy.

evolution	[ivəluʃⁿn, ɛv-]	a process in which animals or plants slowly change over many years
experiment	[ɪkspɛrɪmənt]	a scientific test that you do in order to discover what happens to something; *conduct an experiment*
force	[fɔrs]	the pulling or pushing effect that one thing has on another; *the Earth's gravitational force*
formula (PL) **formulas, formulae**	[fɔrmyələ] [fɔrmyəli]	**1** a group of letters, numbers, or other symbols that represents a scientific rule **2** a description of the chemical elements that a substance contains
fuse	[fyuz]	a small wire in a piece of electrical equipment that stops it from working when too much electricity passes through it
gene	[dʒin]	the part of a cell that controls a person's, an animal's, or a plant's physical characteristics, growth, and development
genetics	[dʒɪnɛtɪks]	the study of how qualities are passed on from parents to children
gravity	[grævɪti]	the force that makes things fall to the ground
hormone	[hɔrmoʊn]	a chemical substance in your body that affects the way your body works
laboratory	[læbrətɔri]	a building or a room where scientific work is done
lens	[lɛnz]	a thin, curved piece of glass or plastic used in things such as cameras and glasses. A lens makes things look larger, smaller, or clearer.
magnet	[mægnɪt]	a piece of special metal that attracts iron or steel towards it

EXAMPLES

He developed a mathematical formula describing the distances of the planets from the Sun.

The Earth's gravity pulls the oceans in daily tides.

microscope	[maɪkrəskoʊp]	a scientific instrument that makes very small objects look bigger
molecule	[mɒlɪkyul]	the smallest amount of a chemical substance that can exist by itself
organism	[ɔrgənɪzəm]	a living thing
physics	[fɪzɪks]	the scientific study of things such as heat, light and sound
power	[paʊər]	energy that can be used for making electricity or for making machines work
radar	[reɪdɑr]	a way of discovering the position of objects when they cannot be seen, by using radio signals
science	[saɪəns]	the study of natural things
scientist	[saɪəntɪst]	someone whose job is to teach or do research in science
spacecraft	[speɪskræft]	a vehicle that can travel in space
specimen	[spɛsɪmɪn]	an example or a small amount of something; *examine a specimen*
test tube	[tɛst tub]	a small tube-shaped container made from glass. Test tubes are used in laboratories.
theory	[θɪəri]	an idea or a set of ideas that tries to explain something
volt	[voʊlt]	a unit used for measuring electricity; *a 12-volt battery*
watt	[wɒt]	a unit for measuring electrical power; *a 60-watt light bulb*

VERBS

dilute	[daɪlut]	to add water to another liquid
dissect	[dɪsɛkt, daɪ-]	to cut open a dead body in order to examine it

EXAMPLES

The system creates enough power to run four lights.
The mystery objects showed up on the plane's radar.
Albert Einstein developed the Theory of Relativity.
Dilute the fruit juice thoroughly.

dissolve	[dɪzɒlv]	to become completely mixed with a liquid
evaporate	[ɪvæpəreɪt]	to change from a liquid into a gas
evolve	[ɪvɒlv]	to gradually develop over a period of time into something different
measure	[mɛʒər]	to find out the size of something
test	[tɛst]	to use something to find out what condition it is in, or how well it works

ADJECTIVES

atomic	[ətɒmɪk]	relating to atoms or to power that is produced by splitting atoms
chemical	[kɛmɪkəl]	relating to chemistry or chemicals; *a chemical reaction*
electric	[ɪlɛktrɪk]	**1** working using electricity; *an electric car* **2** carrying electricity; *electric cables*
nuclear	[nukliər]	relating to the energy that is released when the central parts of atoms are split or combined; *a nuclear power station*
scientific	[saɪəntɪfɪk]	relating to science; *a scientific experiment*

EXAMPLES
Boil the water and sugar until the sugar has dissolved completely.
Water evaporates from the oceans into the atmosphere.
Humans have evolved with the power to hold things.
He spends a lot of time conducting scientific research.

shopping

NOUNS

baker's	[beɪkərz]	a store where bread and cakes are sold
barcode	[bɑrkoʊd]	a set of lines on a product that tell the computer its price
bargain	[bɑrgɪn]	something that is sold at a lower price than usual
bookshop (BRIT)		see **bookstore**
bookstore	[bʊkstɔr]	a store where books are sold (In British English, use **bookshop**)
boutique	[butik]	a small store that sells fashionable clothes, shoes, or jewelry
business hours	[bɪznɪs aʊərz]	the hours that a store is open
butcher's	[bʊtʃərz]	a store where meat is sold
candy store	[kændi stɔr]	a store where candy is sold
carrier bag (BRIT)		see **shopping bag**
cash	[kæʃ]	coins and bills, rather than a check or bank card
catalog	[kætəlɒg]	a list of things you can buy from a particular company
change	[tʃeɪndʒ]	the money that you get back when you pay with more money than something costs
checkout	[tʃɛkaʊt]	the place in a store where you pay
check	[tʃɛk]	a printed piece of paper from a bank that you write an amount of money on and use to pay for things; *pay by check* (In British English, use **cheque**)
chemist's (BRIT)		see **pharmacy**
cheque (BRIT)		see **check**
clothing store	[kloʊðɪŋ stɔr]	a store where you can buy clothes

---

EXAMPLES

I got these cakes from the baker's this morning.
If you go early, you could get a real bargain.
Contact them during their business hours.
I'm afraid we only accept cash.
Here's your change.

complaint	[kəmpleɪnt]	when you say that you are not satisfied with the service or products you have received
credit card	[krɛdɪt kɑrd]	a plastic card that you use to buy goods now and pay for them later; *pay by credit card*
customer	[kʌstəmər]	someone who buys something from a store or a website
department	[dɪpɑrtmənt]	one of the sections in a department store; *the toy department*
department store	[dɪpɑrtmənt stɔr]	a large store that sells many different types of goods
discount	[dɪskaʊnt]	a reduction in the usual price of something
fishmonger's	[fɪʃmʌŋgərz, -mɒŋ-]	a store where fish is sold (*mainly BRIT*)
florist's	[flɔrɪsts]	a store where flowers are sold
gift shop	[gɪft ʃɒp]	a store that sells things that people give as presents
goods	[gʊdz]	things that you can buy or sell; *electrical goods*
greengrocer's	[grɪngroʊsərz]	a store where fruit and vegetables are sold (*mainly BRIT*)
grocery store	[groʊsəri stɔr, groʊsri]	a store that sells food and other things that you need at home
jeweler's	[dʒuələrz]	a store where jewelry is sold (*In British English, use* **jeweller's**)
jeweller's (*BRIT*)		*see* **jeweler's**
line	[laɪn]	a line of people who are waiting for something; *wait in a line* (*In British English, use* **queue**)
mail order	[meɪl ɔrdər]	a system in which you choose goods from a catalog and they are sent to you in the mail
market	[mɑrkɪt]	a place where people buy and sell goods on tables; *a farmers' market*

EXAMPLES
I want to make a complaint.

newsagent's (BRIT)		*see* **newsstand**
newsstand	[nuzstænd]	a place where newspapers and magazines are sold (*In British English, use* **newsagent's**)
online store	[ɒnlaɪn stɔr]	a website with photos and details of goods that customers can buy
pharmacy	[fɑrməsi]	a store that sells medicines and beauty products (*In British English, use* **chemist's**)
price	[praɪs]	the amount of money that you have to pay when you buy something
queue (BRIT)		*see* **line**
receipt	[rɪsit]	a piece of paper that shows that you have paid for something
refund	[rifʌnd]	money that is given back to you when you return goods to a store
sale	[seɪl]	an occasion when a store sells things at a lower price than usual
sales clerk	[seɪlz klɜrk]	someone whose job is to deal with customers in a store (*In British English, use* **shop assistant**)
shoe store	[ʃu stɔr]	a store where shoes are sold
shop (BRIT)		*see* **store**
shop assistant (BRIT)		*see* **sales clerk**
shopping	[ʃɒpɪŋ]	the activity of going to stores to buy things; *go shopping*; *do the shopping*
shopping bag	[ʃɒpɪŋ bæg]	a large bag that is used for carrying things that you have bought (*In British English, use* **carrier bag**)
shopping cart	[ʃɒpɪŋ kɑrt]	a wire or plastic basket on wheels in which you put all the things that you want to buy in a particular store (*In British English, use* **shopping trolley**)

EXAMPLES

The price of bread went up by 20 percent last year.
Please make sure you keep your receipt.
I'd like a refund.
I bought these jeans in the sale.

shopping center	[ʃɒpɪŋ sɛntər]	an area in a town where there are a lot of stores
shopping list	[ʃɒpɪŋ lɪst]	a list of all the things that you want to buy
shopping trolley (BRIT)		see **shopping cart**
size	[saɪz]	how big or small something is
special offer	[spɛʃ^əl ɔfər]	a low price that is offered by a store for a period of time
stationer's	[steɪʃənərs]	a store where you can buy things for writing such as paper, pens, and pencils
store	[stɔr]	a place where you buy things (In British English, use **shop**)
supermarket	[supərmɑrkɪt]	a large store that sells food and other products for the home
till	[tɪl]	a machine that holds money in a store
toy store	[tɔɪ stɔr]	a store where toys are sold
window shopping	[wɪndoʊ ʃɒpɪŋ]	the activity of looking in stores without buying anything

VERBS

browse	[braʊz]	to look at things in a store, without buying anything
buy	[baɪ]	to get something by paying money for it
close	[kloʊz]	when a store closes, it stops being open, so that people cannot go in and buy things
cost	[kɔst]	to have as a price
open	[oʊpən]	when a store opens, people can go in and buy things
pay	[peɪ]	to give someone an amount of money for something that you are buying
return	[rɪtɜrn]	to bring back something you bought because you do not want it any more

EXAMPLES

Do you have this in a smaller size?
How much does it cost?
Can I pay with this card?
You may return any goods within 14 days.

sell	[sɛl]	to have something available for people to buy
spend	[spɛnd]	to use money to buy things
try something on		to put a piece of clothing on in order to see if it fits

ADJECTIVES

cheap	[tʃip]	**1** costing little money or less than you expected **2** costing less money than similar products but often of bad quality
closed	[klouzd]	a store that is closed is not open, so people cannot go in and buy things
expensive	[ɪkspɛnsɪv]	costing a lot of money
in stock	[ɪn stɒk]	available for customers to buy in a store
on sale	[ɒn seɪl]	**1** available for people to buy **2** available to buy at a lower price than usual
open	[oupən]	when a store is open, people can go in and buy things
out of stock	[aut əv stɒk]	no longer available for customers to buy
reduced	[rɪdust]	at a lower price than usual; *a reduced price*
secondhand	[sɛkəndhænd]	already used by another person; not new; *a secondhand car*

PHRASES

"Anything else?"	used by a sales assistant to ask if there are any other things you would like to buy
"Just looking."	used for telling a sales assistant that you do not need any help

EXAMPLES

Do you sell stamps?
Can I try this on?
I'd like something cheaper.
It's too expensive.
I'm afraid we don't have your size in stock.

society and politics

ambassador	[æmbǽsədər]	an important official person who lives in a foreign country and represents his or her own country there; *the American ambassador in Berlin*
army	[ɑrmi]	a large group of soldiers who are trained to fight battles on land
asylum seeker	[əsaɪləm sikər]	someone who asks the government of a foreign country if they can live there, because they are in danger in their own country
capitalism	[kǽpɪtᵊlɪzəm]	an economic and political system in which property, business, and industry are privately owned
capitalist	[kǽpɪtᵊlɪst]	someone who supports the ideas of capitalism
caste	[kǽst]	one of the social classes into which people in a Hindu society are divided
ceasefire	[sisfaɪər]	an agreement to stop fighting for a period of time; *declare a ceasefire*
citizen	[sɪtɪzᵊn]	**1** a person who legally belongs to a particular country **2** a person who lives in a town or a city
civilian	[sɪvɪlyən]	a person who is not a member of the armed forces
civil war	[sɪvᵊl wɔr]	a war that is fought between different groups of people living in the same country
class	[klǽs]	a group of people with the same economic and social position in a society
communism	[kɒmyənɪzəm]	an economic and political system in which property, business, and industry are owned by the state
communist	[kɒmyənɪst]	someone who supports the ideas of communism

---

EXAMPLES

Prince Charlie's army marched on Edinburgh in 1745.
The number of asylum seekers entering the U.S. fell last month.
Ten civilians died in the attack.

community [kəmyuˈnɪti] a group of people who are similar in some way, or have similar interests; *the Muslim community*

council [kaʊnsᵊl] a group of people who are chosen to control a particular area; *the local council*

country [kʌntri] an area of the world with its own government and people

culture [kʌltʃər] the way of life, the traditions, and beliefs of a particular group of people

democracy [dɪmɒkrəsi] a system of government in which people choose their leaders by voting for them in elections

dictator [dɪkteɪtər] a ruler who uses force to keep power in a country

election [ɪlɛkʃᵊn] a process in which people vote in order to choose a person who will hold an official position; *a presidential election*

embassy [ɛmbəsi] **1** a group of officials, headed by an ambassador, who represent their government in a foreign country **2** the building in which these people work

emperor [ɛmpərər] a man who rules an empire

empire [ɛmpaɪər] several separate nations that are all controlled by the ruler of one particular country

globalization [gloʊbəlɪzeɪʃᵊn] the idea that the world is developing a single economy as a result of modern technology and communications

government [gʌvərnmənt] the group of people who control and organize a country, a state, or a city

human rights [hyumən raɪts] the rights that all people in a society should have

immigrant [ɪmɪgrənt] a person who comes to live in a country from another country

---

EXAMPLES
The embassy has confirmed the report.
A police officer was guarding the embassy.
The country has a poor human rights record.

independence	[ɪndɪpɛndəns]	a situation in which one country is not controlled by another country
king	[kɪŋ]	a man from a royal family, who is the head of state of that country
kingdom	[kɪŋdəm]	a country that is ruled by a king or a queen
the middle class	[ðə mɪdᵊl klæs]	the people in a society who are well educated, and who have professional jobs, for example, teachers, doctors, and lawyers
monarchy	[mɒnərki]	a system in which a country has a king or a queen
MP	[ɛm piː]	short for "Member of Parliament:" in Britain, a person in the government who has been elected to represent the people from a particular area
nation	[neɪʃᵊn]	an individual country, its people, and its social and political structures
nationality	[næʃənælɪti]	1 the state of being a legal citizen of a particular country; *Polish nationality* 2 a group of people who have the same race, culture, or language
parliament	[pɑrləmənt]	the group of people who make or change the laws of some countries
party	[pɑrti]	a political organization whose members have similar aims and beliefs; *the Republican Party*
peace	[piːs]	a situation where there is not a war
politics	[pɒlɪtɪks]	the activities and ideas that are concerned with government
population	[pɒpyəleɪʃᵊn]	all the people who live in a country or an area
president	[prɛzɪdənt]	the person who is in charge of a country that has no king or queen

EXAMPLES

We have several different nationalities in our team.

NATO forces were sent to Kosovo to keep the peace.

prime minister	[praɪm mɪnɪstər]	the leader of a government in some countries
queen	[kwin]	**1** a woman from a royal family who rules a country **2** the wife of a king
refugee	[rɛfyudʒi]	a person who has been forced to leave their home or their country, because it is too dangerous for them there
republic	[rɪpʌblɪk]	a country with no king or queen, where the people choose their government
revolution	[rɛvəluʃ°n]	an attempt by a group of people to change their country's government by using force
ruler	[rulər]	the person who rules a country
slave	[sleɪv]	a person who belongs to another person and who is forced to work for them without being paid
soldier	[soʊldʒər]	a member of an army
state	[steɪt]	**1** a country, especially when it is considered politically; *EU member states* **2** a smaller area that some large countries such as the United States are divided into; *the state of Michigan* **3** the government of a country; *a state-owned bank*
territory	[tɛrətɔri]	all the land that a particular country owns
terrorism	[tɛrərɪzəm]	the use of violence to force a government to do something
terrorist	[tɛrərɪst]	a person who uses violence to achieve political aims
the upper class	[ði ʌpər klæs]	the people in a society who have the highest position in society
volunteer	[vɒləntɪər]	someone who works without being paid
war	[wɔr]	a period of fighting between countries or groups

EXAMPLES

In 1818, Argentina was at war with Spain.

| **the working class** | [ðə wɜrkɪŋ klæs] | the people in a society who are less educated, and who have less money than other people |

VERBS

assassinate	[əsæsɪneɪt]	to murder someone for political reasons
break out		when war breaks out, it begins
conquer	[kɒŋkər]	to take complete control of the land of another country or group of people
elect	[ɪlɛkt]	to choose a person to do a particular job by voting for them; *elect a president*
govern	[gʌvərn]	to officially control and organize a country
invade	[ɪnveɪd]	to attack and enter a country
reign	[reɪn]	to rule a country as king or queen
volunteer	[vɒləntɪər]	to work without being paid
vote	[voʊt]	to show your choice officially in an election; *vote in an election*

ADJECTIVES

armed	[ɑrmd]	carrying a weapon, usually a gun; *armed forces*
capitalist	[kæpɪtᵊlɪst]	relating to or supporting capitalism
communist	[kɒmyənɪst]	relating to or supporting communism
democratic	[dɛməkrætɪk]	**1** having or relating to a political system in which the leaders are elected by the people they govern; *democratic elections* **2** based on the idea that everyone has equal rights and should be involved in making important decisions; *a democratic decision*
global	[gloʊbᵊl]	relating to the whole world; *the global economy*
international	[ɪntərnæʃənᵊl]	involving different countries

EXAMPLES
The president was assassinated, and the army took over.
Victoria reigned for over 60 years.

local	[loʊkᵊl]	in or relating to the area where you live
national	[næʃənᵊl]	1 relating to the whole of a country or nation; *a national newspaper* 2 typical of the people or traditions of a particular country or nation; *a national pastime*
patriotic	[peɪtrɪɒtɪk]	feeling love and loyalty towards your country
public	[pʌblɪk]	1 relating to all the people in a country or a community; *public opinion* 2 for everyone to use; *a public swimming pool*
social	[soʊʃᵊl]	relating to society
socialist	[soʊʃəlɪst]	relating to socialism
voluntary	[vɒləntɛri]	voluntary work is done by people who are not paid

IDIOMS

the grass roots	the ordinary people in a society, rather than the leaders
win by a landslide	to win an election by a very large number of votes

sports

NOUN

sport	[spɔrt]	a game or other activity that needs physical effort and skill

TYPES OF SPORTS

aerobics	[ɛəroʊbɪks]	a form of exercise that makes your heart and lungs stronger; *do aerobics*
American football (BRIT)		*see* **football**
badminton	[bædmɪntən]	a game in which two or four players stand on either side of a high net and get points by hitting a small object (called a shuttlecock or birdie) across it using a racket; *play badminton*
baseball	[beɪsbɔl]	a game in which two teams of nine players get points by hitting a ball with a bat and running around four bases in a large field; *play baseball*
basketball	[bɑskɪtbɔl, bæs-]	a game in which two teams of five players each try to throw a large ball through a round net hanging from a high metal ring; *play basketball*
boxing	[bɒksɪŋ]	a sport in which two people fight following special rules
cricket	[krɪkɪt]	a game played by two teams who try to score points by hitting a ball with a wooden bat; *play cricket*
darts	[dɑrts]	a game in which you throw darts (= small pointed objects) at a round board that has numbers on it; *play darts*
football	[fʊtbɔl]	**1** a game in which two teams of eleven players try to get an oval (= egg-shaped) ball to their opponents' end of the field; *play football* (In British English, use **American football**) **2** (BRIT) *see* **soccer**

EXAMPLES

What's your favorite sport?
Terry was the captain of Chelsea Football Club.

golf	[gɒlf]	a game in which you use long sticks (called golf clubs) to hit a small, hard ball into a hole in the ground; *play golf*
gymnastics	[dʒɪmnæstɪks]	a sport that consists of physical exercises that develop your strength and your ability to move easily; *do gymnastics*
hockey	[hɒki]	a sport in which two teams of eleven players use long curved sticks to hit a small hard ball; *play hockey*
horseback riding	[hɔrsbæk raɪdɪŋ]	the sport of riding on a horse; *go horseback riding* (In British English, use **horse-riding**)
horse racing	[hɔrs reɪsɪŋ]	a sport in which riders (called jockeys) race against each other on horses
horse-riding (*BRIT*)		*see* **horseback riding**
ice skating	[aɪs skeɪtɪŋ]	the sport of moving around on ice wearing ice skates; *go ice skating*
jogging	[dʒɒgɪŋ]	the sport of running slowly; *go jogging*
judo	[dʒudoʊ]	a sport in which two people try to throw each other to the ground; *do judo*
karate	[kərɑti]	a Japanese sport in which people fight using their hands, feet, and legs; *do karate*
rugby	[rʌgbi]	a game in which two teams try to get a ball past a line at the end of the field; *play rugby*
skiing	[skiɪŋ]	the sport of traveling over snow on skis; *go skiing*
snooker	[snʊkər]	a game that is played on a special table. Players use a long stick to hit a white ball so that it knocks colored balls into holes around the edge of the table; *play snooker* (*mainly BRIT*)
soccer	[sɒkər]	a game in which two teams of eleven players try to win points by kicking the ball into an area at their opponent's end of the field (In British English, use **football**)
squash	[skwɒʃ]	a game in which two players hit a small rubber ball against the walls of a court; *play squash*
swimming	[swɪmɪŋ]	the sport of moving through water using your arms and legs; *go swimming*

tennis	[tɛnɪs]	a game for two or four players, who use rackets (= special bats) to hit a ball across a net between them; *a game of tennis*; *play tennis*
volleyball	[vɒlibɔl]	a game in which two teams hit a large ball over a high net with their arms or hands; *play volleyball*
windsurfing	[wɪndsɜrfɪŋ]	a sport in which you move across water on a long narrow board with a sail on it; *go windsurfing*

PEOPLE

athlete	[æθlit]	someone who is good at physical sports, exercise, or games, especially in competitions
captain	[kæptɪn]	the leader of a sports team
champion	[tʃæmpiən]	the winner of a sports competition or game; *the world champion*
coach	[koʊtʃ]	someone who is in charge of teaching a person or a sports team
fan	[fæn]	someone who likes a particular sport, team, or player very much; *football fans*
opponent	[əpoʊnənt]	the person who is against you in a sports competition
player	[pleɪər]	a person who takes part in a sport or game
referee	[rɛfəri]	the person who makes sure that players do not break the rules in a match
spectator	[spɛkteɪtər]	someone who is watching a sports event
team	[tim]	a group of people who play a sport against other groups of people
umpire	[ʌmpaɪr]	someone who watches a game such as tennis or baseball to make sure that the players do not break the rules

EXAMPLES

She praised her opponent's ability.
She was a good golfer and tennis player.
The referee blew his whistle to end the game.
The umpire's decision is final.

winner	[wɪnər]	the person who wins a prize, a race, or a competition

PLACES

boxing ring	[bɒksɪŋ rɪŋ]	a square area with ropes around it, where boxing matches take place
court	[kɔrt]	an area for playing a game such as tennis or basketball; *a tennis court*
golf course	[gɒlf kɔrs]	an area of land where people play golf
gymnasium	[dʒɪmneɪziəm]	a room or hall with equipment for doing physical exercise
ice rink	[aɪs rɪŋk]	an area of ice that people can skate on
pitch	[pɪtʃ]	an area of ground that is used for playing a game such as football; *a football pitch*
racetrack	[reɪstræk]	a track that is used for races
stadium	[steɪdiəm]	a large sports field with rows of seats all around it; *a football stadium*
swimming pool	[swɪmɪŋ pul]	a place that has been built for people to swim in

EQUIPMENT AND CLOTHING

ball	[bɔl]	a round object that you kick, throw, or hit in some sports and games
basket	[bɑskɪt, bæs-]	the net that you throw the ball through in basketball
bat	[bæt]	a long piece of wood that is used for hitting the ball in games such as baseball or cricket; *a baseball/cricket bat*
golf club	[gɒlf klʌb]	a long, thin, metal stick that you use to hit the ball in golf
net	[nɛt]	**1** in tennis, and some other sports, the piece of material across the center of the court that the ball has to go over **2** in soccer, the material that is attached to the back of the goal **3** in basketball, the loose material that hangs from the ring

| **racket** | [rækɪt] | a thing with a long handle and a round part with strings stretched across it, used for hitting the ball in some games; *a tennis/badminton racket* |
| **skis** | [skiːz] | long, flat, narrow pieces of wood, metal, or plastic that you fasten to your boots so that you can move easily over snow |

COMPETITIONS

championship	[tʃæmpiənʃɪp]	a competition to find the best player or team in a particular sport or game
competition	[kɒmpɪtɪʃən]	an event in which people try to show that they are best at an activity
final	[faɪnəl]	the last game or race in a series, that decides who is the winner; *play in the final*
foul	[faʊl]	an action that breaks the rules of a particular sport
game	[ɡeɪm]	**1** an activity or a sport in which you try to win; *a game of tennis* **2** one particular occasion when you play a game
goal	[ɡoʊl]	**1** the place, in games such as soccer, where the players try to put the ball in order to win a point for their team **2** a point that is scored when the ball goes into the goal in games such as soccer
halftime	[hæftaɪm]	the short period between the two parts of a game when the players can rest
match	[mætʃ]	a sports game between two people or teams; *a tennis match*
medal	[mɛdəl]	a piece of metal that is give to the person who wins a race or competition; *a gold/ silver/bronze medal*

EXAMPLES

She's competing in the women's basketball championship this month.

Football is such a great game.

Liverpool is in the lead by 2 goals to 1.

Washington led 44-32 at halftime.

point	[pɔɪnt]	a mark that you win in a game or a sport
race	[reɪs]	a competition to see who is the fastest
score	[skɔr]	the result of a game
tie	[taɪ]	an occasion when both teams have the same number of points at the end of a game
tournament	[tʊərnəmənt, tɜr-]	a sports competition in which each player who wins a game plays another game, until just one person or team (the winner) remains
the World Cup	[ðə wɜrld kʌp]	an international soccer tournament that is held every four years in a different country

[**VERBS**]

beat	[bit]	to defeat someone in a race or competition
catch	[kætʃ]	to take and hold a ball that is moving through the air
defend	[dɪfɛnd]	to try to stop the other team from getting points
draw	[drɔ]	to finish a game with the same number of points as the other player or team
hit	[hɪt]	to bat a ball with a lot of force
jump	[dʒʌmp]	to bend your knees, push against the ground with your feet, and move quickly upwards into the air
kick	[kɪk]	to hit a ball with your foot
lose	[luz]	to not win a game
miss	[mɪs]	to not manage to hit or catch something
practice	[præktɪs]	to do a sport regularly in order to do it better (*In British English, use* **pratise**)
practise (*BRIT*)		*see* **practice**
run	[rʌn]	to move very quickly on your legs

EXAMPLES
What's the score?
Switzerland beat the United States two-one.
England drew with Ireland in the first game.

save	[seɪv]	to stop the ball from going into the goal in a sports game; *save a goal*
score	[skɔr]	to get a goal or a point in a sports competition
serve	[sɜrv]	to hit the ball to start part of a game in a tennis match
ski	[skiː]	to move over snow or water on skis
swim	[swɪm]	to move through water by making movements with your arms and legs
throw	[θroʊ]	to use your hand to make a ball move through the air
tie	[taɪ]	if two teams tie, they have the same number of points at the end of a game
train	[treɪn]	to prepare for a sports competition; *train for a match*
win	[wɪn]	to do better than everyone else in a race or a game; *win a game*

ADJECTIVES

| in the lead | [ɪn ðə liːd] | in front of all the other people in a race |
| professional | [prəfɡʃənəl] | doing a particular activity as a job rather than just for pleasure |

EXAMPLES

Can you swim?

Ben Johnson in the lead. Can he hang on? Yes, he's done it!

telephone, post, and communications

NOUNS

address	[ədrɛs]	the number of the building, the name of the street, and the town where you live or work; *name and address*; *mailing address*
area code	[ɛəriə koʊd]	the series of numbers that you have to dial before a phone number if you are making a call from a different area (*In British English, use* **dialling code**)
Blackberry™	[blækbɛri]	a very small device that you can use for receiving and sending e-mails and making phone calls
call	[kɔl]	an occasion when you phone someone; *a phone call*
cellphone	[sɛlfoʊn]	a phone that you can carry with you and use wherever you are (*In British English, use* **mobile phone**)
delivery	[dɪlɪvəri]	an occasion when someone brings letters, packages, or other goods to a particular place; *mail delivery*
dialling code (*BRIT*)		*see* **area code**
directory enquiries (*BRIT*)		*see* **information**
envelope	[ɛnvəloʊp, ɒn-]	the paper cover in which you put a letter before you send it to someone; *a brown envelope*; *a self-addressed envelope*
extension	[ɪkstɛnʃⁿn]	a phone that connects to the main phone line in a building
fax	[fæks]	a copy of a document that you send or receive using a fax machine; *send/receive a fax*
fax machine	[fæks məʃin]	a special machine that you use to send and receive documents electronically

---

EXAMPLES
What is your address?
Please allow 28 days for delivery of your order.
Can I have extension forty-six, please?

form	[fɔrm]	a piece of paper with questions on it and spaces where you should write the answers; *fill in a form*
information	[ɪnfərmeɪʃ°n]	a service that you can call to find out someone's phone number (*In British English, use* **directory enquiries**)
international call	[ɪntərnæʃən°l kɔl]	a phone call made between different countries; *make an international call*
landline	[lændlaɪn]	a phone connection that uses wires, in contrast to a cellphone
letter	[lɛtər]	a message that you write or type on paper and send to someone; *open a letter*; *write/send a letter*
letterbox (BRIT)		*see* **mailbox**
line	[laɪn]	a phone connection or wire
local call	[loʊk°l kɔl]	a phone call to a place that is near; *make a local call*
mail	[meɪl]	**1** the letters and packages that you receive (*In British English, use* **post**) **2** the e-mail that you receive; *a mail server*
mailbox	[meɪlbɒks]	a hole in a door through which mail is delivered, or a box in which mail is delivered; *put something through the mailbox* (*In British English, use* **letterbox** *or* **post box**)
mailman (PL) **mailmen**	[meɪlmæn] [meɪlmɛn]	a man who collects and delivers letters and packages (*In British English, use* **postman**)
mailwoman (PL) **mailwomen**	[meɪlwʊmən] [meɪlwɪmɪn]	a woman who collects and delivers letters and packages (*In British English, use* **postwoman**)
message	[mɛsɪdʒ]	a piece of information that you send or give to someone; *a phone message*; *a voice message*; *send/receive a message*; *leave/take a message*

EXAMPLES

I'll call you later on your landline.

I received a letter from a friend.

Suddenly the telephone line went dead.

There has been no mail in three weeks.

She isn't here yet. Do you want to leave a message?

mobile	[moʊbəl]	same as **mobile phone**
mobile phone (mainly BRIT)		see **cellphone**
operator	[ɒpəreɪtər]	a person who connects phone calls in a place such as an office or a hotel
package	[pækɪdʒ]	something that is wrapped in paper so that it can be sent through the mail
parcel	[pɑrsəl]	same as **package**
phone	[foʊn]	a piece of equipment that you use to talk to someone else in another place; *answer the phone; a pay phone; Can I use the phone?*
phone number	[foʊn nʌmbər]	the number of a particular phone, that you use when you make a call to it
post (BRIT)		see **mail**
postage	[poʊstɪdʒ]	the money that you pay for sending post
post box (BRIT)		see **mailbox**
postcard	[poʊstkɑrd]	a thin card, often with a picture on one side, that you can write on and mail to someone without using an envelope; *send someone a postcard*
postcode (BRIT)		see **zip code**
postman		see **mailman**
post office	[poʊst ɔfɪs]	a building where you can buy stamps and post letters
postwoman		see **mailwoman**
receiver	[rɪsivər]	the part of a phone that you hold near to your ear and speak into; *pick up/lift the receiver*
reply	[rɪplaɪ]	something that you say or write as an answer
ringtone	[rɪŋtoʊn]	the sound that your cellphone makes when someone calls you

---

EXAMPLES

Two minutes later the phone rang.
All prices include postage.
She picked up the receiver and started to dial.
I dialed her number, but there was no reply.

S&H	[ɛs ənd eɪtʃ]	short for "shipping and handling:" the cost of wrapping an item and sending it in the mail
signature	[sɪgnətʃər, -tʃʊər]	your name, written in your own special way
SIM card	[sɪm kɑrd]	a small piece of electronic equipment in a cellphone that connects it to a particular phone network
stamp	[stæmp]	a small piece of paper that you stick on an envelope before you mail it
telephone	[tɛlɪfoʊn]	same as **phone**
text message	[tɛkst mɛsɪdʒ]	a message that you send using a cellphone; *send/receive a text message*
tourist information office	[tʊərɪst ɪnfərmeɪʃⁿn ɔfɪs]	an office that gives information about the local area
voicemail	[vɔɪsmeɪl]	an electronic system that records spoken messages; *a voicemail message*
wrapping paper	[ræpɪŋ peɪpər]	special paper that you use for wrapping presents
writing paper	[raɪtɪŋ peɪpər]	paper for writing letters on
zip code	[zɪp koʊd]	a series of numbers and letters at the end of an address (*In British English, use* **postcode**)

VERBS

answer	[ænsər]	to pick up the phone when it rings
call	[kɔl]	to telephone someone
call someone back		to phone someone in return for a call they made to you

EXAMPLES

Price $12.95 plus $1.95 S&H.
They cost $24.95 including S&H.
She put a stamp on the corner of the envelope.
She didn't answer the phone.
Would you call me as soon as you find out?

deliver	[dɪlɪvər]	to take something to a particular place
dial	[daɪəl]	to press the buttons on a phone in order to call someone; *dial a number*
hang up		to end a phone call
hold the line		to wait for a short time when you are making a phone call
mail	[meɪl]	to send a letter or a package somewhere in the mail (*In British English, use* **post**)
phone	[foʊn]	to contact someone and speak to them on the phone; *Did anybody phone?*; *I phoned the police.*
post (BRIT)		*see* **mail**
reply	[rɪplaɪ]	to write an answer to something that someone writes to you
send	[sɛnd]	to make a message or a package go to someone
sign	[saɪn]	to write your name on a document; *sign your name*; *sign a letter*
text	[tɛkst]	to send someone a text message on a cellphone
write	[raɪt]	to give someone information, ask them something or express your feelings in a letter or an e-mail; *write a letter/an e-mail*

EXAMPLES
Only 90% of first-class mail is delivered on time.
Don't hang up on me!
Could you hold the line, please?
I mailed a letter to Stanley.
I'm mailing you a check.
He never replies to my letters.
Hannah sent me a letter last week.
Mary texted me when she got home.
She wrote to her aunt asking for help.

ADJECTIVES

busy	[bɪzi]	if a phone line is busy, it is already being used by someone else; *The line is busy.* (*In British English, use* **engaged**)
dead	[dɛd]	if a phone line is dead it is no longer working
engaged (*BRIT*)		*see* **busy**
first-class	[fɜrst klæs]	used for describing the fastest and most expensive way of sending letters; *a first-class letter*
second-class	[sɛkənd klæs]	used for describing the slower and cheaper way of sending letters; *a second-class stamp*

PHRASES

best wishes	used at the end of a letter or e-mail, before your name, to someone you know who is not a very close friend
love from	used at the end of a letter or e-mail, before your name, to a friend or relative
sincerely yours	used at the end of a formal letter, before your name, when you have addressed it to someone by their name (*In British English, use* **yours sincerely**)
yours faithfully	used at the end of a formal letter, before your name, when you start the letter with the words "Dear Sir" or "Dear Madam"
yours sincerely (*BRIT*)	*see* **sincerely yours**

EXAMPLES
We tried to call you back but you were busy.
I answered the phone and the line went dead.

television and radio

ad   [æd]   a short film on television or short article on the radio that tells you about something such as a product or an event (*In British English, use* **advert**)

advert (*BRIT*)   *see* **ad**

adverts (*BRIT*)   *see* **commercial break**

aerial (*BRIT*)   *see* **antenna**

antenna   [æntɛnə]   a piece of equipment that receives television or radio signals (*In British English, use* **aerial**)
   (PL) **antennae**   [æntɛni]
   antennas

cable television   [keɪbəl tɛlɪvɪʒən]   a television system in which signals travel along wires

cartoon   [kɑrtun]   a film that uses drawings instead of real people or objects

celebrity   [sɪlɛbrɪti]   someone who is famous; *a TV celebrity*; *a celebrity guest*

channel   [tʃænəl]   a television station; *change channels*; *What channel is it on?*

chat show (*BRIT*)   *see* **talk show**

clip   [klɪp]   a short piece of a film that is shown separately; *a video clip*

commercial break   [kəmɜrʃəl breɪk]   a short interruption in a television or radio program when ads are shown (*In British English, use* **adverts**)

DJ   [di dʒeɪ]   short for "disc jockey:" someone whose job is to play music and talk on the radio; *a radio DJ*

DVD   [di vi di]   short for "digital video disk:" a disk on which a movie or music is recorded; *a DVD player*

EXAMPLES

Have you seen that new ad for Pepsi?
We don't have cable TV.
We watched children's cartoons on TV.
There is a huge number of television channels in America.
They showed a film clip of the Apollo moon landing.

documentary	[dɒkyə-mɛntəri, -tri]	a television program that provides information about a particular subject; *a wildlife documentary*
game show	[geɪm ʃoʊ]	a television program in which people compete to win prizes; *a television game show*
host	[hoʊst]	someone who introduces the different parts of a television or radio program; *a TV/radio host*; *a sports host*
media	[midiə]	television, radio, newspapers, and magazines
news	[nuz]	information about recent events that is reported on the radio or television; *watch/listen to the news*
prime time	[praɪm taɪm]	the time when most people are watching television; *prime-time TV*
program	[proʊgræm, -grəm]	a television or radio show; *a television/radio program*
quiz show	[kwɪz ʃoʊ]	a television or radio program in which people compete in a quiz
radio	[reɪdioʊ]	a piece of equipment that you use in order to listen to radio programs; *listen to the radio*; *on the radio*; *FM/digital radio*
reality TV	[riælɪti ti vi]	a type of television that aims to show how ordinary people behave in everyday life
remote control	[rɪmoʊt kəntroʊl]	the device that you use to control a television or video recorder from a distance
satellite	[sætᵊlaɪt]	a piece of electronic equipment that is sent into space in order to receive and send back information; *satellite television/radio*; *a satellite dish*

EXAMPLES

Did you see that documentary on TV last night?

A lot of people in the media have asked me that question.

Here are some of the top stories in the news.

He wants to watch his favorite TV program.

She reached for the remote control to turn on the news.

screen	[skrin]	a flat surface on a television, where you see pictures or words; *a TV screen*
series (PL) **series**	[sɪəriz]	a set of radio or television programs
set	[sɛt]	a piece of equipment that receives television or radio signals; *a TV set*
sitcom	[sɪtkɒm]	short for "situation comedy:" a series in which a set of characters is involved in various amusing situations; *a TV sitcom*
soap opera	[soup ɒpərə, ɒprə]	a television drama serial about the daily lives of a group of people
station	[steɪʃ°n]	a company that broadcasts programs on radio or television; *a local radio station*
subtitles	[sʌbtaɪt°lz]	the translation of the words of a foreign film or television program that is shown at the bottom of the picture
talk show	[tɔk ʃou]	a television or radio show in which an interviewer talks to guests in a friendly informal way about different topics (*In British English, use* **chat show**)
television	[tɛlɪvɪʒ°n, -vɪʒ-]	**1** a piece of electrical equipment with a screen on which you watch moving pictures with sound; *We bought a new television.* **2** the moving pictures and sounds that you watch and listen to on a television; *What's on television tonight?*
TV	[ti vi]	[INFORMAL] television; *watch TV*
video	[vɪdiou]	a film that you can watch at home
volume	[vɒlyum]	how loud or quiet the sound is on a television or radio

---

EXAMPLES

The long-running TV series is filmed in Chicago.
The dialogue is in Spanish, with English subtitles.
I prefer going to the movies to watching television.
You can rent a video for $3 and watch it at home.
He turned the volume up on the radio.

| **wavelength** | [weɪvlɛŋθ] | the size of a radio wave that a particular radio station uses to broadcast its programs |

VERBS

broadcast	[brɔdkæst]	to send out a program so that it can be heard on the radio or seen on television
fast-forward	[fæst fɔrwɜrd]	to move a video tape forwards quickly
record	[rɪkɔrd]	to put sounds or images onto a CD, DVD, tape, or video so that they can be heard or seen again later
rewind	[riwaɪnd]	to wind a movie back to the beginning
switch something off		to stop electrical equipment from working by operating a switch; *switch off the radio/ television*
switch something on		to make electrical equipment start working by operating a switch; *switch on the radio/television*
tune	[tun]	to adjust a radio or television so that it receives a particular station or program
tune in		to listen to a radio program or watch a television program
turn something off		to make a piece of electrical equipment stop working; *turn off the radio/television*
turn something on		to make a piece of electrical equipment start working; *turn on the radio/television*
watch	[wɒtʃ]	to look at a television for a period of time

EXAMPLES
She found the station's wavelength on her radio.
The concert will be broadcast live on television and radio.
Can you record the movie for me?
The radio was tuned to NPR.
They tuned in to watch the game.
I stayed up late to watch the film.

ADJECTIVES

animated   [ˈænɪmeɪtɪd]   an animated film is one in which puppets or drawings appear to move

digital   [ˈdɪdʒɪtəl]   using information in the form of thousands of very small signals

on-demand   [ɒn dɪˈmænd]   available whenever needed

ADVERBS

live   [laɪv]   used for describing a television or radio program that you watch at the same time that it happens; *watch something live*

on the air   [ɒn ði ɛər]   on radio or television

IDIOMS

channel surfing   a way of watching television in which you keep changing from one channel to another using a remote control

couch potato   a person who spends a lot of time sitting watching television

---

EXAMPLES
Most people now have digital television.
The new video-on-demand service will be available only to those with
  broadband internet connections.
The show went on the air live at 8 o'clock.

theater and cinema

NOUNS

actor [æktər] someone whose job is acting in plays or movies; *a famous actor*

actress [æktrɪs] a woman whose job is acting in plays or movies

audience [ɔdiəns] all the people who are watching or listening to a performance or a movie; *a movie audience*

audition [ɔdɪʃ°n] a short performance that an actor gives so that someone can decide if they are good enough to be in a play or a movie

ballet [bælei] a performance of a type of dancing that tells a story; *go to the ballet*

Bollywood [bɒliwʊd] the Indian film industry; *a Bollywood movie; a Bollywood actor*

box office [bɒks ɔfɪs] **1** the place in a theater or concert hall where the tickets are sold
2 used to refer to the success of a movie or play in terms of the number of people who go to see it

cast [kæst] all the people who act in a play or a movie

character [kærɪktər] one of the people in a story

cinema *(BRIT)* *see* **movie theater**

circus [sɜrkəs] a group of people and animals that travels around to different places and performs shows in a big tent

comedian [kəmidiən] a person whose job is to make people laugh

comedy [kɒmədi] a play or movie that is intended to make people laugh

---

EXAMPLES
She's a really good actress.
They are holding final auditions for presenters.
They collected their tickets at the box office.
The film was a huge success at the box office.
He plays the main character in the movie.
I always wanted to work as a clown in a circus.
The movie is a romantic comedy.

costume	[kɒstum]	a set of clothes that someone wears in a performance; *the costumes and scenery*
curtain	[kɜrtᵊn]	the large piece of material that hangs at the front of the stage in a theater; *the curtain rises/falls*
director	[dɪrɛktər, daɪ-]	the person who tells actors what to do; *a movie director*; *a theater director*
drama	[drɑmə, dræmə]	a serious play or movie
epic	[ɛpɪk]	a long movie about important events
film *(BRIT)*		*see* **movie**
film producer	[fɪlm prədusər]	a person whose job is to produce plays or movies; *a film producer*
film star *(BRIT)*		*see* **movie star**
full house	[fʊl haʊs]	an occasion when there are no empty seats in a theater; *playing to a full house*
Hollywood	[hɒliwʊd]	the American film industry; *Hollywood movie stars*; *a Hollywood movie*
horror movie	[hɔrər muvi, hɒr-]	a type of movie that is very frightening
intermission	[ɪntərmɪʃᵊn]	a short break between two parts of a movie, concert, or show; *during the intermission* (In British English, use **interval**)
interval *(BRIT)*		*see* **intermission**
makeup	[meɪkʌp]	the creams and powders that actors put on their faces to change their appearance; *wear/apply makeup*; *a makeup artist*; *costumes and makeup*
matinee	[mætᵊneɪ]	a performance of a play or a showing of a movie in the afternoon; *a matinee performance*
movie	[muvi]	a story that is told using moving pictures on the television or at a movie theater; *to make/direct a movie*; *to watch a movie* (In British English, use **film**)

EXAMPLES
I'm going to see a movie tonight.
I rarely went to the movies.

the movies	[ðə muviz]	same as **movie theater**; *go to the movies*
movie star	[muvi star]	a famous actor or actress who appears in movies (*In British English, use* **film star**)
movie theater	[muvi θiətər]	a building where people go to watch movies (*In British English, use* **cinema**)
multiplex	[mʌltipleks	a movie theater with several screens; **cinema** sɪnɪmə] *a multiplex cinema*
musical	[myuzɪkəl]	a play or a movie that uses singing and dancing in the story; *a Broadway musical*
opera	[ɒpərə, ɒprə]	a play with music in which all the words are sung; *an opera singer*; *an opera house*
Oscar™	[ɒskər]	a prize given to actors, directors, and other people in the film industry; *get an Oscar*; *She has three Oscars.*
part	[part]	one character's words and actions in a play or movie
performance	[pərforməns]	the activity of entertaining an audience by singing, dancing, or acting; *a concert performance*
play	[pleɪ]	a piece of writing performed in a theater, on the radio, or on television
playwright	[pleɪraɪt]	a person who writes plays
plot	[plɒt]	a series of events that make up the story of a movie
production	[prədʌkʃ°n]	a play or other show that is performed in a theater; *a theater/stage production*; *a film production*
program	[prougræm, -grəm]	a small book or sheet of paper that tells you about a play or concert
review	[rɪvyu]	a report that gives an opinion about something such as a play or a movie

EXAMPLES

He played the part of Hamlet.
They were giving a performance of Bizet's "Carmen."
Hamlet is my favorite play.
Tonight our class is going to see a production of "Othello."
The show received excellent reviews in all the papers.

romance	[roʊmæns, roʊmæns]	a movie or a play about a romantic relationship
rom-com	[rɒmkɒm]	short for "romantic comedy:" a humorous film in which the main story is about a romantic relationship
scene	[siːn]	a part of a play or a movie that happens in the same place; *film/shoot a scene; a love scene*
science fiction	[saɪəns fɪkʃən]	stories and movies about events that take place in the future or in other parts of the universe; *a science fiction movie*
screen	[skriːn]	the flat area on the wall of a movie theater, where you see the movie; *the movie screen*
script	[skrɪpt]	the written words that actors speak in a play or a movie
seat	[siːt]	something that you can sit on in a theater or concert hall
sequel	[siːkwᵊl]	a movie that continues the story of an earlier movie
set	[sɛt]	the place where a movie is made or the scenery that is on the stage when a play is being performed; *a movie set*
show	[ʃoʊ]	a performance in a theater; *a comedy show*
soundtrack	[saʊndtræk]	the music that is played during a movie; *a movie soundtrack*
spotlight	[spɒtlaɪt]	a powerful light in a theater that can be directed so that it lights up a small area
stage	[steɪdʒ]	the area in a theater where people perform; *come on stage; a concert stage; on stage and screen; a stage play*
star	[stɑr]	a famous actor or actress; *a movie star*

EXAMPLES

This is the opening scene of "Hamlet."

Watching a movie on television is not the same as seeing it on the big screen.

We had front-row seats at the concert.

The place looked like the set of a James Bond movie.

How about going to see a show tomorrow?

subtitles	[sʌbtaɪtᵊlz]	the translation of the words of a foreign film that are shown at the bottom of the picture
theater	[θiͅətər]	a place where you go to see plays, movies, or shows; *go to the theater*
thriller	[θrɪͅlər]	an exciting movie or play about a crime
ticket	[tɪͅkɪt]	a small piece of paper that shows that you have paid to go to see a movie or a play; *theater/movie tickets*
tragedy	[trædʒɪdi]	a type of serious play that usually ends with the death of the main character
trailer	[treɪͅlər]	a set of short extracts from a movie that are shown to advertise it

VERBS

act	[ækt]	to have a part in a play or a movie
book	[bʊk]	to buy tickets for a movie or show that you will go to later
clap	[klæp]	to hit your hands together to show that you like something
dance	[dæns]	to move your body to music
play	[pleͅɪ]	to perform the part of a particular character in a play or movie
shoot	[ʃuͅt]	to make a movie
sing	[sɪŋ]	to make music with your voice
star	[staͅr]	**1** to have a famous actor or actress in one of the most important parts in a play or movie **2** to have one of the most important parts in a play or movie

EXAMPLES

The dialogue is in Spanish, with English subtitles.
He acted in many movies, including "Reds."
You can book tickets for the movie theater over the phone.
He played Mr. Hyde in the movie.
He'd love to shoot his movie in Cuba.
The movie stars Brad Pitt.
She stars in the Broadway play.

| watch | [wɒtʃ] | to look at someone or something for a period of time; *watch a movie/play* |

ADJECTIVES

black-and-white	[blæk ənd waɪt]	showing everything in black, white, and gray; *old black-and-white movie footage*
classic	[klæsɪk]	of very good quality, and popular for a long time; *a classic movie*
dubbed	[dʌbd]	having a different soundtrack added with actors speaking in a different language; *cartoons dubbed in Chinese*
low-budget	[loʊ bʌdʒɪt]	made spending very little money; *a low-budget movie*
sold out	[soʊld aʊt]	used to describe a performance for which all the tickets have been sold
subtitled	[sʌbtaɪtəld]	with a translation of the words shown at the bottom of the screen; *a subtitled movie*

THINGS YOU CAN SHOUT

| bravo! | [brɑvoʊ] | an audience shouts "bravo!" to show how much they have enjoyed a performance |
| encore! | [ɒŋkɔr, -kɔr] | an audience shouts "encore!" at the end of a concert to ask for a short extra performance |

IDIOMS

bring the house down	to make everyone laugh or cheer at a performance in the theater
keep you on the edge of your seat	to make you give your full attention to something
steal the show	to attract more attention and praise than other people

EXAMPLES

The movie kept everyone on the edge of their seats.

time

NOUNS

GENERAL

time	[taɪm]	**1** something that we measure in minutes, hours, days, and years; *in a week's time*; *Time passed.* **2** used when you are talking about a particular point in the day, that you describe in hours and minutes
past	[pæst]	the time before the present, and the things that happened then; *in the past*
present	[prɛzᵊnt]	the period of time that is happening now; *live in the present*
future	[fyutʃər]	the time that will come after now; *in the future*

HOURS, SECONDS, AND MINUTES

half an hour	[hæf ən auər]	a period of thirty minutes
hour	[auər]	a period of sixty minutes
minute	[mɪnɪt]	a unit for measuring time. There are sixty seconds in one minute, and there are sixty minutes in one hour.
moment	[moumənt]	a very short period of time; *a few moments later*
quarter of an hour	[kwɔrtər əv ən auər]	a period of fifteen minutes
second	[sɛkənd]	a measurement of time. There are sixty seconds in one minute.

EXAMPLES

I've known Mr. Martin for a long time.
What time is it?
Do you know what time it is?
He was making plans for the future.
I only slept about half an hour last night.
They waited for about two hours.
The pizza will take twenty minutes to cook.
In a moment he was gone.
For a few seconds nobody spoke.

TIMES OF THE DAY

dawn	[dɔn]	the time when the sky becomes light in the morning; *Dawn was breaking.*
sunrise	[sʌnraɪz]	the time in the morning when the sun first appears in the sky; *at sunrise*
morning	[mɔrnɪŋ]	the part of each day between the time that people usually wake up and noon; *tomorrow morning*; *in the morning*; *on Sunday morning*
noon	[nun]	twelve o'clock in the middle of the day; *at noon*
midday	[mɪddeɪ]	same as **noon**
afternoon	[æftərnun]	the part of each day that begins at lunchtime and ends at about six o'clock; *in the afternoon*; *yesterday afternoon*
evening	[ivnɪŋ]	the part of each day between the end of the afternoon and midnight; *yesterday evening*; *in the evening*
sunset	[sʌnsɛt]	the time in the evening when the sun goes down; *at sunset*
dusk	[dʌsk]	the time just before night when it is not completely dark; *at dusk*
night	[naɪt]	**1** the time when it is dark outside, and most people sleep; *during the night* **2** the period of time between the end of the afternoon and the time that you go to bed; *last night*; *ten o'clock at night*
midnight	[mɪdnaɪt]	twelve o'clock in the middle of the night; *at midnight*

DAYS AND WEEKS

day	[deɪ]	a period of twenty-four hours from one midnight to the next midnight; *every day*

EXAMPLES
Nancy woke at dawn.
He stayed in his room all afternoon.
What day is it?

date	[deɪt]	a particular day and month or a particular year
fortnight	[fɔrtnaɪt]	a period of two weeks
week	[wik]	a period of seven days; *last week*
weekday	[wikdeɪ]	any of the days of the week except Saturday and Sunday
weekend	[wikɛnd]	Saturday and Sunday; *on the weekend*

DAYS OF THE WEEK

Monday	[mʌndeɪ, -di]	the day after Sunday and before Tuesday; *a week from Monday*
Tuesday	[tuzdeɪ, -di]	the day after Monday and before Wednesday; *next Tuesday*
Wednesday	[wɛnzdeɪ, -di]	the day after Tuesday and before Thursday; *on Wednesday*
Thursday	[θɜrzdeɪ, -di]	the day after Wednesday and before Friday; *every Thursday morning*
Friday	[fraɪdeɪ, -di]	the day after Thursday and before Saturday; *Friday, November 6*
Saturday	[sætərdeɪ, -di]	the day after Friday and before Sunday; *every Saturday*
Sunday	[sʌndeɪ, -di]	the day after Saturday and before Monday; *on Sunday*

MONTHS

month	[mʌnθ]	one of the twelve parts that a year is divided into
January	[dʒænyuɛri]	the first month of the year; *on January*
February	[fɛbyuɛri, fɛbru-]	the second month of the year

EXAMPLES
What's the date today?
What is he doing here on a weekday?
I had dinner with Tim last weekend.
We go on vacation next month.
We always have snow in January.

March	[mɑrtʃ]	the third month of the year
April	[eɪprɪl]	the fourth month of the year
May	[meɪ]	the fifth month of the year
June	[dʒun]	the sixth month of the year
July	[dʒʊlaɪ]	the seventh month of the year
August	[ɔgəst]	the eighth month of the year
September	[sɛptɛmbər]	the ninth month of the year
October	[ɒktoʊbər]	the tenth month of the year
November	[noʊvɛmbər]	the eleventh month of the year
December	[dɪsɛmbər]	the twelfth and last month of the year

SEASONS

autumn (BRIT)		*see* **fall**
fall	[fɔl]	the season between summer and winter, when the weather becomes cooler and the leaves fall off the trees; *in the fall*; *last/next fall*; *fall leaves* (*In British English, use* **autumn**)
season	[sizᵊn]	a part of the year that has its own typical weather conditions; *the rainy season*
spring	[sprɪŋ]	the season between winter and summer when the weather becomes warmer and plants start to grow again
summer	[sʌmər]	the season between spring and fall, when the weather is usually warm or hot; *a summer's day*
winter	[wɪntər]	the season between fall and spring, when the weather is usually cold

YEARS

| **century** | [sɛntʃəri] | one hundred years; *in the 21st century* |
| **decade** | [dɛkeɪd] | a period of ten years |

EXAMPLES

She was born on September 6th, 1970.
Summer is my favorite season.
They are getting married next spring.
The plant flowers in late summer.

| **leap year** | [lip yɪər] | a year, happening every four years, that has 366 days including February 29 as an extra day |
| **year** | [yɪər] | **1** a period of twelve months, beginning on the first of January and ending on the thirty-first of December; *next/last year*; *a calendar year*
 2 any period of twelve months; *three times a year*; *the academic year* |

MEASURING TIME

alarm clock	[əlɑrm klɒk]	a clock that makes a noise so that you wake up at a particular time; *set the alarm clock*
calendar	[kælɪndər]	a list of days, weeks, and months for a particular year
clock	[klɒk]	a piece of equipment that shows you what time it is
watch	[wɒtʃ]	a small clock that you usually wear on your wrist

(ADJECTIVES)

annual	[ænyuəl]	happening once every year; *an annual meeting*
daily	[deɪli]	appearing or happening every day; *a daily newspaper*; *a daily routine*
early	[ɜrli]	before the usual time; *an early start*
following	[fɒloʊɪŋ]	used for describing the day, week, or year after the one you have just mentioned; *the following morning*
last	[læst]	the most recent; *last July*
late	[leɪt]	after the time that something should start or happen

---

EXAMPLES
He didn't come home last night.
The train was 40 minutes late.

monthly	[mʌnθli]	happening every month; *monthly rent*
next	[nɛkst]	used for talking about the first day, week, or year that comes after this one or the previous one; *the next day*
weekly	[wiːkli]	happening once a week or every week; *a weekly meeting*

ADVERBS

ago	[əgoʊ]	in the past; before now; *two days ago*; *a while ago*
at the moment	[æt ðə moʊmənt]	now
early	[ɜrli]	before the usual time; *get up/arrive early*
immediately	[ɪmidiɪtli]	happening without any delay
late	[leɪt]	after the time that something should start or happen
later	[leɪtər]	used for talking about a time that is after the one that you have been talking about; *two days later*
now	[naʊ]	used for talking about the present time
nowadays	[naʊədeɪz]	now generally, and not in the past
once	[wʌns]	happening one time only
on time	[ɒn taɪm]	arriving at the expected time, and not late; *The train arrived on time.*
soon	[suːn]	after a short time

EXAMPLES
The magazine is published monthly.
She's busy at the moment.
"Call the police immediately!" she shouted.
It started forty minutes late.
I must go now.
Children watch a lot of TV nowadays.
I met Miquela once, at a party.
I'll call you soon.

today	[tədeɪ]	used when you are talking about the actual day on which you are speaking or writing
tomorrow	[təmɔrou]	the day after today
twice	[twaɪs]	two times; *twice a week*
yesterday	[yɛstərdeɪ, -di]	used for talking about the day before today

EXAMPLES
How are you feeling today?
She left yesterday.

tools

NOUNS

ax	[æks]	a tool with a heavy metal blade and a long handle that is used for cutting wood
battery	[bætəri]	a small object that provides electricity for things such as radios
blade	[bleɪd]	the flat, sharp edge of a knife that is used for cutting; *a knife blade*
bolt	[boʊlt]	a long piece of metal that you use with a nut to fasten things together; *nuts and bolts*
bucket	[bʌkɪt]	a round metal or plastic container with a handle, used for holding water; *a bucket of water*
drill	[drɪl]	a tool for making holes; *an electric drill*
file	[faɪl]	a tool that you use for rubbing rough objects to make them smooth
flashlight	[flæʃlaɪt]	a small electric light that you carry in your hand (*In British English, use* **torch**)
glue	[glu]	a sticky substance used for joining things together
hammer	[hæmər]	a tool that is made from a heavy piece of metal attached to the end of a handle, that is used for hitting nails into wood; *a hammer and nails*
handle	[hændᵊl]	the part of a tool that you hold; *a tool handle*
knife	[naɪf]	a sharp flat piece of metal with a handle, that you can use to cut things; *a sharp knife*
ladder	[lædər]	a piece of equipment made of two long pieces of wood or metal with short steps between them, that is used for reaching high places; *climb a ladder*
machine	[məʃin]	a piece of equipment that uses electricity or an engine to do a particular job

---

EXAMPLES
The game requires two AA batteries.
You will need scissors and a tube of glue.

nail	[ne͟ɪl]	a thin piece of metal with one pointed end and one flat end that you hit with a hammer in order to fix things together
needle	[ni͟d³l]	a small, thin metal tool with a sharp point that you use for sewing; *a needle and thread*
nut	[nʌt]	a thick metal ring that you put onto a bolt, that is used for holding heavy things together
paint	[pe͟ɪnt]	a colored liquid that you put onto a surface with a brush
paintbrush	[pe͟ɪntbrʌʃ]	a brush that you use for painting
pliers	[pla͟ɪərz]	a tool with two handles at one end and two flat metal parts at the other that is used for holding or pulling things; *a pair of pliers*
rope	[ro͟ʊp]	a type of very thick string that is made by twisting together several strings or wires; *a piece of rope*
saw	[sɔ͟]	a metal tool for cutting wood; *a saw blade*
scaffolding	[skæ͟fəldɪŋ]	a frame of metal bars that people can stand on when they are working on the outside of a building; *put up/take down scaffolding*
screw	[skru͟]	a small metal object with a sharp end, that you use to join things together
screwdriver	[skru͟draɪvər]	a tool that you use for turning screws
shovel	[ʃʌ͟v³l]	a flat tool with a handle that is used for lifting and moving earth or snow
spade	[spe͟ɪd]	a tool that is used for digging; *a garden spade*
spanner (mainly BRIT)		*see* **wrench**
spring	[sprɪŋ]	a long, spiral piece of metal; *a coiled spring*
stepladder	[ste͟plædər]	a short ladder that you can fold

EXAMPLES

If you want to repair the wheels, you must remove the four nuts.
Each shelf is attached to the wall with screws.
I'll need the coal shovel.

tape measure	[teɪp mɛʒər]	a strip of metal, plastic, or cloth with marks on it, used for measuring
tool	[tul]	anything that you hold in your hands and use to do a particular type of work
toolbox	[tulbɒks]	a box or container for keeping tools in
torch (BRIT)		see **flashlight**
varnish	[vɑrnɪʃ]	a thick, clear liquid that is painted onto things to give them a shiny surface
wire	[waɪər]	a long, thin piece of metal; *a piece of wire*; *a wire fence*
workshop	[wɜrkʃɒp]	a place where people make or repair things
wrench	[rɛntʃ]	a metal tool that you use for turning nuts to make them tighter (*In British English, use* **spanner**)

VERBS

build	[bɪld]	to make something by joining different things together; *build a house/road*
cut	[kʌt]	to use something sharp to remove part of something, or to break it
drill	[drɪl]	to make holes using a drill
fix	[fɪks]	**1** to repair something **2** to attach something firmly or securely to a particular place
hammer	[hæmər]	to hit nails into wood using a hammer
measure	[mɛʒər]	to find out the size of something
mend	[mɛnd]	to repair something
paint	[peɪnt]	to cover a wall or an object with paint; *paint a wall*

EXAMPLES

They cut a hole in the roof and put in a piece of glass.
You'll need to drill a hole in the wall.
This morning, a man came to fix my washing machine.
The clock is fixed to the wall.
She hammered a nail into the window frame.
Measure the length of the table.

| **screw** | [skru] | to join one thing to another thing using a screw |

ADJECTIVES

blunt	[blʌnt]	not sharp or pointed; *a blunt knife*
electric	[ɪlɛktrɪk]	**1** working using electricity; *an electric motor* **2** carrying electricity; *an electric plug/switch*
manual	[mænyuəl]	**1** used for describing work in which you use your hands or your physical strength **2** operated by hand, rather than by electricity or a motor; *a manual pump*
sharp	[ʃɑːp]	very thin and able to cut through things very easily; *a sharp knife/blade*

EXAMPLES

I screwed the shelf on the wall.

He began his career as a manual worker.

towns and cities

bank	[bæŋk]	a place where people can keep their money
beltway	[bɛltweɪ]	a road that goes around a large town to keep traffic away from the center (*In British English, use* **ring road**)
bench	[bɛntʃ]	a long seat made of wood or metal; *a park bench*
bin (BRIT)		*see* **trash can**
bridge	[brɪdʒ]	a structure that is built over a river or a road so that people or vehicles can cross from one side to the other; *a railroad bridge*
building	[bɪldɪŋ]	a structure that has a roof and walls; *new/ old buildings*; *public buildings*; *an office building*
bus station	[bʌs steɪʃ⁽ə⁾n]	a place in a town or a city where a lot of buses stop
bus stop	[bʌs stɒp]	a place on the side of a road, marked by a sign, where a bus stops
café	[kæfeɪ]	a place where you can buy drinks and small meals
capital	[kæpɪtəl]	the city where the government of a country meets; *a capital city*
car park (BRIT)		*see* **parking lot**
castle	[kæsəl]	a large building with thick, high walls that was built in the past to protect people during battles
cathedral	[kəθidrəl]	a large and important church
church	[tʃɜrtʃ]	a building where Christians go to pray; *go to church*
citizen	[sɪtɪzən]	a person who lives in a town or city
city	[sɪti]	a large town; *a big/large/major city*; *the city center*

EXAMPLES

He crossed the bridge to get to school.
Berlin is the capital of Germany.
His father goes to church every day.

crosswalk	[krɔswɔk]	a place where drivers must stop to let people cross a street (*In British English, use* **pedestrian crossing** *or* **zebra crossing**)
crowd	[kraʊd]	a large group of people who have gathered together
directions	[dɪrɛkʃ°nz, daɪ-]	instructions that tell you how to get somewhere
district	[dɪstrɪkt]	a particular area of a city or town; *a business/shopping district*
fire station	[faɪər steɪʃ°n]	a building where fire engines and equipment for stopping fires are kept
guided tour	[gaɪdɪd tʊər]	a short journey around a place of interest with a person who tells you about what you are seeing
hotel	[hoʊtɛl]	a building where people pay to sleep and eat meals; *a luxury/cheap hotel*; *a five-star hotel*; *a hotel room*; *stay in a hotel*
Laundromat™	[lɔndrəmæt]	a place where people pay to use machines to wash and dry their clothes
leaflet	[liflɪt]	a piece of paper containing information about a particular subject
library	[laɪbrɛri]	a place where books are kept for people to use or borrow; *the public/local library*
litter	[lɪtər]	paper or garbage that people leave lying on the ground in public places
map	[mæp]	a drawing of a city, that shows things like roads and important buildings; *a road map*; *a map of the city*
market	[mɑrkɪt]	a place where people buy and sell products
monument	[mɒnyəmənt]	something that you build to help people remember an important event or person; *ancient monuments*

EXAMPLES

A huge crowd gathered in the town square.
She stopped the car to ask for directions.
During the afternoon there's a guided tour of the castle.
Do you have a leaflet about the bus tours around York?
I hate it when I see people dropping litter.

mosque	[mɒsk]	a building where Muslims go to pray
museum	[myuziəm]	a building where you can look at interesting and valuable objects; *visit a museum*
notice	[noutɪs]	a piece of writing in a place where everyone can read it
outskirts	[autskɜrts]	the parts of a town or a city that are furthest away from its center; *live in the outskirts*
park	[pɑrk]	a public area of land in a town with grass and trees, where people go to relax and enjoy themselves; *a public park*
parking lot	[pɑrkɪŋ lɒt]	an area or building where people can leave their cars (*In British English, use **car park***)
parking meter	[pɑrkɪŋ mitər]	a machine in a street that you put money into to pay for leaving your car there
parking space	[pɑrkɪŋ speɪs]	a space where a car can be parked
pavement (*BRIT*)		*see* **sidewalk**
pedestrian	[pɪdɛstriən]	a person who is walking in a town or city
pedestrian crossing (*BRIT*)		*see* **crosswalk**
places of interest	[pleɪsɪz əv ɪntrɪst, -tərɪst]	buildings or parts of a city which are interesting to visit
population	[pɒpyəleɪʃ°n]	all the people who live in an area
post office	[poust ɔfɪs]	a building where you can buy stamps and mail letters
restroom	[rɛstrum, -rʊm]	a room that contains one or more toilets (*In British English, use **toilet***)
restaurant	[rɛstərənt, -tərɑnt, -trɑnt]	a place where you can buy and eat a meal
ring road (*BRIT*)		*see* **beltway**

EXAMPLES

The notice said "Please close the door."
I found a parking space right outside the apartment building.
She visited museums and other places of interest.
Where is the nearest restroom?

road	[roʊd]	a long piece of hard ground that vehicles travel on; *a main road*; *a back road*
season ticket	[siːzᵊn tɪkɪt]	a ticket for a number of journeys, that you usually buy at a reduced price; *a weekly/ monthly/annual season ticket*
shop *(BRIT)*		*see* **store**
shopping center	[ʃɒpɪŋ sɛntər]	an area in a town where a lot of stores have been built close together
sidewalk	[saɪdwɔk]	a path with a hard surface, usually by the side of a road (*In British English, use* **pavement**)
sign	[saɪn]	a piece of wood, metal, or plastic with words or pictures on it that warn you about something, or give you information; *a street sign*
square	[skwɛər]	an open place with buildings around it in a town or city; *the town square*; *the main/ central square*
store	[stɔr]	a place where you buy things; *a local/ corner store*; *a store assistant*; *a store window* (*In British English, use* **shop**)
street	[striːt]	a road in a city or a town; *the main street*; *a side street*; *city streets*
suburb	[sʌbɜrb]	one of the areas on the edge of a city where many people live; *the suburbs*; *a leafy/ wealthy suburb*
subway	[sʌbweɪ]	in a city, the railroad system in which electric trains travel below the ground in tunnels; *take the subway* (*In British English, use* **the underground**)
synagogue	[sɪnəgɒg]	a building where Jewish people go to pray
taxi	[tæksi]	a car that you can hire, with its driver, to take you where you want to go; *take/ catch a taxi*

EXAMPLES

He was hurrying along the sidewalk.
The sign said, "Welcome to Boston."
He lives at 66 Bingfield Street.

taxi rank (BRIT)		*see* **taxi stand**
taxi stand	[tæksi stænd]	a place where taxis wait for customers (*In British English, use* **taxi rank**)
toilet (BRIT)	[tɔɪlət]	**1** a large bowl with a seat that you use when you want to get rid of waste from your body **2** *see* **restroom**
tour	[tʊər]	a trip to an interesting place or around several interesting places; *a bus tour*
tourist	[tʊərɪst]	a person who is visiting a place while on vacations
tower	[taʊər]	a tall, narrow building, or a tall part of another building; *a church tower*
town	[taʊn]	a place with many streets, buildings, and stores, where people live and work; *your home town*; *a seaside town*; *the center of town*
traffic	[træfɪk]	all the vehicles that are on a particular road at one time; *heavy traffic*; *rush hour traffic*
train station	[treɪn steɪʃ°n]	a place where trains stop so that people can get on or off
trash can	[træʃ kæn]	a container that you put garbage in; *put your garbage in the trash can* (*In British English, use* **bin**)
the underground (BRIT)		*see* **subway**
zebra crossing (BRIT)		*see* **crosswalk**
zone	[zoʊn]	an area where something particular happens; *an industrial zone*

VERBS

go shopping	to go to stores to buy things
go sightseeing	to travel around a town to visit famous and interesting places

---

EXAMPLES
Michael took me on a tour of the nearby islands.
I'm going into town.
Where is the train station?

ADJECTIVES

busy	[bɪzi]	full of people who are doing things; *a busy street/road*
clean	[klin]	not dirty
crowded	[kraʊdɪd]	full of people; *crowded streets*; *a crowded bus/train*
dirty	[dɜrti]	covered with unwanted substances such as litter
downtown	[daʊntaʊn]	belonging to the part of a city where the large stores and businesses are; *a downtown hotel*
industrial	[ɪndʌstriəl]	used for describing a city or a country in which industry is very important; *an industrial town/city*
lost	[lɔst]	not knowing where you are; unable to find your way; *I'm lost.*
suburban	[səbɜrbən]	in or relating to the suburbs; *a suburban street/district*
urban	[ɜrbən]	relating to a city or a town; *urban areas*

ADVERBS

left	[lɛft]	opposite the side that most people write with; *turn left*
right	[raɪt]	to the side that is towards the east when you look north; *turn right*
straight ahead	[streɪt əhɛd]	in one direction only; without a curve or bend; *go straight ahead*

PHRASE

no entry		if a sign says "no entry," it means that people are not allowed to go into a particular street or area

EXAMPLES

This is a crowded city of 2 million.

trains

NOUNS

arrival	[əraɪvəl]	the occasion when a train arrives somewhere; *arrivals and departures*
barrier	[bæriər]	a fence or a wall that prevents people or things from moving from one area to another
buffet (*BRIT*)		*see* **dining car**
car	[kar]	one of the sections of a train where people sit; *a railroad/train car*
compartment	[kəmpɑrt-mənt]	**1** one of the separate spaces in a train car (= section of a train); *a first-class compartment* **2** a part of a train that is used for keeping luggage in; *a luggage compartment*
conductor	[kəndʌktər]	a person on a train whose job is to check tickets
connection	[kənɛkʃən]	a train that leaves after another one arrives and allows you to continue your journey by changing from one to the other
departure	[dɪpɑrtʃər]	the occasion when a train leaves somewhere; *a train departure*
destination	[dɛstɪneɪʃən]	the place a train is going to; *arrive at your destination*
dining car	[daɪnɪŋ kɑr]	the part of a train where food and drink is sold (*In British English, use* **buffet**)
driver	[draɪvər]	the person who is driving a train; *a train driver*
engine	[ɛndʒɪn]	the front part of a train that pulls the rest of it
fare	[fɛər]	the money that you pay for a trip in a train; *a train fare*
fast train	[fæst treɪn]	a train that travels very fast, and goes directly to a place, making few stops

---

EXAMPLES

I was afraid that I would miss my connection.
The dining car is now open.

freight train	[freɪt treɪn]	a train that carries goods and not people (*In British English, use* **goods train**)
goods train (*BRIT*)		*see* **freight train**
intercity train	[ɪntərsɪti treɪn]	a fast train that travels long distances between cities, making few stops
journey	[dʒɜrni]	an occasion when you travel from one place to another; *a train journey*
left-luggage office (*BRIT*)		*see* **luggage storage office**
line	[laɪn]	a route that trains move along; *the railroad line*
locker (*BRIT*)		*see* **luggage storage**
lost and found office	[lɔst ənd faʊnd ɔfɪs]	a place at a train station where you can go to look for things that you have lost and that someone else has found
luggage	[lʌgɪdʒ]	the bags that you take with you when you travel; *lost luggage*
luggage rack	[lʌgɪdʒ ræk]	a shelf on a train for putting luggage on
luggage storage	[lʌgɪdʒ stɔrɪdʒ]	a small locker at a train station where you can leave luggage that you want to pick up later (*In British English, use* **locker**)
luggage storage office	[lʌgɪdʒ stɔrɪdʒ ɔfɪs]	a place at a train station where you can pay to leave luggage for a short time (*In British English, use* **left-luggage office**)
one-way	[wʌn weɪ]	a ticket for a journey from one place to another but not back again (*In British English, use* **single**)
passenger	[pæsɪndʒər]	a person who is traveling in a train
platform	[plætfɔrm]	the area in a train station where you wait for a train; *a train platform*
porter	[pɔrtər]	a person whose job is to carry people's luggage in a train station

EXAMPLES

We stayed on the train to the end of the line.
We apologize to any passengers whose journey was delayed today.
The next train to London will depart from platform 3.

railroad	[reɪlroʊd]	a metal track between two places that trains travel along; *railroad tracks* (*In British English, use* **railway**)
railroad crossing	[reɪlroʊd krɔsɪŋ]	a place where a railroad line crosses a road
railway (*BRIT*)		*see* **railroad**
reservation	[rɛzərveɪʃᵊn]	a seat that a transportation company keeps specially for you; *a seat reservation*
return (*BRIT*)		*see* **round trip**
round trip	[raʊnd trɪp]	a ticket for a journey to a place and back again (*In British English, use* **return**)
schedule	[skɛdʒul, -uəl]	a list of the times when trains arrive and depart; *a train schedule* (*In British English, use* **timetable**)
season ticket	[sizᵊn tɪkɪt]	a ticket for a number of train rides, that you usually buy at a cheaper price
seat	[sit]	something that you can sit on; *reserve a seat*
single (*BRIT*)		*see* **one way**
sleeper	[slipər]	**1** a train with beds for passengers on overnight journeys **2** same as **sleeping car**
sleeping car	[slipɪŋ kɑr]	a railroad car with beds in it
slow train	[sloʊ treɪn]	a train that travels slowly, making many stops
station	[steɪʃᵊn]	a place where trains stop so that people can get on or off; *a train station*
steam engine	[stim ɛndʒɪn]	an engine that uses steam as a means of power

EXAMPLES

The road ran beside a railroad.
Is this seat free?
This seat is taken.
I'll take you to the station.
I'll come and pick you up at the station.
In 1941, the train would have been pulled by a steam engine.

subway	[sʌbweɪ]	in a city, the railroad system in which trains travel below the ground; *the New York subway (In British English, use* **the underground**)
suitcase	[su̱tkeɪs]	a case for carrying your clothes when you are traveling; *pack/unpack a suitcase*
ticket	[tɪ̱kɪt]	a small piece of paper that shows that you have paid to travel on a train; *buy a ticket*; *a train ticket*
ticket collector	[tɪ̱kɪt kəlɛktər]	a person who collects the tickets of passengers when they get off a train
ticket office	[tɪ̱kɪt ɔfɪs]	the place where you buy tickets at a train station
timetable (*BRIT*)		*see* **schedule**
track	[træ̱k]	one of the metal lines that trains travel along; *a railroad track*
train	[tre̱ɪn]	a long vehicle that is pulled by an engine along a railroad; *catch a train*; *get on/off a train*; *take the train*; *train travel*
the tube	[ðə tu̱b]	same as **the underground** (*BRIT*)
the underground (*BRIT*)		*see* **subway**
waiting room	[we̱ɪtɪŋ rum]	a room in a train station where people can sit down while they wait
whistle	[wɪ̱sᵊl]	a small tube that you blow into in order to produce a loud sound; *blow a whistle*

VERBS

approach	[əpro̱ʊtʃ]	to move closer to something
arrive	[əra̱ɪv]	to come to a place from somewhere else
book	[bʊ̱k]	to arrange to have or use something at a later time; *book a train ticket*

EXAMPLES
He came to Glasgow by train.
I heard the train approaching.
Their train arrived on time.

cancel	[kænsªl]	to say that a train that should travel will not be traveling
delay	[dɪleɪ]	to make someone or something late; *The train is delayed.*
depart	[dɪpɑrt]	to leave
miss	[mɪs]	to arrive too late to get on a train; *miss your train*

ADJECTIVES

due	[du]	expected to happen or arrive at a particular time; *Find out when the next train is due.*
first-class	[fɜrst klæs]	relating to the best and most expensive seats on a train; *a first-class cabin*; *a first-class ticket*
high-speed	[haɪ spid]	that travels very fast; *a high-speed train*
late	[leɪt]	after the time that something should happen
non-smoking	[nɒn smoukɪŋ]	a non-smoking area is a public place where people are not allowed to smoke
overcrowded	[ouvərkraudɪd]	with too many people
smoking	[smoukɪŋ]	a smoking area is a public place where people are allowed to smoke; *the smoking section/area*

EXAMPLES

Many trains have been canceled.
Thousands of rail passengers were delayed yesterday.
Your train is due to leave in three minutes.
The train is late.

weather

air	[ɛər]	the mixture of gases all around us that we breathe; *fresh air*; *warm/hot air*
atmosphere	[ætməsfiər]	the layer of air or other gases around a planet
climate	[klaɪmɪt]	the normal weather in a place; *a warm/cold climate*; *climate change*
cloud	[klaʊd]	a white or gray thing in the sky that is made of drops of water
darkness	[dɑrknɪs]	the state of being dark, without any light
drought	[draʊt]	a long period of time with no rain
east	[ist]	the direction that is in front of you when you look at the sun in the morning; *The sun rises in the east.*
flood	[flʌd]	an occasion when a lot of water covers land that is usually dry
fog	[fɒg]	thick cloud that is close to the ground
frost	[frɔst]	ice like white powder that forms outside when the weather is very cold
gale	[geɪl]	a very strong wind
hail	[heɪl]	small balls of ice that fall like rain from the sky
heat	[hit]	when something is hot
hurricane	[hɜrɪkeɪn, hʌr-]	a storm with very strong winds and rain
ice	[aɪs]	frozen water

EXAMPLES

Keith opened the window and felt the cold air on his face.

There is an extra hour of darkness on winter mornings.

The drought has killed all their crops.

The car crash happened in thick fog.

A strong gale was blowing.

Our clothes dried quickly in the heat of the sun.

The ground was covered with ice.

lightning	[laɪtnɪŋ]	the very bright flashes of light in the sky that happen during a storm; *thunder and lightning*; *a flash of lightning*
mist	[mɪst]	a lot of tiny drops of water in the air, that make it difficult to see; *mist and fog*; *morning mist*
monsoon	[mɒnsuːn]	the season in Southern Asia when there is a lot of very heavy rain; *the monsoon rains*; *the monsoon season*
north	[nɔːrθ]	the direction that is on your left when you are looking at the sun in the morning
puddle	[pʌdəl]	a small pool of water on the ground
rain	[reɪn]	water that falls from the clouds in small drops; *heavy/pouring rain*; *go out in the rain*
rainbow	[reɪnboʊ]	a half circle of different colors that you can sometimes see in the sky when it rains
raindrop	[reɪndrɒp]	a single drop of rain
sky	[skaɪ]	the space above the Earth that you can see when you stand outside and look upwards; *in the sky*
snow	[snoʊ]	soft white frozen water that falls from the sky
snowflake	[snoʊfleɪk]	one of the soft, white bits of frozen water that fall as snow
south	[saʊθ]	the direction that is on your right when you are looking at the sun in the morning
storm	[stɔːrm]	very bad weather, with heavy rain and strong winds; *violent/severe storms*; *tropical storms*

EXAMPLES

One man died when he was struck by lightning.
In the north, snow and ice cover the ground.
Young children love splashing in puddles.
Outside a light rain was falling.
Today we have clear blue skies.
Six inches of snow fell.

sun	[sʌn]	**1** the ball of fire in the sky that gives us heat and light
		2 the heat and light that comes from the sun
sunshine	[sʌnʃaɪn]	the light and heat that comes from the sun
temperature	[tɛmprətʃər, -tʃʊər]	how hot or cold it is; *warm/cold temperatures*; *average temperature*
thermometer	[θərmɒmɪtər]	an instrument for measuring how hot or cold something is
thunder	[θʌndər]	the loud noise that you sometimes hear from the sky during a storm
thunderstorm	[θʌndərstɔrm]	a very noisy storm
tornado	[tɔrneɪdoʊ]	a storm with strong winds that spin around very fast and cause a lot of damage
tsunami	[tsʊnɑmi]	a very large wave that flows onto the land and destroys things
umbrella	[ʌmbrɛlə]	a thing that you hold over your head to protect yourself from the rain; *put up your umbrella*
weather	[wɛðər]	the temperature and conditions outside, for example if it is raining, hot, or windy; *cold/bad/wet weather*; *hot/warm weather*
weather forecast	[wɛðər fɔrkæst]	a statement saying what the weather will be like for the next few days; *watch/listen to the weather forecast*
west	[wɛst]	the direction that is in front of you when you look at the sun in the evening
wind	[wɪnd]	air that moves

EXAMPLES
The sun is shining.
Suddenly, the sun came out.
They went outside to sit in the sun.
She was sitting outside a cafe in bright sunshine.
What's the weather like?
The sun sets in the west.
A strong wind was blowing from the north.

VERBS

blow	[blou̯]	when a wind or breeze blows, the air moves
freeze	[friːz]	to become solid because the temperature is low
melt	[mɛlt]	to change from a solid substance to a liquid because of heat
rain	[reɪn]	when it rains, water falls from the clouds in small drops
shine	[ʃaɪn]	to give out bright light; *The sun is shining.*
snow	[snou̯]	when it snows, soft white frozen water falls from the sky
thaw	[θɔ]	if snow or ice thaws, it becomes warmer and changes to liquid

ADJECTIVES

cloudy	[klau̯di]	with a lot of clouds in the sky; *a cloudy day/ sky*
cold	[kou̯ld]	without any warmth; *cold weather; cold air*
cool	[kuːl]	having a low temperature, but not cold; *cool air*
dry	[draɪ]	without any rain
freezing	[friːzɪŋ]	very cold
hot	[hɒt]	describing the weather when the temperature is high; *a hot day*

EXAMPLES

The wind is blowing.
Last winter the water froze in all our pipes.
The snow melted.
It's raining.
It snowed heavily all night.
The snow thawed.
The Sahara is one of the driest places in Africa.
It's freezing.
It's too hot to play tennis.

humid	[hyumɪd]	wet and warm; *humid air*; *humid weather/ conditions*
mild	[maɪld]	not too hot and not too cold; *a mild winter*; *mild weather*
rainy	[reɪni]	raining a lot; *a rainy day*
stormy	[stɔrmi]	with strong winds and heavy rain; *stormy weather*
sunny	[sʌni]	with the sun shining brightly
tropical	[trɒpɪkᵊl]	belonging to or typical of the hot, wet areas of the world; *a tropical climate*; *tropical heat*
windy	[wɪndi]	with a lot of wind; *a windy day*

EXAMPLES
The weather was warm and sunny.

geographical place names

Here is a list of the names of well-known places in the world:

Afghanistan /æfgǽnɪstæn, -stɑn/

Africa /ǽfrɪkə/

Albania /ælbéɪniə/

Algeria /ældʒɪ́əriə/

American Samoa /əmérɪkən səmóʊə/

Andorra /ændɔ́rə/

Angola /æŋgóʊlə/

Antarctica /æntɑ́rktɪkə/

Antigua and Barbuda /æntíːgə ənd bɑrbúːdə/

the Arctic /ði ɑ́rktɪk/

Argentina /ɑrdʒəntíːnə/

Armenia /ɑrmíːniə/

Asia /éɪʒə/

the Atlantic /ði ətlǽntɪk/

Australia /ɔstréɪlyə/

Austria /ɔ́striə/

Azerbaijan /æzərbaɪdʒɑ́n/

the Bahamas /ðə bəhɑ́məz/

Bahrain /bɑréɪn/

Bangladesh /bæŋglədéʃ/

Barbados /bɑrbéɪdoʊs/

Belarus /bélərʊs, byɛl-/

Belgium /béldʒəm/

Belize /bəlíːz/

Benin /bɛníːn/

Bhutan /buːtɑ́n/

Bolivia /bəlíːviə/

Bosnia and Herzegovina /bɒzniə ənd hɜrtsəgoʊvíːnə/

Botswana /bɒtswɑ́nə/

Brazil /brəzíl/

Brunei /bruːnáɪ/

Bulgaria /bʌlgéəriə/

Burkina-Faso /bərkíːnəfǽsoʊ/

Burma /bɜ́rmə/

Burundi /bərʊ́ndi/

Cambodia /kæmbóʊdiə/

Cameroon /kæmərúːn/

Canada /kǽnədə/

Cape Verde /keɪp vɜ́rd/

the Caribbean /ðə kærɪ́biən, kərɪ́biən/

the Central African Republic /ðə séntrəl ǽfrɪkən rɪpʌ́blɪk/

Chad /tʃæd/

Chile /tʃíli/

(the People's Republic of) China /(ðə píːpəlz rɪpʌ́blɪk əv) tʃáɪnə/

Colombia /kəlʌ́mbiə/

Comoros /kɒ́məroʊz/

(the Republic of) Congo /(ðə rɪpʌ́blɪk əv) kɒ́ŋgoʊ/

(the Democratic Republic of) Congo /(ðə dɛməkrǽtik rɪpʌ́blɪk əv) kɒ́ŋgoʊ/

Costa Rica /kɒstə ríːkə/

Côte d'Ivoire /koʊt divwɑ́r/

Croatia /kroʊéɪʃə/

Cuba /kyúːbə/

Cyprus /sáɪprəs/

the Czech Republic /ðə tʃɛk rɪpʌ́blɪk/

Denmark /dɛ́nmɑrk/

Djibouti /dʒɪbuːti/

Dominica /dɒmɪniːkə, dəmɪnɪkə/

the Dominican Republic
/ðə dəmɪnɪkən rɪpʌblɪk/

East Timor /iːst tiːmɔːr/

Ecuador /ekwədɔːr/

Egypt /iːdʒɪpt/

El Salvador /ɛl sælvədɔːr/

England /ɪŋglənd/

Equatorial Guinea
/ekwətɔːriəl gɪni/

Eritrea /erɪtriːə/

Estonia /ɛstoʊniə/

Ethiopia /iːθioʊpiə/

Europe /yʊərəp/

Fiji /fiːdʒi/

Finland /fɪnlənd/

France /fræns/

Gabon /gæbɒn/

Gambia /gæmbiə/

Georgia /dʒɔːrdʒə/

Germany /dʒɜːrməni/

Ghana /gɑːnə/

Great Britain /greɪt brɪtən/

Greece /griːs/

Greenland /griːnlənd/

Grenada /grɪneɪdə/

Guatemala /gwɑːtəmɑːlə/

Guinea /gɪni/

Guinea-Bissau /gɪnibɪsaʊ/

Guyana /gaɪɑːnə/

Haiti /heɪti/

Holland /hɒlənd/

Honduras /hɒndʊərəs/

Hungary /hʌŋgəri/

Iceland /aɪslənd/

India /ɪndiə/

Indonesia /ɪndəniːʒə/

Iran /ɪrɑn. ɪræn/

Iraq /ɪrɑk, ɪræk/

(the Republic of) Ireland
/(ðə rɪpʌblɪk əv) aɪərlənd

Israel /ɪzreɪəl/

Italy /ɪtəli/

Jamaica /dʒəmeɪkə/

Japan /dʒəpæn/

Jordan /dʒɔːrdən/

Kazakhstan
/kæzækstæn, kɑːzakstɑn/

Kenya /kɛnyə/

Kiribati /kɪrɪbɑːti/

Kuwait /kuweɪt/

Kyrgyzstan /kɪərgɪstæn, -stɑn/

Laos /laʊs/

Latvia /lætviə, lɑːt-/

Lebanon /lɛbənɒn, -nən/

Lesotho /ləsoʊtoʊ/

Liberia /laɪbɪəriə/

Libya /lɪbiə/

Liechtenstein /lɪktənstaɪn/

Lithuania /lɪθueɪniə/

Luxembourg /lʌksəmbɜːrg/

Macedonia /mæsidoʊniə/

Madagascar /mædəgæskər/

Malawi /məlɑːwi/

Malaysia /məleɪʒə/

the Maldives /ðə mɔːldivz/

Mali /mɑːli/

Malta /mɔltə/

the Marshall Islands
/ðə mɑrʃəl aɪləndz/

Mauritania /mɒrɪteɪniə/

Mauritius /mərɪʃəs/

the Mediterranean
/ðə medɪtəreɪniən/

Mexico /meksɪkoʊ/

Micronesia /maɪkrəniʒə/

Moldova /mɔldoʊvə/

Monaco /mɒnəkoʊ/

Mongolia /mɒŋɡoʊliə/

Montenegro
/mɒntɪnegroʊ, -nigroʊ/

Morocco /mərɒkoʊ/

Mozambique /moʊzæmbik/

Myanmar /myɑnmɑr/

Namibia /nəmɪbiə/

Nauru /nɑuru, nauru/

Nepal /nɪpɔl, -pɑl/

the Netherlands /ðə neðərləndz/

New Zealand /nu zilənd/

Nicaragua /nɪkərɑgwə/

Niger /naɪdʒər, niʒeər/

Nigeria /naɪdʒɪəriə/

Northern Ireland /nɔrðərn
aɪərlənd/

North Korea /nɔrθ kəriə/

Norway /nɔrweɪ/

Oman /oʊmɑn/

the Pacific /ðə pəsɪfɪk/

Pakistan /pækɪstæn, pɑkɪstɑn /

Panama /pænəmɑ/

Papua New Guinea
/pæpyʊə nu ɡini/

Paraguay /pærəgwaɪ, -gweɪ/

Peru /pəru/

the Philippines /ðə fɪləpinz/

Poland /poʊlənd/

Portugal /pɔrtʃəgəl/

Puerto Rico /pwertə rikoʊ, pɔrtə/

Qatar /kɑtɑr, kətɑr/

Romania /roʊmeɪniə/

Russia /rʌʃə/

Rwanda /ruɑndə/

St Kitts and Nevis
/seɪnt kɪts ənd nɪvɪs/

St Lucia /seɪnt luʃə/

St Vincent and the Grenadines /
seɪnt vɪnsənt ənd ðə grenədɪnz,
grenədinz /

Samoa /səmoʊə/

San Marino /sæn mərinoʊ/

São Tomé and Principe
/sau təmeɪ ənd prɪnsɪpeɪ/

Saudi Arabia /saudi əreɪbiə/

Scotland /skɒtlənd/

Senegal /senigɔl/

Serbia /sɜrbiə/

the Seychelles /ðə seɪʃelz/

Sierra Leone /sieərə lioʊn/

Singapore /sɪŋəpɔr/

Slovakia /sloʊvɑkiə, -væk-/

Slovenia /sloʊviniə/

the Solomon Islands
/ðə sɒləmən aɪləndz/

Somalia /səmɑliə/

South Africa /sauθ æfrɪkə/

South Korea /sauθ kəriə/

Spain/speɪn/

Sri Lanka /sri lɑŋkə, læŋkə, ʃri/

Sudan /sudæn/

Suriname /sʊərɪnɑm, -næm/

Swaziland /swɑzilænd/

Sweden /swidən/

Switzerland /swɪtsərlənd/

Syria /sɪəriə/

Taiwan /taɪwɑn/

Tajikistan /tɑdʒikɪstæn, -stɑn/

Tanzania /tænzəniə/

Thailand /taɪlænd/

Togo /toʊgoʊ/

Tonga /tɒŋgə/

Trinidad and Tobago
 /trɪnɪdæd ənd təbeɪgoʊ/

Tunisia /tunɪʒə/

Turkey /tɜrki/

Turkmenistan
 /tɜrkmenɪstæn, -stɑn/

Tuvalu /tuvəlu/

Uganda /yugændə, ugɑndə/

Ukraine /yukreɪn/

the United Arab Emirates
 /ði yunaɪtɪd ærəb ɛmɪrəts/

the United Kingdom
 /ði yunaɪtɪd kɪŋdəm/

the United States of America
 /ði yunaɪtɪd steɪts əv əmerɪkə/

Uruguay /yʊərəgweɪ, -gwaɪ/

Uzbekistan /ʊzbekɪstæn, -stɑn/

Vanuatu /vɑnuɑtu/

the Vatican City /ðə vætɪkən sɪti/

Venezuela /vɛnɪzweɪlə/

Vietnam /vyɛtnɑm, -næm/

Wales /weɪlz/

Yemen /yɛmən/

Zambia /zæmbiə/

Zimbabwe /zɪmbɑbweɪ/

irregular verbs

INFINITIVE	PAST TENSE	PAST PARTICIPLE
arise	arose	arisen
be	was, were	been
beat	beat	beaten
become	became	become
begin	began	begun
bend	bent	bent
bet	bet	bet
bind	bound	bound
bite	bit	bitten
bleed	bled	bled
blow	blew	blown
break	broke	broken
bring	brought	brought
build	built	built
burn	burned or burnt	burned or burnt
burst	burst	burst
buy	bought	bought
catch	caught	caught
choose	chose	chosen
cling	clung	clung
come	came	come
cost	cost	cost
creep	crept	crept
cut	cut	cut
deal	dealt	dealt
dig	dug	dug
dive	dived or dove	dived
do	did	done
draw	drew	drawn
dream	dreamed or dreamt	dreamed or dreamt
drink	drank	drunk
drive	drove	driven

INFINITIVE	PAST TENSE	PAST PARTICIPLE
eat	ate	eaten
fall	fell	fallen
feed	fed	fed
feel	felt	felt
fight	fought	fought
find	found	found
fly	flew	flown
forbid	forbade	forbidden
forget	forgot	forgotten
freeze	froze	frozen
get	got	gotten, got
give	gave	given
go	went	gone
grind	ground	ground
grow	grew	grown
hang	hung	hung
have	had	had
hear	heard	heard
hide	hid	hidden
hit	hit	hit
hold	held	held
hurt	hurt	hurt
keep	kept	kept
kneel	kneeled or knelt	kneeled or knelt
know	knew	known
lay	laid	laid
lead	led	led
lean	leaned	leaned
leap	leaped or leapt	leaped or leapt
learn	learned	learned
leave	left	left
lend	lent	lent

INFINITIVE	PAST TENSE	PAST PARTICIPLE
let	let	let
lie	lay	lain
light	lit or lighted	lit or lighted
lose	lost	lost
make	made	made
mean	meant	meant
meet	met	met
pay	paid	paid
put	put	put
quit	quit	quit
read	read	read
ride	rode	ridden
ring	rang	rung
rise	rose	risen
run	ran	run
say	said	said
see	saw	seen
seek	sought	sought
sell	sold	sold
send	sent	sent
set	set	set
shake	shook	shaken
shine	shined or shone	shined or shone
shoot	shot	shot
show	showed	shown
shrink	shrank	shrunk
shut	shut	shut
sing	sang	sung
sink	sank	sunk
sit	sat	sat
sleep	slept	slept
slide	slid	slid
smell	smelled	smelled

INFINITIVE	PAST TENSE	PAST PARTICIPLE
speak	spoke	spoken
speed	sped *or* speeded	sped *or* speeded
spell	spelled	spelled
spend	spent	spent
spill	spilled	spilled
spit	spit *or* spat	spit, *or* spat
spoil	spoiled	spoiled
spread	spread	spread
spring	sprang	sprung
stand	stood	stood
steal	stole	stolen
stick	stuck	stuck
sting	stung	stung
stink	stank	stunk
strike	struck	struck *or* stricken
swear	swore	sworn
sweep	swept	swept
swell	swelled	swollen
swim	swam	swum
swing	swung	swung
take	took	taken
teach	taught	taught
tear	tore	torn
tell	told	told
think	thought	thought
throw	threw	thrown
wake	woke *or* waked	woken *or* waked
wear	wore	worn
weep	wept	wept
win	won	won
wind	wound	wound
write	wrote	written

measurements

LENGTH

inch (1 in. = 2.54 cm)
foot (1 ft. = 30.48 cm)
yard (1 yd. = 91.44 cm)
millimeter (mm)
centimeter (cm)
meter (m)
kilometer (km)
mile (= 1.61 kilometers)

WEIGHT

ton = 0.9 metric ton
ounce (1 oz. = 28g)
pound (1 lb. = 454g)
milligram (mg)
gram (g)
kilogram (kg)

CAPACITY

pint (= 0.57 liters)
gallon (= 4.55 liters)
milliliter (ml)
liter (l)

EXAMPLES

This tiny plant is only a few inches high.
They drove 600 miles across the desert.
The box weighs 4.5 kilograms.
The boat was carrying 30,000 tons of oil.
Each carton contains a pint of milk.
Adults should drink about two liters of water each day.

numbers/ordinal numbers

1	one
2	two
3	three
4	four
5	five
6	six
7	seven
8	eight
9	nine
10	ten
11	eleven
12	twelve
13	thirteen
14	fourteen
15	fifteen
16	sixteen
17	seventeen
18	eighteen
19	nineteen
20	twenty
21	twenty-one
22	twenty-two
30	thirty
40	forty
50	fifty
60	sixty
70	seventy
80	eighty
90	ninety
100	a/one hundred
101	a/one hundred and one
1,000	a/one thousand
10,000	ten thousand
100,000	a/one hundred thousand
1,000,000	a/one million

NUMBERS OVER 20

We write numbers over 20 (except 30, 40, 50, etc) with a hyphen.

25	twenty-five	45	forty-five
82	eighty-two	59	fifty-nine

A OR ONE?

100	a/one hundred	1,000,000	a/one million
1,000	a/one thousand		

One is more formal, and is often used in order to be very clear and precise.

LARGE NUMBERS

We often use a comma to divide large numbers into groups of three figures.

1,235,578	one million, two hundred and thirty-five thousand, five hundred and seventy-eight

---

EXAMPLES
The total amount was one hundred and forty-nine dollars and thirty cents.
These shoes cost over a hundred dollars.

ORDINAL NUMBERS

1st	first	19th	nineteenth
2nd	second	20th	twentieth
3rd	third	21st	twenty-first
4th	fourth	22nd	twenty-second
5th	fifth	30th	thirtieth
6th	sixth	40th	fortieth
7th	seventh	50th	fiftieth
8th	eighth	60th	sixtieth
9th	ninth	70th	seventieth
10th	tenth	80th	eightieth
11th	eleventh	90th	ninetieth
12th	twelfth	100th	hundredth
13th	thirteenth	101st	hundred and first
14th	fourteenth	200th	two hundredth
15th	fifteenth	$1,000^{th}$	thousandth
16th	sixteenth	$10,000^{th}$	ten thousandth
17th	seventeenth	$100,000^{th}$	hundred thousandth
18th	eighteenth	$1,000,000^{th}$	millionth

EXAMPLES

Kate won first prize in the writing competition.
It's Michael's seventh birthday tomorrow.
My office is on the twelfth floor.
I'm doing a project about fashion in the eighteenth century.
We're celebrating the 200th anniversary of independence next year.
The company announced that it has just served its millionth customer.

people of the world

There are different ways that the noun for a place changes to become the noun for a person from that place, or to become the adjective for that place. For places ending in "-a," the person noun and the adjective usually end in "-an," for example Australia→Australian.

> I live in Australia.
> I am an Australian.
> I am Australian.
> ...the Australian flag.

Here are some other examples of words that work this way:

Place nouns that end in –a → person nouns and adjectives that end in –an
Africa→African, America→American, Asia→Asian, Austria→Austrian, Bulgaria→Bulgarian, Cuba→Cuban, India→Indian, Kenya→Kenyan, Malaysia→Malaysian, Russia→Russian, Slovakia→Slovakian, Slovenia→Slovenian

There is no plural form for "person" words that end in "-s" or "-ese," for example "a Swiss" and "a Chinese". The singular form of these words is also not used very often, and it is more common to say "a Swiss man" or "a Chinese woman."

If there is a language related to a particular country, the name of the language is usually the same as the adjective describing the country, for example *Polish, Japanese, Italian*.

EXAMPLES

Have you ever been to Peru?
She was born in China.
Five Germans and twelve Spaniards were killed in the crash.
Can you speak Welsh?
He is fluent in Vietnamese.
He is English.
...a Mexican restaurant.
...the French president.

Place (noun)	Adjective	Person (noun)
Afghanistan	Afghan	an Afghan
Argentina	Argentinean	an Argentine
Bangladesh	Bangladeshi	a Bangladeshi
Belgium	Belgian	a Belgian
Brazil	Brazilian	a Brazilian
Britain	British	a Briton
Canada	Canadian	a Canadian
Chile	Chilean	a Chilean
China	Chinese	a Chinese
the Czech Republic	Czech	a Czech
Denmark	Danish	a Dane
Egypt	Egyptian	an Egyptian
England	English	an Englishman or an Englishwoman
Europe	European	a European
Finland	Finnish	a Finn
France	French	a Frenchman or a Frenchwoman
Germany	German	a German
Greece	Greek	a Greek
Hungary	Hungarian	a Hungarian
Iceland	Icelandic	an Icelander
Iran	Iranian	an Iranian
Iraq	Iraqi	an Iraqi
Ireland	Irish	an Irishman or an Irishwoman
Italy	Italian	an Italian
Japan	Japanese	a Japanese
Mexico	Mexican	a Mexican
Morocco	Moroccan	a Moroccan
The Netherlands	Dutch	a Dutchman or a Dutchwoman
New Zealand	New Zealand	a New Zealander
Norway	Norwegian	a Norwegian
Pakistan	Pakistani	a Pakistani
Peru	Peruvian	a Peruvian
Poland	Polish	a Pole
Portugal	Portuguese	a Portuguese
Scotland	Scottish	a Scot or a Scotsman or a Scotswoman
Spain	Spanish	a Spaniard
Sweden	Swedish	a Swede
Switzerland	Swiss	a Swiss
Taiwan	Taiwanese	a Taiwanese
Turkey	Turkish	a Turk
Vietnam	Vietnamese	a Vietnamese
Wales	Welsh	a Welshman or a Welshwoman

times and dates

TELLING THE TIME

Here are the most common ways of saying and writing the time.

four o'clock
four
4.00

nine o'clock
nine
9.00

twelve o'clock
twelve
12.00

four in the morning
4 a.m.

nine in the morning
9 a.m.

twelve in the morning
12 a.m.
midday
noon

four in the afternoon
4 p.m.

nine in the evening
9 p.m.

twelve at night
12 p.m.
midnight

half past eleven
eleven-thirty
11.30

quarter after twelve (*American*)
twelve-fifteen
12.15
quarter past twelve (*British*)

twelve forty-five
12.45
quarter to one (*British*)

two twenty-five
2.25
twenty-five past two (*British*))

seven-fifty
7.50
ten to eight (*British*)

EXAMPLES

What time is it? – It's five o'clock.
Excuse me, do you have the time? – Yes, it's eleven-thirty.
The class starts at 11 a.m. and finishes at 1:30 p.m.
We arrived at the airport just after nine.
I'll meet you at seven forty-five.

WRITING DATES

There are several different ways of writing a date.

April 20   20 April
April 20th   20th April

(say "April twentieth" or "the twentieth of April")

If you want to give the year, you put it last.

December 15th, 2012

(say "December fifteenth, twenty twelve")

You can write a date in figures. In American English, you put the month first, then the day, then the year. In British English, you put the day first, then the month, then the year.

In American English, December 15th, 2011 is:

12/15/11   *or*   12.15.11

In British English, December 15th, 2011 is:

15/12/11   *or*   15.12.11

EXAMPLES
The new store opens on February 5th.
I was born on June 15th, 1970.
Date of birth: 6/15/1970.

index

index

A

absent 98, 233
academic 73
accelerate 55
accelerator 49
accessible 147
accident 49, 136, 172
accommodation 149
accountant 167
accounts 43
ache 136
acid 234
acoustic 202
acquaintance 124
acrylic 178
act 271
actor 267
actress 267
ad 43, 262
add 187
addition 183
address 149, 256
adopt 128
adult 124
advert 43, 262
advertise 46
advertising 43
adverts 262
aerial 262
aerobics 249
aeroplane 1
afternoon 274
age 36
agent 43
AGM 43
ago 278
agriculture 88
AIDS 136
air 295
aircraft 1
airline 1
airplane 1
airport 1

airsick 7
air-traffic controller 1
aisle 1
à la carte 119
alarm call 144
alarm clock 277
album 200
alcoholic drink 117
algebra 183
allowance 190
alphabet 217
aluminium 178
aluminum 178
ambassador 243
ambitious 106
ambulance 49, 136
American football 249
anchor 27
anger 105
angle 183
angry 106
animal 9
animated 266
ankle 33
annoyed 106
annual 277
annual leave 93
answer 232, 259
ant 9
antenna 14, 262
antler 14
anxious 106
apartment 149
appetizer 120
apple 131
appliance 155
application 93
apply for a job 97
appointment 136
apprentice 93
approach 293
apricot 131
April 276

aquarium 15
architect 167
area 183
area code 256
arithmetic 183
arm 33
armchair 154
armed 247
army 243
arrest 175
arrival 290
arrivals 1
arrive 293
art 19
artery 33
art gallery 19
article 217
artist 19
arts 68
art school 68
ash 210
ashamed 106
ask 232
aspirin 136
assassinate 247
assault 172, 175
assemble 165
assembly 228
assembly line 162
assignment 68
astronaut 234
astronomy 234
asylum seeker 243
athlete 251
at home 153
ATM 190
atmosphere 295
atom 234
atomic 237
attachment 76
attendance 228
at the moment 278
attic 149